Indian Power Projection
Ambition, Arms and Influence

Shashank Joshi

www.rusi.org

Royal United Services Institute for Defence and Security Studies

Indian Power Projection: Ambition, Arms and Influence
Shashank Joshi
First published 2015

Whitehall Papers series

Series Editor: Professor Malcolm Chalmers
Editors: Adrian Johnson and Ashlee Godwin

RUSI is a Registered Charity (No. 210639)
ISBN 978-1-138-65496-9

Published on behalf of the Royal United Services Institute for Defence
and Security Studies
by
Routledge Journals, an imprint of Taylor & Francis, 4 Park Square,
Milton Park, Abingdon OX14 4RN

SUBSCRIPTIONS
Please send subscription orders to:

USA/Canada: Taylor & Francis Inc., Journals Department, 530 Walnut Street, Suite 850, Philadelphia, PA 19106, USA

UK/Rest of World: Routledge Journals, T&F Customer Services, T&F Informa UK Ltd, Sheepen Place, Colchester, Essex CO3 3LP, UK

Contents

About the Author   iv
Acknowledgements   v
Acronyms and Abbreviations   vi
List of Tables and Figures   viii
Maps   ix

Introduction   1

I. India's Defence Posture   16

II. Air-Power Projection   47

III. Land-Power Projection   76

IV. Enablers: The Sinews of Power Projection   96

V. The Future of Indian Power Projection   119

About the Author

Shashank Joshi is a Senior Research Fellow at the Royal United Services Institute in London and a Research Associate at the Changing Character of War Programme at Oxford University. He is also a PhD candidate in the Department of Government, Harvard University. He specialises in international security in South Asia and the Middle East, with a particular interest in Indian foreign and defence policy. He received his BA from Gonville and Caius College, University of Cambridge and his MA from Harvard, where he was a Kennedy Scholar. He has lectured frequently at the UK Defence Academy and to other diplomatic, military, and academic audiences in the UK and abroad. His work has been published in a variety of peer-reviewed and policy journals, and in British, American and Indian newspapers.

His most recent academic and policy publications include 'India and the Middle East', *Asian Affairs* (Vol. 46, No. 2, 2015); 'India's Nuclear Anxieties: The Debate Over Doctrine, *Arms Control Today* (September 2015); 'An Evolving Indian Nuclear Doctrine?' in Michael Krepon, Joshua T White, Julia Thompson and Shane Mason (eds), *Deterrence Instability and Nuclear Weapons in South Asia* (Washington DC: Stimson Center 2015); 'Assessing Britain's Role in Afghanistan', *Asian Survey* (Vol. 55, No. 2, March/April 2015); 'The Coup-Proofing of India, *Survival* (Vol. 57, No. 2, April–May 2015); 'India's Role in a Changing Afghanistan', *Washington Quarterly* (Vol. 37, No. 2, Summer 2014); 'Looking West: India and the Middle East', *Seminar* (No. 658, June 2014); and 'Iran and the Geneva Agreement: A Footnote to History or a Turning Point?', *RUSI Journal* (Vol. 159, No. 1, 2014).

Acknowledgements

Many people helped with the writing of this Whitehall Paper. Malcolm Chalmers, Sumit Ganguly, Jack Gill and Iskander Rehman were all exceptionally generous with their time and advice. I am also grateful to Air Vice Marshal (Ret) Manmohan Bahadur, Abhijit Iyer-Mitra, Captain Gurpreet Khurana, Walter Ladwig, Antoine Levesques, Frank O'Donnell, Peter Roberts, Jaganath Sankaran, Angad Singh, Vice Admiral Madanjit Singh, Ashley J Tellis and participants at workshops in New Delhi in March 2015 and London in June 2015. The manuscript was much improved by the expert editing of Adrian Johnson and Edward Mortimer.

My greatest thanks go to Hannah Cheetham-Joshi, Sunanda Joshi and Vinit Joshi for their love and support. Finally, my late grandfather Lieutenant Colonel H C Pant served his country for twenty-eight years as an officer in the Indian Army between 1949 and 1977. Appropriately enough, this included his own contribution to Indian power projection, with a posting to the International Control Commission in Vietnam in 1964. I dedicate this book to his memory.

Acronyms and Abbreviations

AAR	Air-to-air refuelling
AEW	Airborne early warning
AEWC	Airborne early warning and control
AFSPA	Armed Forces (Special Powers) Acts
AMCA	Advanced Medium Combat Aircraft
ASEAN	Association of Southeast Asian Nations
ASW	Anti-submarine warfare
AWACS	Airborne Warning and Control System
BJP	Bharatiya Janata Party
BRO	Border Roads Organisation
C4ISR	Command, control, communications, computers, intelligence, surveillance and reconnaissance
CAG	Comptroller and Auditor General
CDS	Chief of the Defence Staff
CEP	Circular error probable
CISMOA	Communications and Information Security Memorandum of Agreement
CTF	Combined Task Force
DAC	Defence Acquisition Council
DFS	Department of Field Support (UN)
DRDO	Defence Research and Development Organisation
ELINT	Electronic intelligence
FAC	Forward air control
FDI	Foreign direct investment
FGFA	Fifth-Generation Fighter Aircraft
GCC	Gulf Cooperation Council
GDP	Gross domestic product
HADR	Humanitarian assistance and disaster relief
HAL	Hindustan Aeronautics Limited
IAF	Indian Air Force
IDS	Integrated Defence Staff
INSAT	Indian National Satellite
IPKF	Indian Peace Keeping Force
IRNSS	Indian Regional Navigation Satellite System
ISAF	International Security Assistance Force
ISR	Intelligence, surveillance and reconnaissance
ITBP	Indo-Tibetan Border Police
JDAM	Joint Direct Attack Munition

LCU	Landing craft, utility
LPD	Landing platform dock
LSA	Logistics Support Agreement
MILSATCOM	Military satellite communications
NATO	North Atlantic Treaty Organization
NSA	National Security Advisor
PGM	Precision-guided munition
PJHQ	Permanent Joint Headquarters (UK)
PLAN	People's Liberation Army Navy
PSI	Proliferation Security Initiative
QDR	Quadrennial Defense Review (US)
RUF	Revolutionary United Front (Sierra Leone)
SAM	Surface-to-air missile
SIPRI	Stockholm International Peace Research Institute
SSBN	Nuclear ballistic-missile submarine
UAE	United Arab Emirates
UAV	Unmanned aerial vehicle
UK	United Kingdom
UN	United Nations
US	United States
USAF	US Air Force
WMD	Weapons of mass destruction

List of Tables and Figures

Table 1:   Examples of Force Projection by Threat
and Persistence   15

Table 2:   Indian Power Projection since 1950   38

Table 3:   IAF Present and Projected Force Structure   52

Table 4:   Sizes of Selected Historical Strike Packages   57

Table 5:   ISR-Relevant Indian UAVs by Type, Number
and Capabilities   105

Table 6:   Selected Military and Dual-Purpose Indian Satellites   109

Figure 1:   Comparative Defence Spending between
Selected States, 1990–2014   21

Figure 2:   Comparative Defence Spending between Selected
States as Percentage of GDP, 1988–2014   21

Figure 3:   Indian Arms Imports, 1990–2014   23

Figure 4:   Indian Arms Imports by Source, 2000–14   25

Figure 5:   India's Peacekeeping Contribution to UN Missions,
1990–2014   34

Figure 6:   Numbers of Indian Naval Assets, 2005–15   39

Figure 7:   IAF Force Structure, 2015–30   49

Figure 8:   Attack, Transport and Multi-Role Helicopter Holdings
of Major States   80

Figure 9:   Perceptions of India in Selected States of
Asia and the US, 2006–15   136

Maps

Map 1: India and Neighbouring Regions.

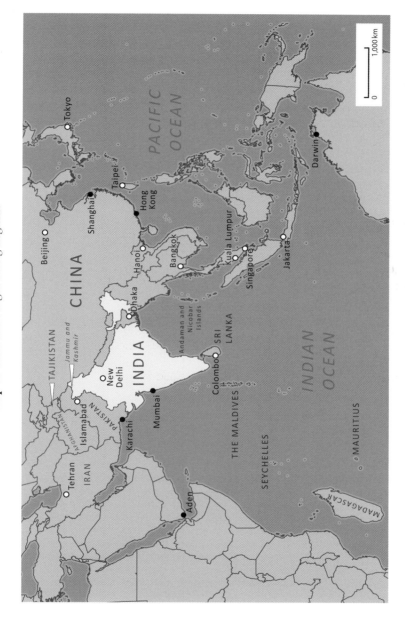

Map 2: Indicative Ranges of Indian Strike Aircraft.

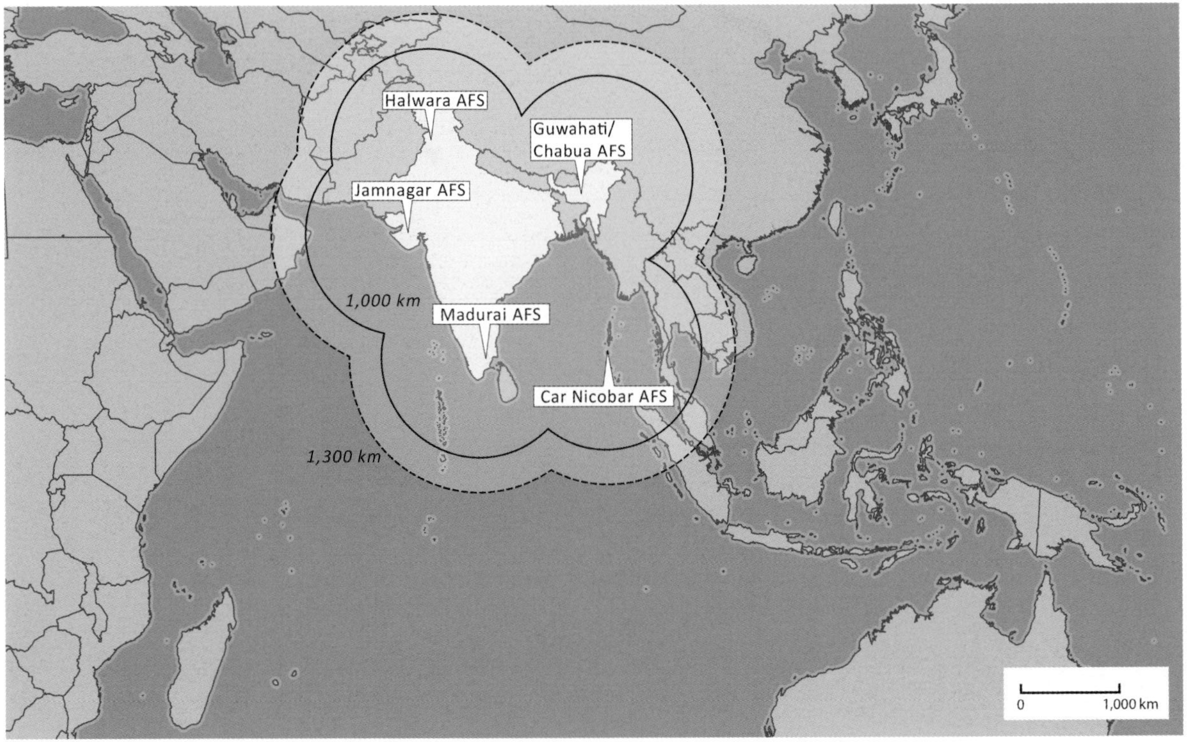

Map 3: Indian Overseas Military-Relevant Facilities.

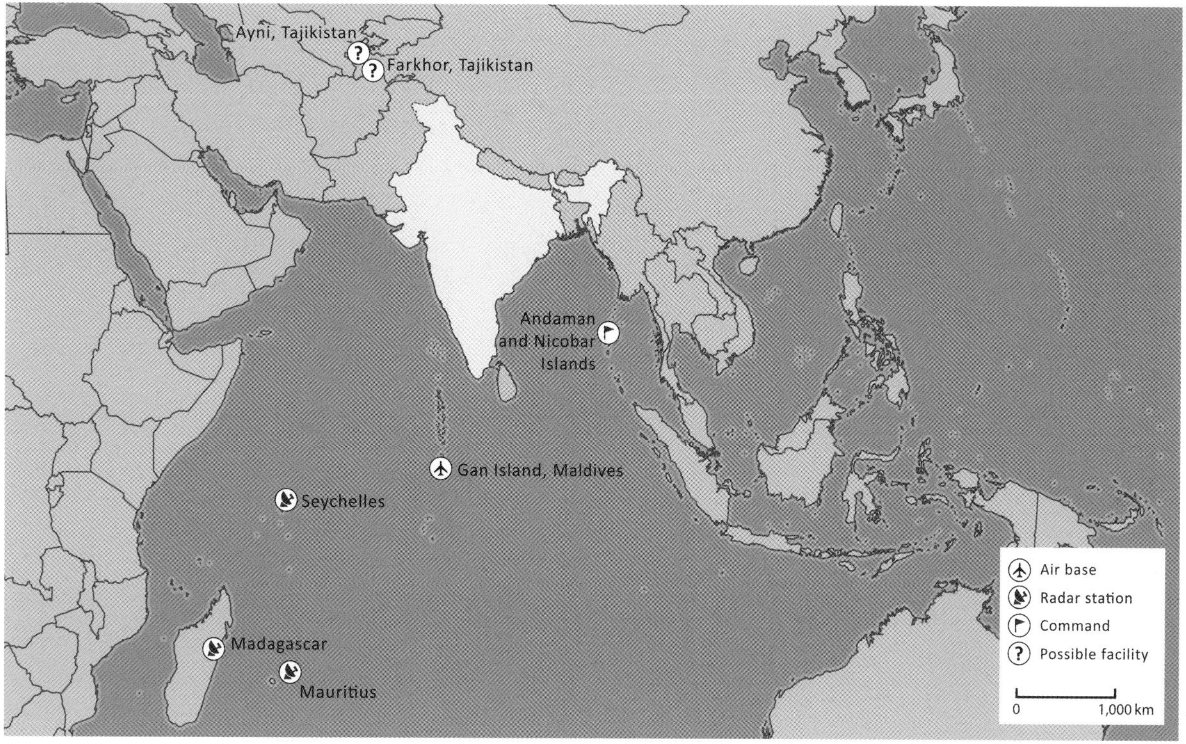

Ayni, Tajikistan

Farkhor, Tajikistan

Andaman and Nicobar Islands

Gan Island, Maldives

Seychelles

Madagascar

Mauritius

Air base
Radar station
Command
Possible facility

0   1,000 km

INTRODUCTION

In the thirty years before India became independent, its army was sent abroad to fight Afghans and Bolsheviks, Germans and Ottomans, Japanese and Iranians. It was a truly expeditionary force, hardened in high-intensity warfare at great distance from Indian soil.[1] But in the nearly seventy years thereafter, Indian military history has been written largely on the country's northern land borders.[2] The three most important exceptions have been numerous UN peacekeeping operations (1947–present), an ill-fated counter-insurgency campaign in Sri Lanka (1987–90) and a modest intervention in the Maldives (1988). But the fiercest, bloodiest and most consequential wars have been local ones. 'India', noted the American scholar George Tanham in a seminal 1992 essay, 'remains a largely land-oriented nation'.[3] 'Indian military power', agreed a major Indian study twenty years later, 'has a continental orientation'.[4]

This is still true. Vast swathes of India's northern and eastern periphery are unsettled: China and India share the longest disputed border in the world; rebels move freely in and out of Myanmar; and the Line of Control that divides India and Pakistan is increasingly violent as the decade-old ceasefire has eroded in recent years. India's military machine – built around roughly three-dozen divisions, around half of which are foot-mobile infantry – is tailored to these traditional theatres of war. In

---

[1] Roy Kaushik (ed.), *The Indian Army in the Two World Wars* (Boston: Brill, 2011).
[2] Sumit Ganguly, *Conflict Unending: India-Pakistan Tensions Since 1947* (New York, NY: Columbia University Press, 2002); Pradeep P Barua, *The State at War in South Asia* (Lincoln: University of Nebraska Press, 2005), parts 4–6; Daniel P Marston and Chandar S Sundaram (eds), *A Military History of India and South Asia: From the East India Company to the Nuclear Era* (Bloomington, IN: Indiana University Press, 2008), chs. 10–11.
[3] George K Tanham, *Indian Strategic Thought: An Interpretive Essay* (Santa Monica, CA: RAND Corporation, 1992), p. vii.
[4] Sunil Khilnani et al., 'Non-Alignment 2.0: A Foreign and Strategic Policy for India in the Twenty First Century', Centre for Policy Research (CPR), 2012, p. 38.

addition, huge paramilitary forces are deployed to fight jihadist, left-wing and separatist militancy across the country.

Yet, in important ways, India is surmounting some of the natural inertia of a large land power. Its policy elite – elected leaders, diplomats, military officers and writers – are still wary of entangling alliances and military adventurism, which they associate with colonial and superpower excess, but they are nevertheless embracing new and more ambitious tasks for the country's growing military. The farthest-reaching of these tasks, figuratively and literally, is military power projection: using force hundreds or even thousands of kilometres beyond the plains of Punjab or mountains of Kashmir, right up to the Indian Ocean littoral and perhaps farther still. Such power projection was, and remains, the preserve of a handful of world powers – largely the US and its two major European allies, Britain and France, conditioned to faraway wars by history, hardware and geography. Other states, like Saudi Arabia and its allies in the Gulf Cooperation Council (GCC), have embraced some types of power projection in recent years – though largely into adjacent territory, with extensive American involvement, and under an American security umbrella. Others still are rediscovering habits of power projection, most notably Russia with its foray into Syria since September 2015.

India is in a significantly different political and strategic position. It lacks political consensus and instinctive national support for long-distance wars, as well as the natural closeness to the US that drives and enables British power projection. Its defence budget, as we shall see, is large and growing, but remains smaller in aggregate than that of every permanent member of the UN Security Council, four-fifths that of Saudi Arabia and scarcely larger than Germany's. Most importantly, its threat perception remains dominated by the allied nuclear powers of Pakistan to the northwest and China to the north that create the daunting possibility of a two-front war.[5] Contrary to commonly held wisdom, India's conventional superiority over Pakistan is largely a myth, given India's long mobilisation times and small munition stockpiles.[6] India, in short, has much on its plate at home. Why, then, is it also sending signals and acquiring combat platforms – aircraft carriers, landing ships, refuelling tankers and transporters – that suggest a broadening of military horizons? And are India's emerging capabilities commensurate with these ambitions or

---

[5] Vinod Anand, 'Review of the Indian Army Doctrine: Dealing with Two Fronts', *CLAWS Journal* (Summer 2010).
[6] Walter C Ladwig III, 'Indian Military Modernization and Conventional Deterrence in South Asia', *Journal of Strategic Studies* (Vol. 38, No. 4, May 2015); Christopher Clary, 'Deterrence Stability and the Conventional Balance of Forces in South Asia', Stimson Center, October 2013.

merely the accoutrements of a rising power more interested in status than combat power?

This introduction seeks to do three things. First, it sets out why India might be investing in military capabilities that, on the face of it, divert resources away from land wars that could directly affect the country's territorial integrity: Why, in short, is India considering power projection at all? Second, it defines power projection as a concept: Why is projecting military power different from using it in the ordinary fashion? Third, it explains the component parts of power projection and therefore the structure of this study: Why is it useful to draw a distinction between air-power projection and land-power projection?

Why Power Projection?

Power Projection in Indian History

Indian power projection has not emerged out of the blue. India's military commitments during both world wars, though under British direction, were among the farthest-flung of any major power. India began sending forces to UN peacekeeping operations from 1950 onward, becoming one of the world's largest troop contributors. Today, India is giving belated attention to its contributions in the World Wars and renewed recognition to its peacekeeping operations – in part as an effort towards its bid for a permanent seat on the UN Security Council.[7] In addition, India also sent forces to both Sri Lanka and the Maldives in the 1980s outside of a UN mandate, though ostensibly at the invitation of host governments, and even despatched a sizeable contingent of paramilitary forces to shield Indian construction workers in Afghanistan after 2001. These episodes are detailed in Chapter I.

India acquired its first aircraft carrier, the INS *Vikrant* (the ex-HMS *Hercules*), in 1961, at a time when its per capita GDP was two-thirds the average for sub-Saharan Africa.[8] India's naval investments dried up after a massive military defeat at China's hands in 1962. But by 1989 – when India made up just 0.5 per cent of world trade and 1.5 per cent of global output,[9] had a per capita GDP still less than that of Pakistan, Liberia

---

[7] Ashok Malik, 'Modi and the World Wars: India Hasn't Yet Understood Its Own Role as International Security Provider', *Times of India*, 2 May 2015.

[8] Calculated from World Bank, 'GDP per Capita (Current US$)', <http://data.worldbank.org/indicator/NY.GDP.PCAP.CD?order=wbapi_data_value_2013+wbapi_data_value+wbapi_data_value-last&sort=asc>, accessed 18 June 2015.

[9] Indian Ministry of Finance, 'Chapter 14: India and the Global Economy', *Economic Survey 2011–12* (New Delhi: Ministry of Finance, 2012), p. 340.

and Ghana,[10] and was about to embark on over a decade of gruelling counter-insurgency in Kashmir[11] – the Indian Navy was operating two aircraft carriers, a fleet of Sea Harriers, and a nuclear-powered submarine leased from the Soviet Union.[12]

These capabilities were outwardly impressive but militarily limited. The civil servant in charge of India's defence ministry noted plaintively at the time that, while he had heard much talk of a blue-water navy, 'he would be happy to have a clear-water navy', suggesting that India's practical reach was quite limited.[13] India's peacekeeping operations were, with a few exceptions, sedate affairs. Some that were not, like Sri Lanka, resulted in abject failure, leaving a cautionary Vietnam-like imprint on its political elite.[14] India's political and economic circumstances – the breakdown of single-party dominance in the 1960s, the suspension of democracy in the 1970s, domestic insurgency and a 'crisis of governability' in the 1980s,[15] and six prime ministers in fewer than ten years in the 1990s[16] – also kept India's ambitions limited. While the late 1980s and 1990s were a time of quiet rapprochement in Sino–Indian relations, Indo–Pakistani relations were in (potentially nuclear) crisis in 1986–87 and 1990; both states fought a small war in 1999; and India faced a Pakistan-backed rebellion in Kashmir throughout the period.[17] India lacked the surplus resources – economic, political and military – to project significant force at a distance. But over the past twenty-five years, these circumstances have changed greatly.[18] India's rise has involved concomitant economic growth, political stability, diplomatic realignment, a re-casting of its international role and military modernisation.

---

[10] World Bank, 'GDP per Capita (Current US$)'.

[11] Sumantra Bose, *Kashmir: Roots of Conflict, Paths to Peace* (Cambridge, MA: Harvard University Press, 2003), ch. 3.

[12] International Institute for Strategic Studies, *Military Balance 1989–1990* (London: IISS/Brassey's, 1989).

[13] Tanham, *Indian Strategic Thought*, p. 66, footnote 22.

[14] P A Ghosh, *Ethnic Conflict in Sri Lanka and Role of Indian Peace Keeping Force (I.P.K.F.)* (New Delhi: APH Publishing, 1999), chs. 6–7.

[15] Atul Kohli, *Democracy and Discontent: India's Growing Crisis of Governability* (Cambridge: Cambridge University Press, 1990), pp. 3–9.

[16] Ramachandra Guha, *India after Gandhi: The History of the World's Largest Democracy*, 1st ed. (New York, NY: Ecco, 2007), p. 665.

[17] Kanti P Bajpai et al., *Brasstacks and Beyond: Perception and Management of Crisis in South Asia* (New Delhi: Manohar, 1995); P R Chari, Pervaiz Iqbal Cheema, and Stephen P Cohen, *Four Crises and a Peace Process: American Engagement in South Asia* (Washington, DC: Brookings Institution Press, 2007).

[18] For a survey, see Stephen P Cohen, *India: Emerging Power* (Washington, DC: Brookings Institution Press, 2001).

Drivers of Indian Power Projection

The most important of these enabling conditions is the first: economic growth. During 1990–91, Iraq's invasion of Kuwait and the resulting crisis caused a spike in oil prices, and in turn a balance-of-payments crisis in India's weak and unproductive economy.[19] India responded by partially liberalising its economy. In the forty years before that point, India's annual GDP growth had averaged 4 per cent; in the period since, it has averaged 6.7 per cent.[20] Between 2003 and 2010, a period that roughly coincides with the first term (2004–09) of the Congress Party-led government headed by Prime Minister Manmohan Singh, India underwent the most dramatic and sustained expansion in its modern history even as the global financial crisis hit Western economies from 2007.[21]

More resources enabled more to be spent on hard power. As detailed in Chapter I, real-terms Indian defence spending more than doubled between 1990 and 2014, growing at a faster rate than all the large military powers other than Saudi Arabia and China. India spent more of this on procurement and less on salaries and other expenditure, enabling it to invest more in the large and increasingly costly platforms necessary for modern power projection. Some plans, such as that for an indigenously built Indian aircraft carrier, pre-dated economic liberalisation, but were nevertheless buoyed by it. Others followed. In 1994, for instance, New Delhi opened talks with Moscow to buy the aircraft carrier *Admiral Gorshkov*, finally receiving the ship a decade later in 2014.

As India has grown in wealth and military power, so too have its interests. As the American analyst Ashley Tellis observes, 'India's rising national power has sensitized New Delhi to its larger interests throughout the vast Indo-Pacific region – from the east coast of Africa to the Persian Gulf to the Southeast Asian straits and even beyond, to the distant East Asian rimlands.'[22] This is unsurprising: as powers rise, they typically acquire new interests, and attach greater importance to – and, in due course, sometimes defend – previously marginal ones. The US between the late nineteenth century and the early twentieth century presents a number of examples of this phenomenon.[23] Crises that might once have

---

[19] Vijay Joshi and I M D Little, *India's Economic Reforms, 1991–2001* (Oxford: Clarendon Press, 1996), pp. 1–2, 14–15, 44–45.

[20] Surjit S Bhalla, 'The How and Why of Economic Growth in India, 1950–2012', in Robert E Looney (ed.), *Handbook of Emerging Economies* (London: Routledge, 2014), p. 61.

[21] *Ibid.*, p. 75.

[22] Ashley J Tellis, 'Making Waves: Aiding India's Next-Generation Aircraft Carrier', Carnegie Endowment for International Peace, April 2015, p. 5.

[23] Fareed Zakaria, *From Wealth to Power: The Unusual Origins of America's World Role* (Princeton, NJ: Princeton University Press, 1998).

been viewed as safely distant become transformed, by the alchemy of prosperity and power, into more pressing threats to vital national interests. As Fareed Zakaria argues, however, this process can be slow and halting, with 'crises and galvanizing events' resulting in reassessments of national power and bursts of expansion or activity.[24]

The clearest manifestation of this shift is the way in which Indian politicians have described the domain of Indian interests. In the late 1990s, 'Aden to Malacca' became popular shorthand, invoked by Indian officials up to the prime minster himself.[25] In 2004, Prime Minister Singh told a conference of Indian military commanders that 'our strategic footprint covers the region bounded by the Horn of Africa, West Asia, Central Asia, South-East Asia and beyond, to the far reaches of the Indian Ocean', and that 'awareness of this reality should inform and animate our strategic thinking and defence planning'.[26] In 2006, Foreign Minister Pranab Mukherjee described this as India's 'extended frontier'. In October 2014, Prime Minister Narendra Modi told commanders that he envisaged India as 'one of the anchors of regional and global security'.[27] Such language has come to be seen as normal, but it represents a rupture from the rhetoric of the 1980s and early 1990s.

What are those Indian interests that supposedly span such a large distance? They include a mixture of the old and the new, the explicit and the unstated. Some reflect longstanding concerns which India was previously less able to influence, while others arise from the country's deepening integration into the global economy and the changing balance of power in Asia.

Some of the most important interests might be grouped into five categories, in no particular order.[28] First is the regional balance of power. This includes Pakistani and Chinese influence and presence in the region,

---

[24] *Ibid.*, p. 11.

[25] C Raja Mohan, 'Looking beyond Malacca', *Indian Express*, 11 October 2011.

[26] Extracts from Prime Minister's Address, Combined Commanders Conference 2004', *Press Information Bureau, Government of India*, 26 October 2004, <http://bit.ly/1RYtqZ2>; quoted in Walter C Ladwig III, 'India and Military Power Projection: Will the Land of Gandhi Become a Conventional Great Power?', *Asian Survey* (Vol. 50, No. 6, November 2010), p. 1170.

[27] PM India, 'PM's Address at the Combined Commanders Conference', news updates, 17 October 2014, <http://pmindia.gov.in/en/news_updates/pms-address-at-the-combined-commanders-conference/>, accessed 19 October 2015.

[28] These categories are distilled from studies including Atul Kohli and Prerna Singh (eds), *Routledge Handbook of Indian Politics* (Oxford: Routledge, 2013), chs. 27–28, 31–32; David Scott (ed.), *Handbook of India's International Relations* (London: Routledge, 2011), chs. 12–18, 23–25; Kanti Bajpai, Saira Basit and V Krishnappa (eds), *India's Grand Strategy: History, Theory, Cases* (New Delhi: Routledge, 2014), part III.

and adverse political shifts in third countries that might affect this. Second is transnational terrorism that could target India, notably in Afghanistan and Pakistan, but stretching beyond those two states. Third is economic security, including reliable energy flows and the security of Indian capital overseas. Fourth is the security and status of Indian diasporas abroad. Fifth is the so-called global commons, ranging from sea-lane security to the other types of policing and stabilisation. A sixth factor – more a means than an end – is the flourishing of the Indo–US relationship in the past ten to twenty years. While this does not drive Indian power projection, it plays a role in Indian debates over it, and is therefore considered here too.

The first of these five factors – India's interest in maintaining a favourable regional balance of power – is especially affected by the fundamental change in China's position. Between 2005 and 2015 alone, China's economy grew four times larger, while its military spending tripled. 'Never before in history', writes the Harvard scholar Graham Allison, 'has a nation risen so far, so fast, on so many dimensions of power'.[29] The growth of Chinese power has broadened the traditional scope of the Sino–Indian rivalry from continental to maritime dimensions, and therefore lent new importance to power projection. The sustained growth of China's economy through the 2000s coincided with a period of heightened antagonism over the Sino–Indian border, likely fanned by Chinese concerns over the stability of Tibet and the implications of Indo–US rapprochement. India grew increasingly worried about the widening economic gap as well as China's military modernisation. Part of the Indian response was a localised military build-up, such as the construction of new roads and airstrips near the border, and investment in new, mountain-oriented units. But India also sought alternative means to counter Chinese strength, one of which was exploiting China's dependence on long, vulnerable sea lanes that pass through numerous chokepoints. Some Indian analysts, for instance, argue that India could 'shut down the Indian Ocean shipping lanes whenever it chooses', and that investment in the power-projection platforms necessary for this mission against the 'Chinese jugular' ought to be prioritised over land power.[30]

It is also important to recognise that India's armed forces have translated these new interests into new roles, with greater or lesser degrees of enthusiasm. The Indian Army, the most focused on traditional fronts of all three services, has done so haltingly and with little zeal. The

---

[29] Graham Allison, 'The Thucydides Trap: Are the U.S. and China Headed for War?', *The Atlantic*, 24 September 2015.
[30] Shashank Joshi, 'Can India Blockade China?', *The Diplomat*, 12 August 2013.

air force has been more eager, and the navy, the most intrinsically expeditionary, most of all. Army doctrines of 2004 and 2009 both make reference to power projection, while the latter lists 'out of area contingencies' as of one of five major priorities.[31] Successive statements of Indian Navy doctrine and strategy, notably in 2007 and 2009, list power projection as a task and define 'primary areas of maritime interest' to include the Persian Gulf, the Cape of Good Hope and the Strait of Malacca and Singapore.[32] The Indian Air Force's (IAF) doctrine of 2012 places 'force projection within India's strategic area of influence' in its basic vision statement.[33] That same year, India's twelfth defence plan published by the Defence Acquisition Council (DAC), a body headed by the defence minister, and whose decisions are implemented by three boards, notes that its naval objectives are, inter alia, to 'build adequate stand off capability for sea lift and expeditionary operations to achieve desired power projection force levels'.[34] The growing salience of power projection to the military is taken up in Chapter I.

One last factor is worth considering: growing Indo–US alignment, and American support for India as a regional security provider. This is not a major driver of Indian capabilities, but it might support them, both directly and indirectly. Beginning in the late 1990s, accelerating in the early 2000s and surging after a major Indo–US defence agreement was signed in 2005, many American observers have viewed India as a partner, or 'natural ally'.[35] This rapprochement, coming after decades of Indo–Soviet partnership and Indo–US estrangement, was related to broad, structural factors – the shift of economic power towards the Asia-Pacific, the sustained economic growth of China and various American efforts to manage the effects of China's rise in Asia – as well as key policy initiatives taken by successive American presidents, notably George W Bush.[36]

---

[31] Headquarters Army Training Command, 'Indian Army Doctrine', October 2004, pp. 6, 9–10; Anand, 'Review of the Indian Army Doctrine', p. 259.

[32] Integrated Headquarters, Ministry of Defence (Navy), 'Freedom to Use the Seas: India's Maritime Military Strategy', May 2007; Integrated Headquarters, Ministry of Defence (Navy), 'Indian Maritime Doctrine', 2009, p. 68.

[33] Indian Air Force, 'Basic Doctrine of the Indian Air Force: 2012', 2012, p. 1.

[34] Indian Ministry of Defence, 'Demands for Grants (2012–2013)', fifteenth report to the Standing Committee on Defence, April 2012, p. 70.

[35] Rudra Chaudhuri, *Forged in Crisis: India and the United States since 1947* (Noida, Uttar Pradesh: HarperCollins Publishers India, 2014), part III; Evan A Feigenbaum, 'India's Rise, America's Interest: The Fate of the U.S.–Indian Partnership', *Foreign Affairs* (Vol. 89, No. 2, March/April 2010); C Raja Mohan, *Crossing the Rubicon: The Shaping of India's New Foreign Policy* (New York, NY: Palgrave Macmillan, 2004).

[36] Teresita C Schaffer, *India and the United States in the 21st Century: Reinventing Partnership* (Washington, DC: CSIS Press, 2009), pp. 65–88.

One central feature of American perceptions of India has been the notion that India's economic and military rise allows it to 'provide' security to a much broader area than before, rather than simply protect its own national borders. When then-Secretary of State Colin Powell underwent confirmation hearings in 2001, for instance, he told the US Senate, 'India has the potential to help keep the peace in the vast Indian Ocean area and its periphery'.[37] The 2006 US National Security Strategy (NSS) declared: 'India now is poised to shoulder global obligations in cooperation with the United States in a way befitting a major power'.[38] In 2009, then-Secretary of Defense Robert Gates announced, 'we look to India to be a ... net provider of security in the Indian Ocean and beyond', phrasing that was repeated in the next year's Quadrennial Defense Review (QDR).[39] Then in 2015, the NSS endorsed 'India's role as a regional provider of security' in more explicit terms than ever before.[40] Others have echoed this language. Ashley Tellis, who played an important role in this process a decade ago, writes that 'if India can achieve the economic and geopolitical success it seeks for its own development, it could in time become a security provider in the Indian Ocean basin, easing U.S. burdens there'.[41]

Indians themselves have accepted and echoed this language, though not without significant reservations. In 2013, Prime Minister Manmohan Singh agreed that 'we are well positioned ... to become a net provider of security in our immediate region and beyond'.[42] In 2015, India's foreign minister took this a step further and declared at the UN General Assembly that 'India has emerged as a net security provider' (though tellingly, she cited only non-combat humanitarian and evacuation operations in Nepal and Yemen).[43]

---

[37] Committee on Foreign Relations, 'Nomination of Colin L. Powell to Be Secretary of State', Hearing before the Committee on Foreign Relations, United States Senate, S HRG 107–114, January 2001, p. 34.

[38] White House, 'The National Security Strategy of the United States of America', March 2006, p. 39.

[39] Anit Mukherjee, 'India as a Net Security Provider: Concept and Impediments', Policy Brief, S Rajaratnam School of International Studies, August 2014, p. 1.

[40] White House, 'National Security Strategy', February 2015), p. 25.

[41] Ashley J Tellis, 'Kick-Starting the U.S.-Indian Strategic Partnership', Carnegie Endowment for International Peace, September 2014.

[42] Vinay Kumar, 'India Well Positioned to Become a Net Provider of Security: Manmohan Singh', *The Hindu*, 23 May 2013.

[43] Sushma Swaraj, 'Speech by External Affairs Minister at the General Assembly of the United Nations – The UN at 70: A Time for Action', Ministry of External Affairs, Government of India, 1 October 2015, <http://www.mea.gov.in/Speeches-Statements.htm?dtl/25878/English_rendering_of_Speech_by_External_Affairs_

Net security provision, nebulous as the term is, would seem to include at least the possibility of India contributing military forces to address threats to the regional or global 'commons', such as patrolling sea lanes, or contributing to multinational military operations to protect or restore the status quo, even where Indian interests may not directly be at risk. To be sure, Indian elites continue to reject any notion of a formal military alliance. India is not interested in deputising for the US as a junior partner, as Britain is sometimes seen to have done.[44] But the willingness of the Modi government to all but endorse the US rebalance to Asia and to invoke the South China Sea dispute in successive top-level communiqués is a powerful indication of India's willingness to align its rhetoric on security with that of Washington. This may well influence its future decisions about power projection. India rejected joining the US war in Iraq in 2003 after giving it serious consideration, and again rejected participation in air strikes in Iraq and Syria in 2014, but it may look upon other more modest or regionally focused requests in the future with greater favour. The US, in turn, has offered unprecedented military technology transfers to India, including assistance with India's indigenous aircraft carrier, which would meaningfully augment India's power-projection capabilities.[45]

Understanding These Drivers
These factors – economic and military growth, broadening interests, the rise of China and the military's willing adoption of new roles – have been among the primary drivers of Indian interest and investment in power-projection capabilities. A sixth related factor, US support for India as a regional security provider, is shaping the Indian and international debate around India's military roles. These factors are clearly interrelated. For instance, parochial pressures for service-specific prestige platforms can shape a country's force structure and that, in turn, can generate incentives to find rationales for the new capabilities. This is a military variant of the hammer-nail problem: a country with long-range capabilities might 'learn' to fear more distant threats that do not trouble lesser-endowed peers. Britain and France, for instance, are far more militarily active in the Middle East than equally large economies with similar equities in the region.

It is also far from clear how, exactly, India plans to prioritise that long list of interests, which spans the highly specific to the very general, and the modest to the ambitious. Patrolling sea lanes is relatively straightforward

---

Minister_at_the_General_Assembly_of_the_United_Nations__The_UN_at_70_A_ Time_for_Action>, accessed 19 October 2015.
[44] Chaudhuri, *Forged in Crisis*, pp. 255–65.
[45] Shishir Gupta, 'US Offers India State-of-the-Art Gear for New Aircraft Carrier', *Hindustan Times*, 6 June 2015.

and will be interpreted by smaller powers in benign terms; targeting terrorists in Central Asia or joining a multinational stabilisation force in Southeast Asia is much harder and more likely to elicit questions about India's ambitions. Beyond its immediate neighbours, India is currently seen as a largely – though certainly not exclusively – benign military actor, and a more activist defence posture could erode that status, particularly among those smaller states that sit closer to India than China and have in the past been at the sharp end of Indian power.

We can, however, deduce some answers to the question of prioritisation by looking at the shape and direction of India's power-projection capabilities, taken up in Chapters II, III and IV. What is clear is that Indian elites have often defined Indian objectives in aspirational terms, while making specific policy choices that point to more modest aims in practice. While Indian capabilities are growing at a quickening pace, investments have nevertheless been incremental, limited and have an emphasis on 'dual-use' capabilities that have applications in local wars (for instance, transport aircraft). India is currently more interested in soft power-projection missions – such as disaster relief or anti-piracy – than harder and more demanding missions. It can perform some more demanding missions, but only – as this study shows – in a narrow range of circumstances. Of course, even these limited investments lay the groundwork for a more ambitious turn to power projection, should future Indian governments opt for this.

What is Power Projection?

Why Power Projection Matters
There are plenty of books and journal articles on India's armed forces, many of them providing in-depth analysis of how India's military is structured and how it might fare in a war with Pakistan. Is power projection different?

For one thing, military history and modern strategic studies have tended to treat the use of force differently depending on whether it occurs within or adjacent to national borders, or beyond. This is in part a legacy of the distinction between interior and exterior lines of communication: the presumed ease of movement and supply of armed forces within one's own terrain relative to doing so on neutral or hostile terrain.[46] The distinction between types of force also stems from a related, but distinct, idea, popularised by the American academic John Mearsheimer, of the 'stopping power of water': the notion that the power of armies is sharply

---

[46] Carl von Clausewitz, *On War*, revised edition, edited and translated by Peter Paret and Michael Eliot Howard (Princeton, NJ: Princeton University Press, 1984), pp. 345–47.

limited, in number and firepower, when traversing large bodies of water to hostile territory.[47] One might add to this the stopping power (or, more properly, resistance) of spatial distance in general.[48] In other words, it is harder for states to move armed forces over water than land, harder to move them over territory that is not theirs, and harder to move over longer distances than shorter ones. Naturally, it would be harder for India to fight a war deep inside Tibet or on the Arabian shoreline than on the edges of the country – much as, other things being equal, it is harder for NATO to fight in Afghanistan than on the North German Plain.

As a consequence, many scholars accord a special status to those states capable of surmounting these difficulties. Jack Levy, for instance, defines a great power as one that possesses not just 'relative self-sufficiency with respect to security', but also 'the ability to project military power beyond its borders in pursuit of its interests.'[49] Great powers are distinguished in this projection by 'the total amount of power projected, the logistical ability to sustain it over an extended period, and the ability to affect the overall distribution of power at the systemic level' – that is, between the top handful of states.[50] In his 1993 article 'The Unipolar Illusion', Christopher Layne described the central feature of US hegemony – and of the responses of other large powers to it – largely in terms of power projection.[51] Popular discussions of the great-power status of the UK, France and China frequently invoke possession of aircraft carriers. Power projection, then, allows a state to influence developments and exert leverage at a greater distance, and is associated with a particular status in world politics, which can itself bring particular benefits, such as inclusion at the proverbial 'top tables' and privileged relationships with smaller powers. Despite this, the component parts of power projection remain under-theorised.

Defining Power Projection
The US Department of Defense defines power projection as 'the ability of a nation to apply all or some of its elements of national power – political, economic, informational, or military – to rapidly and effectively deploy

---

[47] John J Mearsheimer, *The Tragedy of Great Power Politics* (New York, NY: WW Norton, 2003), ch. 4.
[48] Patrick Porter, *The Global Village Myth: Distance, War, and the Limits of Power* (London: Hurst, 2015), p. 10.
[49] Jack S Levy, *War in the Modern Great Power System: 1495–1975* (Lexington, KY: University Press of Kentucky, 2015), p. 14.
[50] *Ibid.*
[51] Christopher Layne, 'The Unipolar Illusion: Why New Great Powers Will Rise', *International Security* (Vol. 17, No. 4, Spring 1993), pp. 5, 35–39.

and sustain forces in and from multiple dispersed locations'.[52] This is a confusing and over-broad definition, one that would include nearly any use of military force, whether in neighbouring territory or on the other side of the globe, as well as non-military power. Power projection is better understood as the use of different elements of national power beyond – and typically a significant distance from – one's immediate land and maritime borders.[53] British doctrine accordingly defines 'expeditionary warfare' – here, synonymous with power projection – as 'the projection of military power over extended lines of communication into a distant operational area to accomplish a specific objective'.[54] This would exclude purely non-kinetic instruments, such as sanctions. It should also presume the possibility of conflict: deploying platforms into wholly permissive environments, such as friendly port calls, is better understood as *influence* projection rather than power projection. Other environments, where direct combat is unlikely, but resistance and opposition of some kind are possible – such as Iran's use of naval vessels to challenge the Saudi-led coalition's blockade of Yemen in 2015[55]– lie within my definition.

We should also distinguish between conventional and unconventional power projection. The latter would include the use of cyber-weapons, information warfare or support for non-state actors. Each of these activities has proved important in modern conflicts. Examples, respectively, include the kinetic effect the US achieved with its use of the Stuxnet malware against the Iranian nuclear programme from 2007 onwards; Russia's sophisticated disinformation campaign to accompany its invasion and annexation of Ukrainian territory in 2014; and the 2001 US air campaign in Afghanistan in aid of the Northern Alliance.[56] These are examples of enduring and important elements of national power, capable

---

[52] Barry Leonard (ed.), 'Department of Defense Dictionary of Military and Associated Terms', amended through April 2010, Joint Publication 1-02, January 2011, p. 367.

[53] For a similar definition, see Dennis C Blair, 'Military Power Projection in Asia', in Ashley J Tellis, Mercy Kuo and Andrew Marble (eds), *Strategic Asia 2008–09: Challenges and Choices* (Washington, DC: National Bureau of Asian Research, 2008), pp. 398–403.

[54] Robert Fry, 'Expeditionary Operations in the Modern Era', *RUSI Journal* (Vol. 150, No. 6, December 2005), p. 60.

[55] Ladane Nasseri, Nafeesa Syeed, and Deema Almashabi, 'Iranian Aid Ship Nears Yemen, Raising Risk of Saudi Showdown', *Bloomberg*, 17 May 2015.

[56] See, respectively, Ivanka Barzashka, 'Are Cyber-Weapons Effective? Assessing Stuxnet's Impact on the Iranian Enrichment Programme', *RUSI Journal* (Vol. 158, No. 2, March/April 2013); Sam Jones, 'Ukraine: Russia's New Art of War', *Financial Times*, 28 August 2014. See also Stephen D Biddle, 'Allies, Airpower, and Modern Warfare: The Afghan Model in Afghanistan and Iraq', *International Security* (Vol. 30, No. 3, Winter 2005/06).

of being used independently or in aid of conventional power projection. In this study, they are relevant insofar as they enable and enhance conventional military power projection, something explored in Chapter IV.

A Typology of Power Projection

Having defined power projection, it is necessary to specify its different elements. Walter Ladwig, in his assessment of Indian power projection, breaks the concept down in two ways: first into three components of military power (sea, land and air); and second into nine different missions (from 'soft', such as non-combatant evacuation, to 'hard', such as armed intervention abroad).[57] In the interests of parsimony and generalisability, I propose disaggregating power projection somewhat differently, into two broad and more fundamental categories of capability: air-power projection and land-power projection.

Almost all types of power projection can be distilled down into these two forms, because kinetic effect is, in the vast majority of cases, ultimately *delivered* by air (air power) or ground forces (land power) even if it is *conveyed* by air, land and sea.[58] Air-power projection refers to destroying targets at long range using air-delivered platforms and munitions. This includes land-based and naval strike aircraft, as well as ground-, air- and sea-launched missiles. Land-power projection refers to sending ground forces to the target. This includes both the combat forces themselves – including air-assault, airborne-assault and amphibious forces – as well as the transport platforms that deliver and supply them, such as transport aircraft and ships.

There are three caveats to this schema. First, I avoid the term sea power in this study, because its relevant aspects – aircraft carriers and amphibious forces – can be subsumed under each of these two respective headings. In almost all cases, sea power is ultimately delivered from the air (as with carrier-based strike) or by ground forces (as with amphibious operations). This is an unorthodox categorisation, but it confers the advantage of allowing us to analyse comparable platforms, such as land-based and naval aircraft, alongside one another. Second, and in part as a result, I have avoided discussing sea control and sea denial. The former might be better understood as a prerequisite to power projection, rather than being projection in its own right, and is closely linked to naval air power; the latter, in an offensive sense, refers to strikes against a very specific range of targets (ships), and is addressed briefly and partially in Chapter II in the context of India's modest submarine fleet. Nevertheless, I acknowledge that the narrow case of interdiction and blockade deserves greater discussion than has been possible here. Third, I recognise that these are not clearly distinct categories. As I

---

[57] Ladwig, 'India and Military Power Projection'.

[58] One exception would be shore bombardment by sea-based guns.

Table 1: Examples of Force Projection by Threat and Persistence.

	High Persistence	Low Persistence
High Threat	**Longer Range** Iraq War, 2003–08	**Longer Range** Falklands War, 1982 US raid on Osama bin Laden's hideout in Pakistan, 2011

	Shorter Range
	Indian intervention in Sri Lanka,
	  1987–90
	Israeli intervention in Lebanon,
	  1982
		Shorter Range
		Israeli strike on Iraq, 1981

Low Threat	**Longer Range**
	NATO-led intervention in Libya,
	  2011
		Longer Range
		US strikes on Afghanistan and
		  Sudan, 1998

	Shorter Range Australian-led intervention in East Timor, 1999–2000	**Shorter Range** US intervention in Grenada, 1983

discuss in Chapter III, naval air power is an important component of virtually any amphibious operation, and air-assault or airborne forces are dependent on broader air-lift capabilities. Notwithstanding these issues, this schema provides a structure to assess the power-projection capabilities of any state, including India, in a systematic manner. It splits up capability by what is being projected (air strikes or land power), rather than the service doing it or the specific mission (showing the flag or a major amphibious assault).

Power-projection capabilities can also be assessed in terms of the threat, persistence and range of any given operation. Threat refers to the degree of enemy resistance to the projected combat forces; persistence to the time for which the force has to be projected and sustained; and range to the geographical and effective distance involved. This division, summarised in Table 1, is worth bearing in mind as we consider the potential applications of Indian power projection in subsequent chapters. The number and type of Indian capabilities point more to short- and medium-term operations in the lower row, and particularly in the bottom-right cell.

The remainder of this study proceeds as follows. Chapter I places India's defence posture in historical and regional context. Chapter II then assesses India's air-power projection, including air strikes, while Chapter III turns to land-power projection, including amphibious operations. Chapter IV examines the role of enablers – such as inter-service jointness and intelligence – in turning platforms into a capability. Chapter V concludes the study by asking why, where, and how India might use its power-projection capabilities in the future – and how other states might view this.

I. INDIA'S DEFENCE POSTURE

India is an emerging twenty-first-century power stuck in the groove of twentieth-century conflicts. Even as its influence spreads wider, its likeliest wars will be on its doorstep. This mismatch shapes and constrains its defence posture. No discussion of India's power-projection forces could be meaningful without first understanding the nature of India's armed forces and what they see as their priorities. This chapter begins by setting out the basic size and shape of India's military and trends in its recent development. It then explores some of the most pressing questions confronting the military today: its relationship to the civilian leadership and that between service arms; readiness and standards; and the enduring problem of limited war under Pakistan's increasingly low nuclear thresholds. Finally, the chapter describes how the role of power projection has evolved in India's thinking about defence and India's practical experience in this regard.

By way of context, India has fought four wars with Pakistan: over Kashmir in 1947–49 and 1965; over then-East Pakistan (now Bangladesh) in 1971; and over the Kargil sector of Kashmir in 1999. The latter two were resounding victories, and the former operational successes but strategic draws. India suffered a major and traumatising defeat at the hands of China in 1962.[1] It has also engaged in more limited operations, most recently a cross-border strike in Myanmar by special forces; multiple domestic counter-insurgency campaigns, most prominently in Jammu and Kashmir and in the northeastern states; and, as described below, a series of operations further from India's borders.

Basic Size and Shape

India's armed forces are built around a 1.1-million-strong army, virtually unchanged in size over the past thirty years, as well as a 180-ship navy and

---

[1] Daniel P Marston and Chandar S Sundaram (eds), *A Military History of India and South Asia: From the East India Company to the Nuclear Era* (Bloomington, IN: Indiana University Press, 2008) chs. 10–11; Pradeep P Barua, *The State at War in South Asia* (Lincoln: University of Nebraska Press, 2005), pp. 159–266.

880-plane air force. A ninety-ship coast guard and 1.4-million-strong paramilitary forces – largely tasked to India's various domestic insurgencies – supplement these, as do 300,000 first-line army reservists and half a million with less onerous commitments.[2] In 2014, India's annual military expenditure was approximately $50 billion: the seventh-highest in the world; 2.8 per cent of the world total;[3] and a relatively modest 2.4 per cent of GDP.[4]

The army has six operational commands that control thirteen corps in total. Three of these, I, II and XXI, are strike corps, tasked with leading offensive thrusts into Pakistan. Under this are an estimated thirty-four active manoeuvre combat divisions, with four more (all mountain divisions) at various stages of being risen.[5] In 2009, at a time of rising concern over China, India began raising two new mountain divisions to be based in the northeast,[6] and in 2013 announced the creation of a long-mooted mountain strike corps, also oriented towards China, with three further divisions to be in place by 2018–19 (though the latter was slashed for budgetary reasons in April 2015).[7]

The Indian Air Force's numbers are in a period of flux as a generation of Soviet-era fighters is retired, while their replacements erratically trickle in. The backbone of the fleet – just under a third of the total number of combat aircraft – and its primary air-superiority platform consists of the Su-30MKI, an export variant of the Russian Su-30 Flanker, first acquired in 2002 and with more expected over the next several years.[8] India has also settled on the French Dassault

[2] International Institute for Strategic Studies (IISS), *The Military Balance 2015* (London: Routledge/IISS, 2015), p. 247. Unless otherwise specified, military data quoted hereafter should be assumed to come from this source.

[3] Stockholm International Peace Research Institute (SIPRI), 'The Share of World Military Expenditure of the 15 States with the Highest Expenditure in 2014', 2015, <http://goo.gl/EfYtxt>, accessed 20 October 2015.

[4] SIPRI, 'SIPRI Military Expenditure Database 1988–2014', 2015, <http://www.sipri.org/research/armaments/milex/milex_database>, accessed 20 October 2015.

[5] Richard A Rinaldi and Ravi Rikhye, *Indian Army Order of Battle* (General Data LLC, 2011), pp. 12–15; on Re-organised Army Plains Infantry Division (RAPID), see Amit Gupta, *Building an Arsenal: The Evolution of Regional Power Force Structures* (Westport, CT: Praeger, 1997), pp. 58–59. This excludes three artillery divisions.

[6] *Times of India*, 'Army Plans to Raise Arunachal and Sikkim Scouts for China Border', 18 May 2010; Subir Bhaumik, 'India to Deploy 36,000 Extra Troops on Chinese Border', *BBC News*, 23 November 2010.

[7] Nitin A Gokhale, 'So It's Going to Be 17 Mountain Corps?', NewsWarrior, 16 November 2013, <http://nitinagokhale.blogspot.co.uk/2013/11/so-its-going-to-be-17-mountain-corps.html>, accessed 20 October 2015; Rajat Pandit, 'Fund Crunch Hits Army's New Strike Corps', *Times of India*, 16 April 2015.

[8] Gareth Jennings, 'India to Review Safety of Su-30MKI Fighter Fleet', *IHS Jane's Defence Weekly*, 28 May 2015.

Rafale as a more flexible multi-role fighter, though it remains unclear whether it would build on a small order placed in early 2015. The IAF's strength fell to thirty-two combat squadrons by the end of 2015 – roughly the same as a decade ago, but at the low end of the 35–40 fielded from the 1970s to 2000s.[9] In 2011, the IAF asked to build up to forty-five combat squadrons, around 810 aircraft, in response to what it calls a 'two front collusive threat' from what could be 1,500 fourth-generation Pakistani and Chinese fighters, but the government has approved just forty-two squadrons and Defence Minister Manohar Parrikar suggests that 'at least' thirty-seven squadrons might be satisfactory.[10] The Indian parliament's Defence Committee in 2014 assessed the gap between sanctioned and existing strength as 'very grim' and 'dismal'.[11] In practice, the IAF's numerical strength over the next decade is more likely to climb back to the average of the past thirty years, rather than to jump to new heights as some hope. However, as Chapters II and III show, this stagnation in numbers obscures some important shifts in capability.

The Indian Navy shows a similar trend: stagnation in some areas, with growing capability in others. The navy currently operates around fifteen submarines and 125 surface ships.[12] Senior officers once spoke of becoming a 160-ship navy by 2022, and now aim for 200 ships by 2027 – though such boasts are aspirational.[13] The number of India's principal surface combatants, twenty-seven, was exactly the same in 2015 as in 1990 – but it has around twice as many destroyers, more maritime strike aircraft, more advanced maritime patrol aircraft and, for the first time since 1986–1996, two aircraft carriers. Indian shipbuilding is a rare success story for indigenous defence production, with the new *Kolkata-* and *Visakhapatnam*-class destroyers some of the cheapest per tonne

---

[9] Ajay Banerjee, 'IAF Combats Lowest Fighter Strength', *Tribune*, 5 July 2015; George K Tanham and Marcy Agmon, *The Indian Air Force: Trends and Prospects* (Santa Monica, CA: RAND Corporation, 1995), p. 60.

[10] For the estimate of Chinese and Pakistani aircraft numbers, see Ashley J Tellis, 'Dogfight! India's Medium Multi-Role Combat Aircraft Competition Decision', Carnegie Endowment for International Peace, January 2011, pp. 1, 18; Ajai, Shukla, 'India Could Also Buy Light Fighter to Replace MiG-21: Parrikar', *Business Standard*, 14 April 2015.

[11] Indian Ministry of Defence, 'Demands for Grants (2014–2015) Navy and Airforce Demand (Demand No. 23 & 24)', fourth report to the Standing Committee on Defence, December 2012, p. 36.

[12] *IHS*, 'Jane's World Navies: India', 7 May 2015, p. 2; Pradip R Sagar, '4 More French Submarines to Meet Indian Navy's Requirement', *New Indian Express*, 6 October 2015.

[13] Manu Pubby, 'With Six New Nuclear Attack Submarines, India Officially Opens up on its Undersea Aspirations', *Economic Times*, 15 July 2015.

anywhere in the world,[14] and 4–5 new ships being added every year. However, submarine numbers have stalled, falling steadily from nineteen boats in 2005 to fourteen today – the lowest level in almost thirty years. This is well above Taiwan and Vietnam (four apiece), Pakistan (eight), and Australia (nine), but below Japan (eighteen), South Korea (twenty-three) and China (seventy). Despite plans for expansion, Indian submarine numbers will plateau at twenty boats in the 2020s, compared to China's fifty-plus.[15]

Trends

Defence Spending
The first, most prominent and most significant trend in the Indian military has been the rapid growth in defence spending over the past twenty-five years.

According to the Stockholm International Peace Research Institute (SIPRI) figures, real-terms Indian defence spending more than doubled from just under $19 billion in 1990 to around $50 billion in 2014, representing an average annual growth rate of 4.4 per cent (but compared to an average annual growth rate in GDP of 6.6 per cent). This outstrips all other large military spenders over this period other than Saudi Arabia and China (whose budgets grew more than threefold and tenfold respectively).[16] In the most recent figures available, India's 2015/16 budget allocated a little under 247 trillion rupees for defence – just over $38 billion at present exchange rates.[17] (The large discrepancy between this

---

[14] Ajai Shukla, 'INS Visakhapatanam Shows Growing Indian Ability to Build Warships Economically', Broadsword, 21 April 2015, <http://ajaishukla.blogspot.co.uk/2015/04/ins-visakhapatanam-shows-growing-indian.html>, accessed 20 October 2015.

[15] Ajai Shukla, 'A Powerful Surface Navy Lacks Submarine Punch', Broadsword, 2 October 2014, <http://ajaishukla.blogspot.co.uk/2014/10/a-powerful-surface-navy-lacks-submarine.html>, accessed 20 October 2015.

[16] SIPRI, 'SIPRI Military Expenditure Database 1988–2014'. Spending measured in US dollars at constant 2011 prices and exchange rates; note that India excludes defence pensions, paramilitary forces, border security and many import-related costs from its official defence budget, to the point where some argue the true number may be one-third to one-half higher than is reported. See George J Gilboy and Eric Heginbotham, *Chinese and Indian Strategic Behavior: Growing Power and Alarm* (Cambridge: Cambridge University Press, 2012), p. 119.

[17] Laxman K Behera, 'India's Defence Budget 2015–16', Institute for Defence Studies and Analyses, 2 March 2015, <http://www.idsa.in/issuebrief/IndiasDefenceBudget2015–16_lkbehera_020315.html>, accessed 20 October 2015. Calculated at rates prevailing on 9 October 2015.

and the SIPRI figure of $50 billion may arise in part because of the large fall in the rupee's value over the past several years, deflating the dollar value of India's spending, as well as SIPRI's inclusion of spending on paramilitary forces and military pensions.[18] India allocated around $8.4 billion to military pensions for 2014/15 and a recent politically charged decision to boost many retirees' pensions, known as One Rank One Pension, adds a further burden of $4.3 million.[19] These amounts are excluded in official defence-spending figures.) If we accept the SIPRI figure for ease of cross-country comparison, India's present spending is less than a quarter of China's and 8 per cent that of the US, but amounts to nearly 60 per cent of Russia's and over 80 per cent of France's and Britain's.

Economic Growth

Second, India's economic growth has allowed defence spending to rise in absolute terms even as it consumes an ever-smaller share of GDP. India routinely spent above 3 per cent of GDP on defence prior to the 1990s, but now spends a near all-time low of 2.4 per cent. Indian parliamentary committees and commentators have urged that this slide be reversed, but successive governments have been content with the growth in aggregate spending.

Composition of Spending

Third, the balance between different forms of expenditure in Indian defence spending has also shifted. India makes a distinction between revenue, which 'does not result in creating permanent assets' – what in a Western context might be called operating expenditure – and capital, which includes 'permanent assets like land, buildings, and machinery'.[20] While imperfect, the proportion of capital expenditure in overall spending can therefore serve as a very rough indicator of modernisation.[21] Official data suggest

---

[18] On SIPRI's measure, see SIPRI, *SIPRI Yearbook 2011: Armaments, Disarmament and International Security* (Oxford: Oxford University Press, 2011), p. 167. Note that between 2009 and 2014 India's rupee-denominated spending rose by about 63 per cent, while spending in constant (2011) US dollars rose by less than 2 per cent because of the depreciation of the rupee. The latter measure therefore distorts Indian defence spending, much of which is relatively insensitive to inflation in tradeable sectors that shapes the prevailing exchange rate.

[19] Ajai Shukla, 'Army's Manpower Costs Give Reason to Rethink Policy', Broadsword, 9 September 2015, <http://ajaishukla.blogspot.co.uk/2015/09/armys-manpower-costs-give-reason-to.html>, accessed 20 October 2015.

[20] P R Chari, 'India's Defence Expenditure: Can It Be Reduced?', RCSS Policy Studies 12, Regional Centre for Strategic Studies, 2000.

[21] Amiya Kumar Ghosh, *India's Defence Budget and Expenditure Management in a Wider Context* (New Delhi: Lancer Publishers, 1996), pp. 98–99, 106.

Figure 1: Comparative Defence Spending between Selected States, 1990–2014.

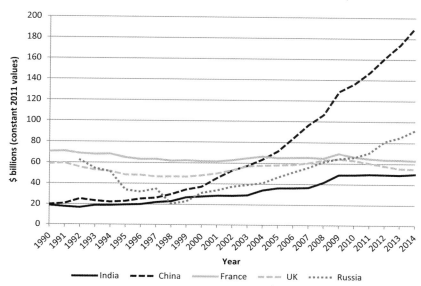

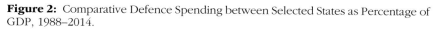

Source: *SIPRI, 'SIPRI Military Expenditure Database 1988–2014'.*

Figure 2: Comparative Defence Spending between Selected States as Percentage of GDP, 1988–2014.

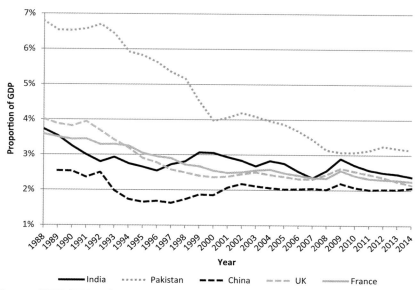

Source: *SIPRI, 'SIPRI Military Expenditure Database 1988–2014'.*

that capital expenditure jumped from under a quarter of spending in 2003 to over a third by 2004, and has hovered around 40 per cent in the decade since.[22] It is possible that this growth is an artefact of accounting changes or growth in spending on areas with little to do with military capability. Without a further breakdown of spending, it is impossible to be sure.

However, it is clear that Indian arms imports – most of which, by value, have been combat platforms – have grown more than overall spending. For instance, between 2005 and 2015, Indian arms imports grew by a factor of 3.6, while overall defence spending grew by just 1.4.[23]

Fourth, there has been a modest rebalancing between the three services – away from the army and towards the navy and, to a lesser extent, the air force.[24] The army in the late 1960s consumed well above 70 per cent of expenditure, but in the second half of the 2000s its share has hovered around 50 per cent. The navy, allocated as little as 2 per cent in the 1960s, and averaging 13 per cent over the 1990s, reached an all-time high of 19 per cent in 2012/13. The air force shows no strong trend, with the average share rising slightly from 24 per cent over the period 1995–2004 to 26 per cent during the period 2005–15. (These numbers do not sum to 100 per cent; the residuals are made up of spending on defence R&D and ordnance factories.) The army continues to be the most expenditure-intensive of the services. In 2015/16, it spent 80 per cent of its allocation on revenue, compared with just 38 and 41 per cent for the navy and air force respectively.[25]

Even on this trend, India remains a land-dominated power. The US defence budget for 2015/16, for instance, allocated under a quarter of spending to the army, against 30 per cent for the navy and 28 per cent for the air force.[26] As of 2005, Japan was spending only 38 per cent on the

---

[22] Laxman Kumar Behera, 'India's Inadequate Defence Budget 2008–09', Institute of Peace and Conflict Studies, 26 March 2008, <http://www.ipcs.org/article/defence/indias-inadequate-defence-budget-2008–09-2521.html>, accessed 20 October 2015; Behera, 'India's Defence Budget 2015–16'. See also the relevant Annual Reports of the Indian Ministry of Defence, available at <http://www.mod.nic.in/forms/List.aspx?Id=57&displayListId=57>.
[23] SIPRI, 'SIPRI Arms Transfers Database 1950–2014', n.d., <http://www.sipri.org/databases/armstransfers>, accessed 20 October 2015.
[24] Pre-1989 data are drawn from Raju G C Thomas, *Indian Security Policy* (Princeton, NJ: Princeton University Press, 1986), p. 191.
[25] Behera, 'India's Defence Budget 2015–16'.
[26] Department of Defense, 'DoD Releases Fiscal Year 2016 Budget Proposal', news release, 2 February 2015, <http://www.defense.gov/Releases/Release.aspx?ReleaseID=17126>, accessed 20 October 2015. Here, as with the Japanese example below, the nature of the residual is unknown.

Figure 3: Indian Arms Imports, 1990–2014.

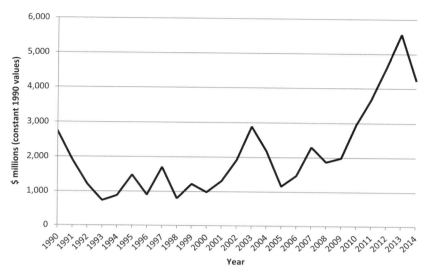

Source: SIPRI, 'SIPRI Arms Transfers Database 1950–2014'.

army, against 23 per cent on both the navy and air force.[27] Nevertheless, the rebalancing between Indian services represents a gradual and modest shift in India's defence posture, favouring more outward-facing forces better configured for power projection. In China, another historically land-focused power, recent White Papers and acquisitions suggest that budget priority is also being given to the navy and air force.[28]

Equipment Purchases

A fifth developing trend, which is likely to become more significant, is the shift, particularly since 2012, from Soviet or Russian weaponry to American and Western hardware, reflecting the Indo–US rapprochement from 2005 onwards. In the mid-1990s, 80 per cent of transport aircraft and helicopters were of Soviet design.[29] Reflecting this procurement legacy,

---

[27] Evan S Medeiros et al., *Pacific Currents: The Responses of U.S. Allies and Security Partners in East Asia to China's Rise* (Santa Monica, CA: RAND Corporation, 2008), p. 51.
[28] Bernard D Cole, *The Great Wall at Sea: China's Navy in the Twenty-First Century* (Annapolis, MD: Naval Institute Press, 2010), p. 58; Andrew J Nathan and Andrew Scobell, *China's Search for Security* (New York, NY: Columbia University Press, 2012), p. 288.
[29] Tanham and Agmon, *The Indian Air Force*, p. 84.

today 79 per cent of India's combat-aircraft squadrons and 96 per cent of its main battle tanks are still of Soviet design.[30] But American arms sales to India have begun picking up in the past four years, exceeding 10 per cent of all Indian arms imports in 2013 and reaching a high of 27 per cent in 2014. Over the same period between 2012 and 2014, Russia's share of Indian arms imports fell from 85 per cent to 51 per cent, reflecting a 45 per cent fall by value.[31] In 2014, the Indian defence minister reported even more dramatic figures, suggesting that the US had actually overtaken Russia in the previous three years, supplying around $5 billion worth of arms against Russia's $4 billion.[32]

This would be a short period over which to draw strong inferences, were it not for the significant progress in the Indo–US relationship and the particular military importance of the specific platforms being transferred (landing ships, transport aircraft and maritime surveillance aircraft) or under negotiation (attack and transport aircraft, light artillery and advanced carrier technology).[33] Ashley Tellis argues that the defence relationship is 'achieving the kind of strategic intimacy last seen in 1962', when New Delhi turned to Washington for help after defeat by China, and that military-to-military co-operation 'exceeds anything India achieved with the Soviet Union during the latter half of the Cold War'.[34] While differences remain – over the conditions of technology transfer and Indian faith in American wartime reliability – the relationship has shown strong signs of growth under Modi.

Russia will continue to be an important provider of technology and platforms, most notably the Fifth-Generation Fighter Aircraft (FGFA), but it is highly unlikely to restore the dominance it once held – particularly in light of Indian concerns with recent Indo–Russian deals and projects.[35] India has already slashed its prospective orders of the FGFA and complained about its financial burden and marginal role in the project.

---

[30] Author's calculations, from IISS, *The Military Balance 2015*, pp. 248, 251.

[31] SIPRI, 'SIPRI Arms Transfers Database 1950-2014'.

[32] Rajat Pandit, 'US Pips Russia as Top Arms Supplier to India', *Times of India*, 13 August 2014.

[33] Ajai Shukla, 'India–US Defence Ties Grow with Assertive Modi Govt', *Business Standard India*, 21 January 2015.

[34] Ashley J Tellis, 'Beyond Buyer-Seller', *Force*, August 2015, p. 6.

[35] Ajai Shukla, 'The Ghost of Gorshkov', Rediff News, 25 July 2015, <http://www.rediff.com/news/report/defence-news-the-ghost-of-gorshkov/20150725.htm>, accessed 20 October 2015; Ajai Shukla, 'Russia Can't Deliver on Fifth Generation Fighter Aircraft: IAF', *Business Standard India*, 21 January 2014; for a sanguine view of Indo–Russian friction, see Vijainder K Thakur, 'IAF's FGA Project Entering a Death Spiral?', Thum! Kaun Aata Hai?, 7 October 2015, <http://thumkar.blogspot.in/2015/10/iafs-fga-project-entering-death-spiral.html>, accessed 20 October 2015.

Figure 4: Indian Arms Imports by Source, 2000–14.

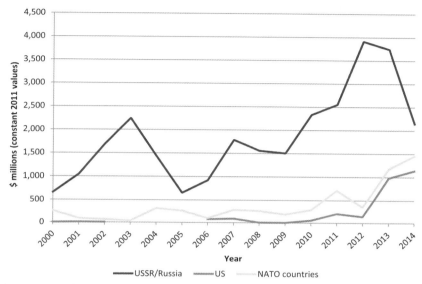

Source: SIPRI, 'SIPRI Arms Transfers Database 1950–2014'.

India's interest in maintaining diverse suppliers will also benefit other states, like France and Israel.

Challenges

Compared with fifteen years ago, when it successfully reversed a Pakistani attack on part of Kashmir, India's armed forces are better funded and equipped with Western equipment once out of their reach. But they continue to face a number of material, institutional and strategic challenges – each of which constrains India's ability to project power.

Readiness and Standards

The first major issue concerns readiness and standards. Successive reports by parliamentary committees and the Comptroller and Auditor General (CAG) – a constitutionally mandated body – as well as writing by serving and retired military officers, have pointed to problems with procurement, manpower, ammunition holdings, readiness rates and safety. In a leaked 2012 letter, army chief General V K Singh wrote to Prime Minister Manmohan Singh warning that the state of the armed forces was 'alarming', tank regiments were 'devoid of critical ammunition to defeat enemy tanks', air defence systems were '97 per cent obsolete', and there existed 'large scale voids' in surveillance and night-fighting capabilities across infantry and special-forces battalions.[36] Singh's remarks may have been a plea for resources, but they were consistent with independent accounts. A recent CAG report has noted that of the different types of Indian ammunition stocks, one half – including large-calibre artillery ammunition – would not last for ten days of 'intense' fighting.[37]

The IAF reportedly meets the NATO standard of 180 flying hours per pilot per year.[38] But the Soviet-heavy fleet has an accident rate of 6–7 per 100,000 flight hours, compared with 4–5 for NATO air forces, losing the equivalent of one fighter squadron (about 16–18 fighters) to crashes every two years.[39] But it is an improvement. Between 1993 and 2002, the accident rate for India's ageing MiG-21 Fishbed fleet reached around twenty-five per 100,000 hours, worse than that of other states that operate the same aircraft.[40] In 1993, 'almost all' of India's then modern MiG-29s were grounded for want of Russian-supplied lubricants.[41] Availability rates today range from 21 per cent for the admittedly decrepit Sea Harrier, to 55 per cent for the newer Su-30MKI.[42] In January 2015, as little as two-fifths of the Su-30MKI fleet was operationally available.[43] An internal IAF assessment notes that overall availability across the combat, transport and helicopter fleets averaged 60 per cent from 2012 to 2015, with the fighters the lowest at 55 per cent.[44] In 2015, a report by the Defence Committee

[36] Smita Gupta, 'Army Chief's Leaked Letter to PM Puts Centre in a Fix', *The Hindu*, 28 March 2012.

[37] Union Government, Defence Services, 'Report of the Comptroller and Auditor General of India on Ammunition Management in Army (for the Year Ended March 2013)', PA 19, May 2015, p. 10.

[38] IISS, *The Military Balance 2015*, p. 251.

[39] Strategy Page, 'Attrition: Pakistan Air Force Crumbling Away', 27 December 2012, <http://www.strategypage.com/htmw/htatrit/20121227.aspx>, accessed 20 October 2015; Ajai Shukla, 'IAF Crashes Lose One Fighter Squadron Every 2 Yrs', *Business Standard*, 21 March 2013.

[40] Miguel Vasconcelos, 'Civil Airworthiness Certification: Former Military High-Performance Aircraft', Federal Aviation Administration, September 2013, pp. 2–3.

[41] Damon Bristow, 'India's New Armament Strategy: A Return to Self-Sufficiency?', *Whitehall Paper* (London: Royal United Services Institute for Defence Studies, 1995), p. 31.

[42] S Anandan, 'INS Viraat to Be Decommissioned in 2016', *The Hindu*, 12 February 2015; Rahul Bedi, 'India Defence Minister Admits Su-30 Serviceability Issues', *IHS Jane's Defence Weekly*, 18 March 2015.

[43] Rahul Bedi, 'HAL Hands Back First Overhauled Su-30MKI to Indian Air Force', *IHS Jane's Defence Weekly*, 11 January 2015.

[44] *IHS Jane's Defence Weekly*, 'Briefing – Fettered Flight: Indian Air Force Procurement and Capabilities', 28 January 2015.

also noted that the IAF's fighter aircraft to pilot ratio had fallen to 1:0.81, considerably less than the authorised level of 1:1.25.[45]

As to the navy, a parliamentary report in 2014 expressed concern about a 'spurt of naval accidents', one of which resulted in the navy chief's resignation; a growing shortage of over 2,000 officers (20 per cent of the required total) and over 14,000 sailors (22 per cent); and the 'snail pace of commissioning of vessels'.[46] These problems have tied India's hands in even the most significant crises of the past fifteen years – notably against Pakistan, as explored below – and they would likely constrain power-projection operations too.[47]

Civil-Military and Inter-Service Relations

The Indian military exists under an unusual level of civilian control – unusual both relative to modern democracies, such as the UK or the US, and relative to what might be expected for a state with large armed forces, multiple domestic insurgencies and long and disputed borders.[48] One authoritative study of the Indian Army goes as far as to argue that 'no other democracy in the world has so tightly constrained its officer corps'.[49]

Coup-proofing measures have included lowering the army's status relative to civil servants; abolishing the office of commander-in-chief (roughly equivalent to a chief of the defence staff – CDS) and replacing it with three weaker, co-equal service chiefs; assigning the intelligence services to monitor serving and retired senior officers; ensuring that no single ethnic or religious group dominates the upper ranks; and building up paramilitary forces to handle internal security and balance against the army.[50] Evidence of civilian mistrust burst into the public consciousness in January 2012, when allegedly irregular movements of

---

[45] Rahul Bedi, 'Indian Parliamentary Committee Says IAF Facing Crisis in Combat Pilot Numbers', *IHS Jane's Defence Weekly*, 29 April 2015.

[46] Indian Ministry of Defence, 'Demands for Grants (2014–2015) Navy and Airforce Demand (Demand No. 23 & 24)'.

[47] Rahul Bedi, 'A Strike Staunched', *Frontline* (Vol. 19, No. 12, June 2002); Manoj Joshi, 'We Lack the Military That Can Deter Terrorism', *Mail Today*, 26 November 2009; Siddharth Srivastava, 'Indian Army "Backed Out" of Pakistan Attack', *Asia Times*, 21 January 2009.

[48] Paul Staniland, 'Explaining Civil-Military Relations in Complex Political Environments: India and Pakistan in Comparative Perspective', *Security Studies* (Vol. 17, No. 2, 2008).

[49] Stephen P Cohen, *The Indian Army: Its Contribution to the Development of a Nation*, Revised. (Delhi: Oxford University Press, 2001), pp. 226, xi.

[50] Steven I Wilkinson, *Army and Nation: The Military and Indian Democracy since Independence* (Cambridge, MA: Harvard University Press, 2015), pp. 103–08, 140–46.

mechanised infantry and paratroopers around New Delhi provoked alarm in the government, which – adding to tensions – was at the time locked in an ugly legal dispute with the army chief General V K Singh.[51]

Civilian domination has a number of consequences. It inhibits military planning, constrains operations and results in a less-than-smooth relationship between the three services.

The first problem is what the scholar Anit Mukherjee describes as an 'absent dialogue' between politicians, officers and a non-expert bureaucracy that acts as a buffer between the two.[52] Indian officers therefore have less sway over issues like threat assessment and arms procurement than they might in other countries, despite the willingness of successive governments to allocate increasingly large shares of resources to defence.

Second, this civilian control has intruded into some operational issues. Examples include the ban on the IAF crossing the Line of Control in the Kargil War,[53] the aversion to giving the military sole custody of nuclear weapons,[54] and the removal of a corps commander for unauthorised movements during the 2001–02 stand-off with Pakistan.[55] This should not be exaggerated, however. In at least two important areas – the granting of legal immunity to troops in domestic counter-insurgency through the Armed Forces (Special Powers) Acts (AFSPA) and some territorial disputes with Pakistan – governments have given strong, if not overwhelming, consideration to the army's position.[56] While Indian military leaders would undoubtedly obey a shift in policy in these areas, the historical weight

---

[51] Shekhar Gupta, Ritu Sarin, and Pranab Dhal Samanta, 'The January Night Raisina Hill Was Spooked: Two Key Army Units Moved towards Delhi without Notifying Govt', *Indian Express*, 20 September 2013.

[52] Anit Mukherjee, 'The Absent Dialogue', Seminar, July 2009, <http://www.india-seminar.com/2009/599/599_anit_mukherjee.htm>, accessed 20 October 2015.

[53] Benjamin Lambeth, *Airpower at 18,000': The Indian Air Force in the Kargil War* (Washington, DC: Carnegie Endowment for International Peace, 2012), p. 13. This echoed an earlier restriction on the Indian Navy in the 1965 war, which was forbidden from going more than 200 miles beyond Bombay or north of the parallel of Porbandar. 'The Navy', wrote Admiral S N Kohli, 'had gone to war with their hands tied behind their backs'. See G M Hiranandani, *Transition to Triumph: History of the Indian Navy, 1965–1975* (New Delhi: Lancer Publishers, 2000), p. 52.

[54] Gaurav Kampani, 'New Delhi's Long Nuclear Journey: How Secrecy and Institutional Roadblocks Delayed India's Weaponization', *International Security* (Vol. 38, No. 4, Spring 2014), p. 102; Anit Mukherjee, George Perkovich and Gaurav Kampani, 'Correspondence: Secrecy, Civil-Military Relations, and India's Nuclear Weapons Program', *International Security* (Vol. 39, No. 3, Winter 2014/15).

[55] V K Sood and Pravin Sawhney, *Operation Parakram: The War Unfinished* (New Delhi: Sage Publications, 2003), p. 80.

[56] Srinath Raghavan, 'Civil–Military Relations in India: The China Crisis and After', *Journal of Strategic Studies* (Vol. 32, No. 1, 2009).

accorded to their institutional views gives them a degree of authority that may be overlooked.

Third, and perhaps most importantly, the state of civil-military relations directly affects inter-service relations, and therefore the spirit and practice of jointness that go to the heart of modern military operations, something explored further in Chapter IV. Despite a string of official committees stretching back decades that have urged India to reverse its post-independence reforms and create a chief of the defence staff, bureaucrats and politicians – from all parties – have remained wary of creating such a powerful post.[57] The result is that individual services have separate procurement channels (sometimes for the very same platform), write their own, independent doctrines and have no effective joint institutions.[58] This is of profound importance in considering how Indian military capabilities described in subsequent chapters cohere into power-projection capabilities – or fail to do so. Chapter IV examines this point in more detail.

Indian Defence Posture: Pakistan and China

India's single most probable military contingency remains a limited war with Pakistan – most likely resulting from a terrorist attack originating in Pakistan and attributed to that country's intelligence services.[59] Recent Indian thinking on limited war was first spurred by the Pakistan-initiated Kargil War in 1999, which proved that nuclear weapons had not ruled out localised conflict, and then by terrorist attacks by Pakistan-backed groups in 2001–02, which resulted in a major, though inconclusive, stand-off between the two countries.[60] These crises showed that future wars could not unfold like the large campaigns that India had won in the 1960s and

---

[57] Anit Mukherjee, *Failing to Deliver: Post-Crises Defence Reforms in India, 1998–2010* (New Delhi: IDSA, 2011), pp. 28–30; Wilkinson, *Army and Nation*, p. 219; Anit Mukherjee, 'Closing the Military Loop', *Indian Express*, 1 April 2015.

[58] P S Das, 'Jointness in India's Military: What it Is and What it Must Be', *Journal Of Defence Studies* (Vol. 1, No. 1, 2007; Anit Mukherjee, 'India's Joint Andaman and Nicobar Command is a Failed Experiment', *Asia Pacific Bulletin* No. 289, East-West Center, November 2014; Vijai Singh Rana, 'Enhancing Jointness in Indian Armed Forces: Case for Unified Commands', *Journal of Defence Studies* (Vol. 9, No. 1, January 2015); Patrick Bratton, 'The Creation of Indian Integrated Commands: Organisational Learning and the Andaman and Nicobar Command', *Strategic Analysis* (Vol. 36, No. 3, May 2012).

[59] George Perkovich and Toby Dalton, 'Modi's Strategic Choice: How to Respond to Terrorism from Pakistan', *Washington Quarterly* (Vol. 38, No. 1, Spring 2015).

[60] Rajesh M Basrur, 'Kargil, Terrorism, and India's Strategic Shift', *India Review* (Vol. 1, No. 4, 2002); S Kalyanaraman, 'Operation Parakram: An Indian Exercise in Coercive Diplomacy', *Strategic Analysis* (Vol. 26, No. 4, 2002).

1970s: wars had to start quickly once a crisis had begun, lest major powers intervene to restrain India; and they had to end quickly and remain limited, to keep Pakistan's nuclear forces out of play. No more the 'toe-to-toe slugging match … on a division-by-division basis'.[61] No more the armoured thrusts across the Indus, towards Afghanistan.

In 2004, the Indian Army announced a new doctrine, part of which became colloquially known as 'Cold Start'. This was associated with three elements: smaller, more mobile units in place of India's traditionally large, slow land formations; quicker mobilisation to pre-empt international pressure in a crisis; and shallow thrusts into Pakistani territory, designed to punish or grab land as a bargaining chip without triggering Pakistani nuclear use.[62] Indian civilians – motivated in part by the civil-military concerns outlined above – denied that they had approved such a plan, the air force dismissed it as a 'non-starter' and American diplomats described it as a 'mixture of myth and reality'.[63]

India's passivity after the 2008 Mumbai terrorist attacks suggested that these assessments were correct and that Pakistan's emphasis on tactical nuclear weapons has further complicated India's calculus.[64] Moreover, recent research emphasises that India's supposed conventional advantage against Pakistan is in fact highly limited in short wars, owing to a combination of terrain that favours defenders; a lack of strategic surprise; slower mobilisation times; the relative distance of Indian forces from the border; and the aforementioned issues around readiness.[65] India's

---

[61] Ashley J Tellis, 'The Naval Balance in the Indian Subcontinent: Demanding Missions for the Indian Navy', *Asian Survey* (Vol. 25, No. 12, December 1985), p. 1186.

[62] Walter C Ladwig III, 'A Cold Start for Hot Wars? The Indian Army's New Limited War Doctrine', *International Security* (Vol. 32, No. 3, Winter 2007/08).

[63] Pinaki Bhattacharya, 'Army and IAF Face Off over New War Plan', *India Today*, 14 December 2009; Tim Roemer, 'Cold Start: A Mixture of Myth and Reality', Ref: IIR684401010, 1 October 2010, US Embassy, New Delhi, available at <http://www.theguardian.com/world/us-embassy-cables-documents/248971>.

[64] Vipin Narang, 'Posturing for Peace? Pakistan's Nuclear Postures and South Asian Stability', *International Security* (Vol. 34, No. 3, Winter 2009/10); David O Smith, 'The US Experience with Tactical Nuclear Weapons: Lessons for South Asia', Stimson Center, March 2013; Shashank Joshi, 'Pakistan's Tactical Nuclear Nightmare: Déjà Vu?', *Washington Quarterly* (Vol. 36, No. 3, Summer 2013); Rajuram Nagappa, Arun Vishwanathan, and Aditi Malhotra, *Hatf-IX/Nasr – Pakistan's Tactical Nuclear Weapon: Implications for Indo-Pak Deterrence* (Bangalore, India: National Institute of Advanced Studies, 2013). Note that as of October 2015, US officials estimated that Pakistan had built but not deployed tactical nuclear weapons. See David E Sanger, 'U.S. Exploring Deal to Limit Pakistan's Nuclear Arsenal', *New York Times*, 15 October 2015.

[65] Christopher Clary, 'Deterrence Stability and the Conventional Balance of Forces in South Asia', Stimson Center, October 2013; Walter C Ladwig III, 'Indian Military

operational and strategic environment had changed beyond recognition, but Indian leaders were unwilling or unable to countenance policies – such as defence reform towards jointness, investment in logistics and more forward deployment – that might have addressed these.[66] MIT scholar Vipin Narang goes as far as to argue that 'major conventional war – even in retaliation – is no longer a viable option for India'.[67]

It is clear that Indian leaders are exploring alternative means of responding to future terrorist attacks, including air strikes or – particularly the Modi government – covert action, which are less likely to risk escalation to the nuclear level.[68] In August 2015, India's hawkish National Security Advisor (NSA) Ajit Doval, who had previously written of the importance of covert warfare, stated that 'the days of wars in the service of statecraft are coming to an end. Wars are no longer a viable mechanism for achieving political and strategic objectives in a cost effective way'.[69] However, the army is understandably unwilling to give up a core mission and Indian leaders will continue to seek ways to use land forces and air power in limited, flexible ways for punitive and coercive purposes. Given the deep roots, longstanding state sponsorship and multifaceted nature of the threat from jihadist groups in Pakistan, this is likely to remain a high priority for Indian military forces.[70]

Over the past decade, India has also paid greater attention to China after a period of relative military neglect in the 1990s. This change was related to a variety of political and strategic shifts – including US overtures to India, instability in Tibet and Chinese anxieties over Indian leverage, and a flaring up of the Sino–Indian border dispute in rhetoric and reported incursions.[71] In 2006, there began 'the largest permanent build-up of Indian military forces at the border since the 1960s', prompted by China's improving lines of communication in Tibet.[72] These changes were reflected in the so-called Raksha Mantri's [Defence Minister's] Operational

Modernization and Conventional Deterrence in South Asia', *Journal of Strategic Studies* (Vol. 38, No. 4, May 2015).

[66] Shashank Joshi, 'India's Military Instrument: A Doctrine Stillborn', *Journal of Strategic Studies* (Vol. 36, No. 4, August 2013).

[67] Narang, 'Posturing for Peace?', p. 64.

[68] Swami, Praveen, 'India's New Language of Killing', *The Hindu*, 1 May 2014; Perkovich and Dalton, 'Modi's Strategic Choice'; Praveen Swami, 'Both Active and Effective: A Short History of Indian Special Ops', *Indian Express*, 11 June 2015.

[69] Samrat Chakrabarti, 'It's Time to be More Assertive: Doval', *The Hindu*, 5 August 2015.

[70] Christrophe Jaffrelot, *The Pakistan Paradox: Instability and Resilience* (New York, NY: Oxford University Press 2015), pp. 562–96.

[71] Jeff M Smith, *Cold Peace: China–India Rivalry in the Twenty-First Century* (Lanham, MD: Lexington Books, 2013), pp. 19–70.

[72] *Ibid*., pp. 41–42.

Directive, a sporadically issued document in which the defence minister sets out priorities for the service chiefs.[73]

In 2006–07, the government approved the construction of seventy-three strategic roads along the Sino-Indian border, reversing an earlier policy of avoiding such roads lest they facilitate Chinese advances into India.[74] Beginning in 2009, Indian military and civilian officials began speaking of the threat of a 'two-front' war involving both Pakistan and China.[75] They also suggested that India's posture to China was moving from 'dissuasive deterrence' to the more ambitious 'active deterrence', a shift that involved the re-opening of dormant landing strips, the forward deployment of two squadrons of Su-30MKI strike aircraft and the raising of a new strike corps oriented towards China rather than, as with India's previous three strike corps, to Pakistan.[76] In 2014, India also began introducing the first of six squadrons of the indigenous Akash anti-aircraft system to the northeast.[77] Concurrently, broader Chinese naval activities in the Indian Ocean – including nuclear-submarine forays and agreements with regional powers like Sri Lanka – have caused significant concern in New Delhi, though these are perceived as evolving challenges rather than immediate threats.[78] Indian analysts do not think conflict with China is imminent. They also recognise that India's conventional inferiority will take years to address. While there is periodic frustration at the Indian government's unwillingness to push back in prominent or escalatory ways to small Chinese provocations on the border – which are often timed to coincide with high-level bilateral visits – India's approach is to manage the

---

[73] A K Lal, *Transformation of the Indian Armed Forces 2025: Enhancing India's Defence* (New Delhi: Vij Books, 2012), p. 47.

[74] Sudhi Ranjan Sen, 'Only 20 Per Cent of India-China Strategic Border Roads Ready Till Now', *NDTV*, 27 February 2015. A decision adopted in 1959 had earlier prohibited roads and airfields from being constructed within thirty miles of the border with China. See John W Garver, *Protracted Contest: Sino-Indian Rivalry in the Twentieth Century* (Seattle, WA: University of Washington Press, 2001), p. 99.

[75] Rajat Pandit, 'Army Reworks War Doctrine for Pakistan, China', *Times of India*, 30 December 2009; PTI, 'Unsure of China's Motives, but 1962 Repeat Not Possible: VK Singh', *Times of India*, 7 November 2010; Rajat Pandit, 'Two-Front War Remote, but Threat from China Real', *Times of India*, 12 October 2012; *Hindustan Times*, 'NSA Ajit Doval: India Must Prepare for a Two-Front War', 25 November 2014; ABP Live, 'India Must Be Prepared for a Two-Front War, Says Air Marshal Reddy', 5 January 2015, <http://www.abplive.in/india/2015/01/05/article469273.ece/India-must-be-prepared-for-a-two-front-war-says-Air-Marshal-Reddy>, accessed 20 October 2015.

[76] Ali Ahmed, 'Ongoing Revision of Indian Army Doctrine', IDSA Comment, IDSA, January 2010.

[77] Rajat Pandit, With Eye on China, India Deploys Akash Missiles in Northeast', *Times of India*, 22 August 2014.

[78] C Raja Mohan, 'Samudra Manthan: Sino-Indian Rivalry in the Indo-Pacific', Brief, Carnegie Endowment for International Peace, 2012.

conflict diplomatically while building up its capabilities. The geography of the Sino-Indian 'fronts' – the adverse terrain of the Himalayan-Tibetan massif and the expanse of the Indo-Pacific – means that this build-up is likely to favour military capabilities well suited to power projection.[79]

The previous sections have sketched the broad outlines of India's defence posture. India is a large and growing military power, but with key weaknesses in readiness, civil-military relations, and inter-service integration. Its defence priorities are shaped primarily by conventional threats on its disputed western and northern borders, namely threats arising from Pakistan-based terrorist groups with links to Pakistani intelligence, as well as a larger and broader, though longer-term, challenge from China. Absent a drastic change in China's growth trajectory or Pakistani policies, these threats are likely to remain the most important influences on Indian military capabilities and doctrines. By contrast, extra-regional threats have been a relatively minor influence. Nevertheless, India does have some experience with power projection.

Indian Experience with Power Projection

Excluding India's experience during both World Wars and some operations within local wars, such as the use of paratroopers in East Pakistan in 1971, four examples of Indian power projection are worth considering in more detail. Most of this experience is decades old and few active military officers will have had direct involvement with the operations discussed below. The exceptions – humanitarian assistance and disaster relief (HADR) over the past decade or so – are also the least operationally taxing, and therefore the least illuminating in terms of power projection into anything other than highly permissive environments. I have excluded some relatively minor threats of force, such as India's use of a truncated infantry battalion to secure Sri Lanka's airport in 1971 or the deployment of an Indian destroyer to the Seychelles in 1986.[80]

UN Peacekeeping Operations (1950–present)
First, India has been the largest troop contributor to UN peacekeeping operations since their inception.[81] 180,000 troops have participated in

---

[79] The phrase is Garver's, in *Protracted Contest*, p. 24.

[80] V P Malik, *India's Military Conflicts and Diplomacy: An Inside View of Decision Making* (Noida, Uttar Pradesh: HarperCollins Publishers India, 2013), p. 3; David Brewster, *India's Ocean: The Story of India's Bid for Regional Leadership* (London: Routledge, 2014), p. 77.

[81] Permanent Mission of India to the UN, 'India and United Nations Peacekeeping and Peacebuilding', n.d., <https://www.pminewyork.org/pages.php?id=1985>,

Figure 5: India's Peacekeeping Contribution to UN Missions, 1990–2014.

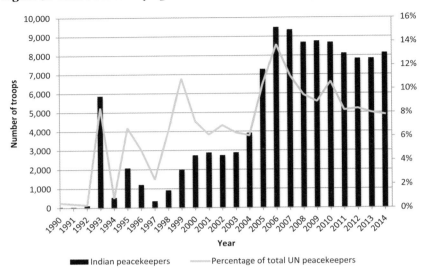

Indian peacekeepers ——— Percentage of total UN peacekeepers

Source: *Data collated from monthly summaries of troop and police contributors, United Nations Peacekeeping, <www.un.org/en/peacekeeping/resources/statistics/contributors. shtml>, accessed 11 November 2015.*

over forty-four missions, with over 156 deaths. Over the last twenty-five years, numbers peaked in 2006 when India was supplying over 9,000 troops comprising around 14 per cent of total UN peacekeepers globally. In 2014, India was the second-largest contributor with 8,123 personnel across twelve missions.[82] In September 2015, India, possibly spurred on by new Chinese commitments to UN peacekeeping, announced it would add an additional battalion of 850 troops to existing or new operations, three additional police units, more technical personnel and additional training for peacekeepers.[83]

Although peacekeeping is not comparable to conventional war, Indian contributions have included brigade-sized commitments, in addition to warships and attack helicopters.[84] In Somalia (1993–95),

---

accessed 20 October 2015; Indian Ministry of Defence, 'Annual Report 2013–14', n.d., pp. 27–28.
[82] This includes 991 police personnel.
[83] Geetanjali Chopra, 'Rise of the Indian Peacekeepers', *Pioneer*, 22 October 2015; 'Full Text of PM Modi's Statement at the UN Peacekeeping Summit', *NDTV*, 29 September 2015.
[84] Permanent Mission of India to the UN, 'India and United Nations Peacekeeping and Peacebuilding'.

for instance, India held 'operational responsibilities for one third of Somalia (173,000 km^2), the largest ever held by any UN contingent'.[85] Sushant K Singh and Richard Gowan note that some of these have 'blurred the boundary between peacekeeping and peace enforcement', including medical support to US airborne forces in the Korean War, the enforcement of a no-fly zone and bombardment of rebel airfields in the Congo in the 1960s, and the use of 'unprecedented' force in the decades-later UN mission in the Democratic Republic of the Congo.[86] India played an especially prominent role in the multinational Operation *Khukri* in 2000, when mainly Indian forces broke a two-month siege by the Revolutionary United Front (RUF) in Sierra Leone over three days of combat.[87]

The Indian Army currently maintains a 4,000-strong Standby Brigade Group for peacekeeping operations, capable of deploying an infantry battalion group within a month and the rest of the brigade in under eight weeks.[88] However, India has largely been able to deploy and supply forces in these theatres of war in relatively permissive conditions, making them weak precedents for more demanding types of power projection. The UN provides assistance with peacekeeping logistics through its Department of Field Support (DFS), including a permanent logistics base, in Italy.[89] Moreover, the UN itself acknowledges that 'the system of [UN] logistics is not well-designed to support high-tempo, short-notice military operations'.[90]

Sri Lanka (1987–90)

India deployed forces to Sri Lanka as part of the Indian Peace Keeping Force (IPKF) between 1987 and 1990, which was 60,000-strong (possibly as high

[85] Sushant K Singh, 'Peacekeeping in Africa: A Global Strategy', *South African Journal of International Affairs* (Vol. 14, No. 2, December 2007), p. 74.

[86] Sushant K Singh and Richard Gowan, 'India and UN Peacekeeping: The Weight of History and a Lack of Strategy', in Waheguru Pal Singh Sidhu, Pratap Bhanu Mehta and Bruce Jones (eds), *Shaping the Emerging World: India and the Multilateral Order* (Washington, DC: Brookings Institution Press, 2013), pp. 178, 181.

[87] See 'Chapter 5: Operation Khukri: The Hazards of UN Peacekeeping' in Malik, *India's Military Conflicts and Diplomacy*, pp. 157–78.

[88] Singh, 'Peacekeeping in Africa', p. 77.

[89] Don Leslie, 'Operational Logistical Support of UN Peacekeeping Missions: Intermediate Logistics Course', Peace Operations Training Institute, August 2011, p. 13; Katharina P Coleman, 'Overcoming Logistics Difficulties in Complex Peace Operations in Remote Areas', presentation given at the International Forum for the Challenges of Peace Operations, Beijing, 14 October 2014.

[90] UN Department of Peacekeeping Operations and Department of Field Support, 'United Nations Peacekeeping Operations: Principles and Guidelines', 2008, p. 76.

as 105,000) at its peak.[91] Operation *Pawan*, which opened the campaign with an assault on Jaffna, involved amphibious and air-assault operations with varying degrees of success.[92] The IPKF was a large force tasked with counter-insurgency/stabilisation operations.

However, the comparatively short distance between the Indian mainland and Sri Lanka – the Palk Strait is as little as 35 km wide – renders this a special case, given that the distinctive quality of force projection is the difficulty of applying force over long distances. It might be argued that, in military terms, the IPKF, however demanding its task, and despite the novel challenge of maritime logistics, had more in common with India's domestic counter-insurgency deployments than other operations. Nevertheless, Chapter IV raises some of the lessons that might apply in future Indian deployments. Finally, it should also be noted that the IPKF is often remembered in extremely negative terms, both because of the substantial number of Indian casualties and perceived lack of political direction – and is sometimes described as 'India's Vietnam'.[93] In 2000, when the Sri Lankan government once more faced severe rebel pressure in the Jaffna peninsula, India declined to intervene.[94] The cautionary Sri Lanka analogy is likely to come up in any future Indian debate over prolonged foreign intervention.

Maldives (1988)

In the late 1980s, India undertook a limited intervention in the Maldives, named Operation *Cactus*. India initially projected a much smaller quantity of force than in Sri Lanka (400 paratroopers) over a much longer distance (from Agra to Hulhule, 2,500 km) and against a much smaller force (between just 80–400 Tamil militants), in order to reverse a coup against the government of the Maldives in November 1988.[95] This was not an airborne assault, which was precluded by the small size of the drop zone,

---

[91] 60,000 is widely cited, but Sri Lankan military intelligence put the Indian Peace Keeping Force (IPKF) at 100,000, and others higher still. See P A Ghosh, *Ethnic Conflict in Sri Lanka and Role of Indian Peace Keeping Force (IPKF)* (New Delhi: APH Publishing, 1999), p. 108.

[92] A K Tiwary, *Indian Air Force in Wars* (Atlanta, GA: Lancer Publishers LLC, 2013), ch. 8; Ken Conboy and Paul Hannon, *Elite Forces of India and Pakistan* (Oxford: Osprey Publishing, 2012), pp. 15–16.

[93] Rediff, 'India's Vietnam', 23 March 2000, <http://www.rediff.com/news/2000/mar/23lank.htm>, accessed 20 October 2015.

[94] Celia W Dugger, 'A Wary India Prepares to Step Back into Sri Lanka's War', *New York Times*, 25 May 2000.

[95] Devin T Hagerty, 'India's Regional Security Doctrine', *Asian Survey* (Vol. 31, No. 4, April 1991), pp. 358–59.

but a semi-clandestine landing involving a degree of co-ordination with ground officials, albeit marked by uncertainty over the status of the surrounding area.[96] The first forces were landed within thirteen hours of the order being given.[97] The airlifting of 3,000 troops was ordered, but only 1,650 were needed.[98]

Humanitarian and Disaster Relief
India has developed significant experience in HADR and associated activities, notably the evacuation of Indian nationals and others from conflict zones.[99] These activities involve a significant, sometimes dominant, civilian component, but rely on many of the same instruments as power projection, notably airlift and sealift. Key moments in the recent evolution of this capability include India's responses to:

- Foreign disasters, including the Indian Ocean tsunami of 2004; Hurricane Katrina in 2005; Cyclone Sidr in Bangladesh in 2007; Cyclone Nargis in Myanmar in 2008; the nuclear disaster in Fukushima, Japan, in 2011; search and rescue efforts for the missing Malaysian airliner flight MH370 in 2014; and the Nepal earthquake in 2015[100]
- Domestic crises, including an earthquake in Gujarat in 2001; and floods in Uttarakhand in 2013 and in Kashmir in 2014[101]

---

[96] A G Bewoor, 'Indian Armed Forces Defeat Coup in Maldives', *CLAWS Journal* (Autumn 2014), pp. 150–56; A G Bewoor, 'Op Cactus: Reminescenses [sic]', n.d., <https://goo.gl/e5qlly>.
[97] Tiwary, *Indian Air Force in Wars*, p. 295.
[98] *Ibid.*, pp. 295–98.
[99] For good surveys, see Claudia Meier and C S R Murthy, 'India's Growing Involvement in Humanitarian Assistance', GPPi Research Paper, Global Public Policy Institute (GPPi), March 2011; Rahul Parmar, 'HADR in the IOR & the Indian Navy', Integrated Headquarters of Ministry of Defence, n.d., <http://goo.gl/CKEtEi> (cached version), accessed 20 October 2015; C Raja Mohan, 'Indian Military Diplomacy: Humanitarian Assistance and Disaster Relief', Working Paper No. 184, Institute of South Asian Studies, March 2014; Sarabjeet Singh Parmar, 'Humanitarian Assistance and Disaster Relief (HADR) in India's National Strategy', *Journal of Defence Studies* (Vol. 6, No. 1, January 2012).
[100] Indian Ministry of Defence, Press Information Bureau, 'HADR Exercise by Indian Navy', press release, 10 February 2015, <http://pib.nic.in/newsite/PrintRelease.aspx?relid=115326>, accessed 20 October 2015.
[101] Ashok K Chordia, 'Airlift during Disasters: The Uttarakhand Experience', Issue Brief, Centre for Air Power Studies, July 2013.

Table 2: Indian Power Projection since 1950.

	Threat	Persistence	Range
UN peacekeeping	Low–high	High	High
IPKF	Medium–high	High	Low
Operation *Cactus*	Low–medium	Low	Medium–high
HADR	Low	Low–medium	Low–high

- Large-scale evacuation efforts, from Iraq in 1991 (176,000 evacuees); Lebanon in 2006 (2,280); Libya in 2011 (15,000); and Yemen in 2015 (5,600).[102]

These operations play an important role in relating Indian military capabilities to the country's self-identity as an increasingly active regional power in a concrete yet conspicuously benign way. For instance, when India's foreign minister, Sushma Swaraj, echoed US language of India as a 'net provider of security' in her 2015 address to the UN General Assembly, she invoked the examples of Yemen and Nepal. HADR has also played an important role in consolidating the bilateral and multilateral military-to-military relationships between India, the US, Japan and other regional powers, such as the *Malabar* and *Milan* exercise series, explored further in Chapter V.[103] Given India's aversion to military alliances, this experience would be crucial for inter-operability if India chose to enter expeditionary military coalitions in the future.

India's four sets of experience are summarised in Table 2.

Power Projection in Indian Defence Posture

Although India's defence posture is configured for local threats on India's immediate borders, it is also true that extra-regional interests and threats – and therefore power-projection capabilities – have grown in importance over time. The Indian Navy, both because of the intrinsic reach and flexibility of navies and its limited role in India's land wars, embraced power projection the earliest and with the most enthusiasm. But the air

---

[102] K P Fabian, 'Oral History: Biggest Ever Air Evacuation in History', *Indian Foreign Affairs Journal* (Vol. 7, No. 1, January–March 2011), p. 92; Manmohan Bahadur, 'What India Needs to Learn from #YemenEvacuation', *Economic Times*, 23 April 2015; Mohan, 'Indian Military Diplomacy', pp. 7–8.

[103] Mohan, 'Indian Military Diplomacy', pp. 9–12.

Figure 6: Numbers of Indian Naval Assets, 2005–15.

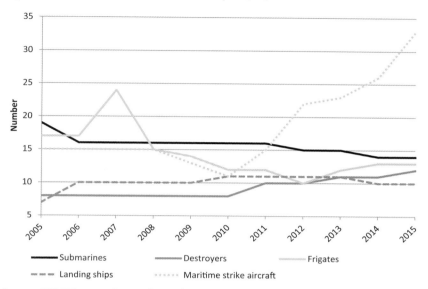

Source: *IISS Military Balance editions from 2005 to 2015, with some corrections.*

force and army are catching up. The following sections briefly survey how trends in procurement and doctrine reflect the increased prominence of power projection. Some aspects of these trends – notably doctrine – reflect service-specific visions, rather than points of national consensus guided and endorsed by India's political leadership. Doctrines may represent one way for services to seek prestige, autonomy, strategic roles and resources. However, they also guide training, planning, procurement and ways of thinking.

The Indian Navy

As explained in the previous chapter, India procured its first aircraft carrier, the *Vikrant*, in 1961; its second, the *Viraat* (the former HMS *Hermes*), in 1988; and the third, the *Vikramaditya* (the former *Admiral Gorshkov*) in 2014.[104] To fly off these platforms, it acquired the Sea Hawk in 1961, Sea Harrier in 1983 and the MiG-29 K Fulcrum in 2010.[105] Until the 1960s,

---

[104] G M Hiranandani, *Transition to Eminence: The Indian Navy 1976–1990* (New Delhi: Lancer Publishers, 2005), p. 91.

[105] Stephen Skinner, *Hawker Siddeley Aviation and Dynamics: 1960–77* (Ramsbury: Crowood, 2014), ch. 3; Chris Smith, *India's Ad Hoc Arsenal: Direction or Drift in Defence Policy?* (Oxford: Oxford University Press, 1994), p. 119; Rediff

however, these platforms were coupled to relatively modest views of sea power. This began to change in the 1970s, following military victory over Pakistan in 1971 (when America despatched the carrier USS *Enterprise* to the Bay of Bengal to intimidate New Delhi) and the increasing presence of superpower navies in the Indian Ocean.[106] This precipitated what has been described as India's 'radial turn ... toward a sea-denial strategy'[107] – seen for example in a corresponding focus on submarines (from four in 1970, to eight in 1980 and to nineteen in 1990).

More recently, however, Indian submarine numbers have stagnated, falling by one-fifth in the past decade, while the number of destroyers has risen by one-half. Maritime strike aircraft have doubled over the same period and the number of major landing ships is up tenfold over twenty years. Though the number of India's principal surface combatants was virtually unchanged between 1991 and 2011, their aggregate tonnage grew by nearly 30 per cent and the number of missile cells fivefold.[108] Although many of these capabilities have obvious power-projection applications, one naval officer observes that a pivotal moment came in 2005 when then-navy chief Admiral Arun Prakash specifically 'made a strong pitch for real-time and robust expeditionary capabilities', instructing the navy's planning section to prepare urgent requirements for helicopter carriers.[109] That same year, India agreed to buy the amphibious ship USS *Trenton*, larger than anything in its inventory at the time.[110] This was followed with plans for further amphibious procurement, described in Chapter III.

From the late 1990s and through the 2000s, the navy also released a series of statements of Indian naval thinking: the Strategic Defence Review in 1998; Maritime Doctrine in 2004 and 2009; and Maritime Military Strategy in 2007.[111] Although these writings did not prioritise different Indian missions, they did formally lay out the service's emphasis on

---

News, 'Navy to Induct Russia's MiG-29K Fighter Jets', 2 February 2010, <http://news.rediff.com/report/2010/feb/02/navy-to-induct-russias-mig-29k-fighter-jets.htm>, accessed 20 October 2015.
[106] Hiranandani, *Transition to Triumph*, pp. 17–19.
[107] Stephen P Cohen and Sunil Dasgupta, *Arming without Aiming: India's Military Modernization* (Washington, DC: Brookings Institution Press, 2010), p. 75.
[108] Walter C Ladwig III, 'Drivers of Indian Naval Expansion', in Harsh V Pant (ed.), *The Rise of the Indian Navy: Internal Vulnerabilities, External Challenges* (Burlington, VT: Ashgate, 2012), pp. 3–4.
[109] Abhijit Singh, 'The Indian Navy's "New" Expeditionary Outlook', ORF Occasional Paper No. 37, Observer Research Foundation, October 2012, p. 5.
[110] Sandeep Unnithan, 'With Open Arms', *India Today*, 1 August 2005.
[111] Iskander Rehman, 'India's Aspirational Naval Doctrine', in Harsh V Pant (ed.), *The Rise of the Indian Navy: Internal Vulnerabilities, External Challenges* (Burlington, VT: Ashgate, 2012), p. 71.

power projection in ways that would previously have been considered diplomatically inadvisable (see Chapter V). The 2009 doctrine, for instance, listed 'power projection' and 'expeditionary ops' as sixth and seventh on a list of core missions, directly below 'sea control', 'sea denial' and 'blockade'.[112] Equally importantly, successive navy chiefs, while tactfully emphasising their potential contribution to local land wars, have stressed the importance of blue-water reach and 'longevity in distant theatres'.[113] In practice, it is hard to disambiguate local and blue-water capabilities, because naval forces tend to be especially mobile and therefore fungible. But the navy is least yoked to the spectre of Indo-Pakistani war and most directly challenged by the growth of Chinese diplomatic and military power – and therefore most likely to emphasise, in its platforms and doctrine, the use of force at greater distances from Indian territory.

The Indian Air Force

The IAF has been characterised as 'for most of its history ... an air defence force', which continues to have 'limited offensive capability' or, even more harshly, 'little more than a support entity for the Indian Army'.[114] The IAF has, however, had some strategic missions. These have included strategic reconnaissance of important targets, strategic bombing and, from the 1980s onward, nuclear delivery (now largely superseded by ballistic missiles). However, these were configured towards local contingencies, and in large part towards Pakistan rather than China.[115]

This configuration is most evident in India's failure to acquire long-range fighters or reconnaissance aircraft, deep-strike theatre bombers and, until 1985, long-range refuelling aircraft.[116] The navy has operated four Tu-142 maritime reconnaissance and anti-submarine warfare (ASW) aircraft since 1988, adapted from the Tu-95 bomber, but there is no evidence that any are adapted for strike roles. In the late 1990s, the navy attempted, but failed, to acquire four Tu-22M Backfire supersonic strategic bombers (reportedly first offered by Moscow in the 1970s), with one Indian analyst framing this as a naval effort 'to appropriate the manned

---

[112] Integrated Headquarters, Ministry of Defence (Navy), 'Indian Maritime Doctrine', 2009, pp. 92, 125.

[113] Rajat Pandit, '"Blue-Water Navy is the Aim"', *Times of India*, 1 November 2006.

[114] Cohen and Dasgupta, *Arming without Aiming*, pp. 76, 96; Benjamin S Lambeth, 'India's Air Force Evolves', *Air Force Magazine* (March 2015), p. 62.

[115] Tanham and Agmon, *The Indian Air Force*, p. 45.

[116] R K Pal and A P Mote, *Sentinels of the Sky: Glimpses of the Indian Air Force* (New Delhi: Ritana Books, 1999), p. 50.

strategic bombing role for itself'.[117] It was later reported that India planned to lease Tu-160 Blackjack supersonic strategic bombers – with over twice the range of the Tu-22 – from Russia, though nothing came of this either;[118] nor did a mooted 'strategic air command' come to fruition.[119]

Since the turn of the millennium, however, the IAF's long-range capabilities have expanded with the acquisition of the Su-30MKI in 2002; Il-78 refuelling aircraft in 2003;[120] Phalcon AWACS in 2009; and C-130 Super Hercules[121] and C-17 Globemaster transport aircraft in 2010 and 2013, respectively. This was in parallel to a shift in doctrine. In 1995, the IAF formulated its first-ever air-power doctrine, according offensive operations the same priority as air defence.[122] In mid-2007 – presumably informed by the US and Allied examples during Kosovo, Afghanistan and Iraq – the IAF revised its doctrine, emphasising 'potent strategic reach' and signalling its intention to become an 'expeditionary force' and 'global player'.[123] Senior, serving IAF officers, acknowledging the force's 'tactically oriented' history, began exhorting further investment in a 'credible strategic aerial-intervention capability'.[124] In 2009, the former commander of the IAF's Western Command, Air Marshal V K Bhatia, described the service's 'growing aspirations to transform itself from a mere sub-continental tactical force to an intercontinental strategic aerospace power in conformity with other leading air forces in the world'.[125]

In 2012, the IAF released an unclassified Basic Doctrine. This stated that the IAF's vision was to 'enable force projection within India's strategic area of influence', a large territorial area extending well beyond India's

---

[117] Carlo Kopp, 'Backfires for China?', *Australian Aviation* (September 2004), p. 42; Bharat Karnad, *Nuclear Weapons and Indian Security: The Realist Foundations of Strategy* (New Delhi: Macmillan, 2002), pp. 663–64.

[118] Bharat Karnad, *India's Nuclear Policy* (Westport, CT: Praeger Security International, 2008), p. 100.

[119] *International Defence Digest*, 'India's First Airpower Doctrine Takes Shape', 6 January 1997.

[120] *IHS Jane's Defence Weekly*, 'India Receives Il-78 Tankers', 3 July 2003.

[121] Lockheed Martin, 'Indian Air Force Receives First Lockheed Martin C-130J Super Hercules', press release, 16 December 2010, <http://www.lockheedmartin.com/us/news/press-releases/2010/december/IndianAirForceReceivesFir.html>, accessed 20 October 2015.

[122] Bhashyam Kasturi, 'Force Structuring and Doctrines of the IAF', *Air Power Journal* (Vol. 3, No. 2, Summer 2008), p. 10.

[123] Rajat Pandit, 'IAF Plans War Doctrine to Expand "Strategic Reach"', *Times of India*, 2 August 2007.

[124] Arjun Subramaniam, 'The Strategic Role of Airpower: An Indian Perspective on How We Need to Think, Train, and Fight in the Coming Years', *Air & Space Power Journal* (Vol. 22, No. 3, Fall 2008).

[125] Lambeth, 'India's Air Force Evolves', p. 63.

borders (discussed later in this chapter).[126] The doctrine emphasised the role of aerial refuelling and AWACS in permitting 'long range strikes without the need to stage through airfields', but also noted that 'the IAF will be required to ... if possible, operate from air bases in our neighbourhood'. That the doctrine would allude to airbases on foreign soil is especially significant, given India's longstanding sensitivity to the issue of foreign military basing.

The Indian Army

Among all the services, the Indian Army is most constrained in its approach by the enduring problem of disputed land borders, the possibility of war with Pakistan and domestic insurgency. Its overwhelming focus is to the immediate north and west, and its training, equipment and structures are configured for local land wars. The army's first public doctrine in 2004 did pay lip service to India's 'considerable interests in the areas stretching from West Asia through Central Asia and South Asia to South East Asia' and the importance of the Indian Ocean. Among five 'major tasks' listed, it included, as fourth and fifth, participation in UN peacekeeping operations and the requirement to 'be prepared to render military assistance to friendly countries when required to do so'.[127] A 2009 revision of the doctrine reportedly included 'out of area contingencies' as one of its five major priorities.[128] At the time of its release, the army chief noted that it 'would enable us to protect our island territories [and] also give assistance to the littoral states in the Indian Ocean Region'.[129] In practice, however, army officers have given far less attention to power-projection themes in their doctrine than air force and navy officers have in theirs.

The army now trains over 5,000 foreign armed forces personnel every year – notably including over 1,000 Afghans in 2014.[130] The development of the army's power projection-specific forces – air assault, airborne assault, amphibious infantry and special forces – is detailed in Chapters III and IV, but it is worth noting that the army began re-raising an amphibious formation, formerly the 91 Infantry Brigade, in 2009 and Indian special forces, though weak in several regards, were expanded in 2014.

---

[126] Indian Air Force, 'Basic Doctrine of the Indian Air Force: 2012', 2012, p. 10.

[127] Headquarters Army Training Command, 'Indian Army Doctrine', October 2004 p. 10.

[128] Vinod Anand, 'Review of the Indian Army Doctrine: Dealing with Two Fronts', *CLAWS Journal* (Summer 2010), p. 259.

[129] Pandit, 'Army Reworks War Doctrine for Pakistan, China'.

[130] Indian Ministry of Defence, 'In Defence of the Nation' March 2015, p. 7; Amitabh Pashupati Revi, 'In Major Policy Shift, Afghanistan Sends Army Cadets for Training in Pakistan', *NDTV*, 6 February 2015.

Civilian Limits

These shifts in military attitudes towards power projection were matched – and in part enabled – by changes in civilian attitudes, articulated by politicians, diplomats and other officials. While military doctrine was written with relative autonomy by particular groups of officers within each service, probably with quite limited civilian input, it nevertheless required a certain degree of civilian acceptance. Nor could India have acquired platforms with strong power-projection applications without buy-in from the bureaucracy and elected leaders.

An interrelated combination of growing resources, widening interests, competition with China and Indo–US convergence have contributed to a more ambitious, active and assertive vision for Indian security policy than in previous decades. One aspect of this policy is the way India frames its area of interest. The scholar David Scott shows that the idea of an 'extended neighbourhood' – stretching beyond continental South Asia – came into increasingly wide usage from 1998 onwards among Indian officials.[131] In 2004, India's foreign minister stated that this extended neighbourhood 'stretches from the Suez Canal to the South China Sea and includes within it West Asia [the Middle East], the Gulf, Central Asia, South East Asia, East Asia, the Asia Pacific and the Indian Ocean Region'. This ambitious formulation has been repeated over the subsequent decade – with small variations – by ministers and officials from both India's centre-left and centre-right, and explicitly tied to economic, energy and security interests.[132] Over this same period, outsiders, notably officials in the US, have endorsed this growing Indian footprint, in striking contrast to their sensitivity over Chinese activity.[133] And while Indian officials have been guarded in their references to power projection, preferring to emphasise non-combat or peacekeeping missions, this caution has on occasion slipped. In 2008, for instance, then-Defence Minister AK Antony told journalists that, 'as the experience of the British in [the] Falklands or that of [NATO] in Afghanistan demonstrate[s], security forces have to be ready for force projection far beyond their national boundaries to secure and maintain national as well as international peace and stability'. In December 2015, Modi made what was probably the starkest prime-ministerial intervention on this subject to date, in an address to his combined military commanders aboard the carrier INS *Vikramaditya*,

---

[131] David Scott, 'India's "Extended Neighborhood" Concept: Power Projection for a Rising Power', *India Review* (Vol. 8, No. 2, 2009).
[132] David Scott, 'India's Aspirations and Strategy for the Indian Ocean: Securing the Waves?', *Journal of Strategic Studies* (Vol. 36, No. 4, February 2013), pp. 485–87.
[133] Ely Ratner et al., 'More Willing & Able: Charting China's International Security Activism', Center for a New American Security, May 2015.

stating that 'as our security horizons and responsibilities extend beyond our shores and borders, we must prepare our forces for range and mobility'.[134]

To be sure, Indian foreign policy remains marked by opposition to foreign (and particularly Western) military intervention – sometimes even when it has had the imprimatur of the UN.[135] In 1991, India opposed the US-led coalition's war to expel Iraq from Kuwait *despite* UN Security Council approval.[136] The Bharatiya Janata Party (BJP)-led government in 2003 briefly considered the possibility of deploying an infantry division to northern Iraq – a contingent that would have been the second largest in the country behind that of the US – but eventually dismissed this possibility in the absence of Security Council authorisation.[137] Although New Delhi was eager to advance the Indo–US relationship, it would not do so at the cost of its traditional commitment to multilateralism and what India's then-prime minister called 'an honest non-aligned policy'.[138] The subsequent Congress Party-led government vociferously opposed NATO's 2011 intervention in Libya against the regime of Colonel Muammar Qadhafi, which unfolded during the Indian presidency of the UN Security Council.[139] In 2014–15, the BJP government refused to join the multinational coalition against Daesh (also known as the Islamic State of Iraq and Syria) in Iraq despite the group having killed nearly forty Indian citizens and having recruited potentially hundreds more.[140]

India's Considered Approach

These are cautionary examples. While India is developing a broad range of military capabilities that permit it to project force throughout the area it has defined as its extended neighbourhood, Indian commitments to sovereignty,

---

[134] *Rediff News*, 'Protect Tamils in LTTE-Held Areas, India Tells Lanka', 15 September 2015; Press Information Bureau, Government of India, 'PM Chairs Combined Commanders Conference on Board INS Vikramaditya at Sea', media release, 15 December 2015, <pib.nic.in/newsite/PrintRelease.aspx?relid=133265>, accessed 17 December 2015.
[135] C Raja Mohan, 'Balancing Interests and Values: India's Struggle with Democracy Promotion', *Washington Quarterly* (Vol. 30, No. 3, Summer 2007), pp. 103, 113–14; Siddharth Mallavarapu, 'Democracy Promotion circa 2010: An Indian Perspective', *Contemporary Politics* (Vol. 16, No. 1, March 2010), pp. 53–60.
[136] Fabian, 'Oral History', pp. 94–95.
[137] Rudra Chaudhuri, *Forged in Crisis: India and the United States since 1947* (Noida, Uttar Pradesh: HarperCollins Publishers India, 2014), p. 202.
[138] *Ibid.*, p. 207.
[139] Vijay Prashad, 'Syria, Libya and Security Council', *Frontline* (Vol. 29, No. 5, March 2012)
[140] Anindita Sanyal, 'India Won't Join Military Action Against IS, Will Help US Control Terror', *NDTV*, 1 October 2014.

non-intervention and caution in the use of force will surely constrain the use of these power-projection capabilities. Anyone moderately familiar with the assumptions, ideas and attitudes of India's intellectual and political elites will understand that, even into the long term, India will not intervene with the ease or frequency of today's power-projecting states.

On the other hand, it would be naive to think that India will abjure power projection altogether. Indian grand strategy is in flux. India's relationship with the US could be entering its second major phase of maturation, potentially driving greater Indian involvement in regional security. This involvement may be extremely limited at first, but it could grow in line with Indian power and in response to changes in the international environment, such as a weakening of American leadership in Asia. Indian leaders are assertive, confident, and ambitious – even, some would argue, hubristic.[141] Chapter V will look at how India's widening interests might indicate where it projects power in the future. But first, the next three chapters take a closer look at how Indian capabilities are evolving.

---

[141] C Raja Mohan, *Modi's World: Expanding India's Sphere of Influence* (Noida, Uttar Pradesh: HarperCollins Publishers India, 2015), ch. 10.

II. AIR-POWER PROJECTION

Over the past twenty-five years, the use of air power – broadly conceived, to include sea- and land-based aircraft, and long-range missiles[1] – has become an increasingly important part of Western power projection. The precise and successful use of air power in Iraq and Bosnia in 1991–95; its refinement in Serbia, Afghanistan and Iraq during 1999–2003; and the widespread and sustained use of remotely piloted strike aircraft across the Middle East, Africa and Asia from 2002 to the present have all contributed to a renaissance in air power.[2] Over this period, missiles have largely been used as precursors or accompaniments to strikes by aircraft, but have on occasion been used in isolation – most notably by the US against targets linked to Al-Qa'ida in Sudan and Afghanistan in August 1998 in retaliation for bombings of the US embassies in Kenya and Tanzania.[3] While many have argued that the independent, strategic effect of air power has been exaggerated, its appeal has largely grown in recent years following disillusionment with manpower-heavy interventions viewed as strategic failures, notably Afghanistan (2001–present) and Iraq (2003–11). This process has been compounded by a perception that domestic public opinion in would-be intervening democracies is casualty-averse, and therefore a belief that air power will meet with greater political support than the deployment of ground forces.[4]

---

[1] In this chapter, 'missiles' largely refers to long-range missiles rather than air-launched variants, with the latter subsumed within the discussion of air strikes.

[2] Benjamin S Lambeth, *The Transformation of American Air Power* (Ithaca, NY: Cornell University Press, 2000), ch. 9; Martin Van Creveld, *The Age of Airpower* (New York, NY: PublicAffairs, 2012), ch. 20; Micah Zenko, *Reforming U.S. Drone Strike Policies* (New York, NY: Council on Foreign Relations, 2013), pp. 6–8.

[3] Micah Zenko, *Between Threats and War: U.S. Discrete Military Operations in the Post-Cold War World* (Stanford, CA: Stanford University Press, 2010), ch. 4.

[4] Christopher Gelpi, Peter D Feaver and Jason Reifler, *Paying the Human Costs of War: American Public Opinion and Casualties in Military Conflicts* (Princeton, NJ: Princeton University Press, 2009), pp. 65–66; Richard C Eichenberg, 'Victory Has Many Friends: US Public Opinion and the Use of Military Force, 1981–2005', *International Security* (Vol. 30, No. 1, Summer 2005), p. 166.

Since the Second World War, air power has been used and combined in a variety of wars: 'discretely', to achieve an independent and limited effect, short of capturing territory or defeating an army;[5] in conjunction with third-party ground forces; or in conjunction with one's own ground forces.[6] Examples of 'discrete' air power include American retaliatory air strikes against the Qadhafi regime in Libya in 1986; Emirati and Egyptian air strikes in the same country to degrade Islamist rebels in 2014; and the aforementioned drone and missile strikes. Examples of air strikes in conjunction with third-party ground forces – albeit with a small presence of the intervener's special forces – include US air strikes in aid of the Northern Alliance in 2001 or the Saudi and Emirati-led coalition's air strikes in Yemen in 2015 in aid of anti-Houthi Yemeni government forces. Examples of air strikes to support one's own forces include air operations in Britain's recapture of the Falkland Islands in 1982 or Coalition operations in Iraq in 2003.[7]

These missions generate different demands on air power. One-off strikes on large, static targets to punish an adversary are, of course, easier than sustained bombardments against dense and sophisticated air-defence systems, or close air support of unfamiliar and irregular ground forces. But the basic challenge – delivering munitions to a distant target, typically through combat forces deployed away from home bases – is the same, and a small set of platforms, mainly aircraft and missiles, lies at its centre. These are discussed in turn, beginning with land-based aircraft and the platforms that extend their range, then turning to carrier-based aircraft and finally examining missiles.

Land-Based Aircraft

The IAF through its history has largely been configured for the air defence of India, and only secondarily for strike missions, whether local or long range. This legacy has shaped its present force structure.

At the high-end of air combat, three MiG-29 Fulcrum and nine Su-30MKI Flanker squadrons serve primarily as air-superiority fighters, though the Flanker has a range and payload suitable for strike missions. At the lower-end, a large fleet of ageing MiG-21 Fishbed variants, of which six squadrons are the Bison variant upgraded in 2006, serves in

---

[5] Zenko, *Between Threats and War*.
[6] Stephen D Biddle, 'Allies, Airpower, and Modern Warfare: The Afghan Model in Afghanistan and Iraq', *International Security* (Vol. 30, No. 3, Winter 2005/06).
[7] The role of ground forces, including their transport to the theatre of conflict and the use of special forces, is examined in Chapters III and IV.

Figure 7: IAF Force Structure, 2015–30.

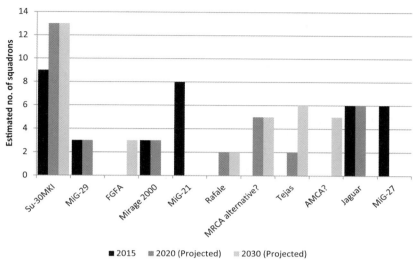

Source: *See Table 3.*

particular as an interceptor designed for area defence.[8] In the strike role, India employs the six squadrons of the MiG-27 Flogger and four squadrons of the deep-penetration Jaguar. Three squadrons of the Mirage 2000, upgraded in 2014–15, serve in both air-combat and (secondarily) strike roles. Both the Jaguar and Mirage are thought to be nuclear-capable. As discussed in the previous chapter, the IAF does not possess a traditional strategic bomber and shows little interest in acquiring one.

India plans to replace its MiG-21s with the indigenously built light multi-role HAL Tejas. The early version of the Tejas, the Mark 1, is disliked by many in the IAF and was expected to be procured only in very small numbers (one or two squadrons by 2020); but the IAF has indicated it might order three to four squadrons of a slightly upgraded variant, the Mark 1A – so 120 Mark 1s and 1As in all – and four further squadrons of a higher-end Mark 2 later.[9] India had also planned to order eight squadrons of the Rafale as part of a tender for a medium multi-role

---

[8] Ashley J Tellis, 'Dogfight! India's Medium Multi-Role Combat Aircraft Competition Decision', Carnegie Endowment for International Peace, January 2011, p. 76.
[9] Ajai Shukla, 'Parrikar Cuts Gordian Knot to Boost Tejas Line', *Business Standard*, 2 October 2015.

combat aircraft, but after unexpectedly ordering two squadrons in fly-away condition in April 2015, it cancelled the overall tender, leaving open the question of how it would make up a shortfall of ninety aircraft.[10] On present trends, which depend on orders and production of the Tejas as well as the choice of supplement to the Rafale, the IAF's overall strength is unlikely to grow significantly over the next five years and looks incredibly unlikely to meet the sanctioned level of forty-two combat squadrons – over 750 airframes.

Nor is the shape of its force structure likely to change. The loss of dedicated strike aircraft in the 2020s could open up a major capability gap, but it is possible that the IAF will decide the Su-30MKI and other multi-role aircraft are sufficiently versatile to take on the strike role. This would be one indicator of a lower priority on power projection. Finally, India also hopes to develop an advanced medium combat aircraft – a stealthy medium-weight fifth-generation aircraft – but this is at least fifteen years (and likely 20–25 years) away from completion.[11] Table 3 shows the IAF's present holdings in different categories of aircraft, with roughly estimated figures for 2020 and 2030 based on expected procurement. Given the history of Indian procurement – delayed, erratic and usually short of expectations – this should be taken with the appropriate caution.

These aircraft are equipped with a range of air-to-surface weapons, of which a growing but unknown proportion comprises precision-guided munitions (PGMs).[13] Air-power expert Benjamin Lambeth suggests that 'the IAF still remains only in the early stages of its precision revolution and is now about where the US Air Force stood at the time of Operation Desert Storm in 1991'.[14] More recent anecdotal accounts suggest the IAF has made extremely slow progress on building up PGM stockpiles and that this could limit the sustainability of any air campaign. India first used laser-guided bombs, the US-made Paveway II, in June 1999 during the Kargil War, and their use, only twice, had a significant impact on the

---

[10] *Times of India*, '"Make in India" for 90 Medium Combat Jets', 2 August 2015.
[11] Abhijit Iyer-Mitra and Pushan Das, 'The Advanced Medium Combat Aircraft: A Technical Analysis', ORF Issue Brief No. 105, Observer Research Foundation, September 2015; Ajai Shukla, 'Indian Air Force Chief Expects Full Strength of 42 Squadrons by 2027', Broadsword, 5 October 2015, <http://ajaishukla.blogspot.co.uk/2015/10/indian-air-force-chief-expects-full.html>, accessed 21 October 2015; Ajai Shukla, 'From Tejas to AMCA', *Business Standard*, 6 July 2015.
[12] Atul Chandra, 'Future Planning', *Force*, October 2014.
[13] Pramod K Mehra, 'The Indian Air Force of Tomorrow', in Rajesh Basrur, Ajaya Kumar Das, and Manjeet Singh Pardesi (eds), *India's Military Modernization: Challenges and Prospects* (New Delhi: Oxford University Press, 2014), pp. 70–71.
[14] Benjamin S Lambeth, 'India's Air Force Evolves', *Air Force Magazne*, March 2015, p. 63.

campaign.[15] The specific range of air-to-surface weaponry is also relevant, given the obvious advantages of stand-off strikes from beyond the range of adversary air-defence networks. For instance, a number of Israeli strikes into Syria in recent years are understood to have struck ten miles into Syria from the relatively safety of Lebanese airspace using loft-bombing.[16] In March 2015, India began receiving the first of forty-two modified Su-30MKIs adapted to launch the 300 km-range BrahMos cruise missile, previously reserved for the navy.[17] More broadly, while India has experience with integrating multinational avionics into its airframes – combining Russian, French, Israeli and indigenous systems in the Su-30MKI, for instance – the details of air-to-ground-relevant avionics are hard to gauge.[18] Some ISR-related issues are taken up in Chapter IV.

India's Reach

How far can India's land-based aircraft be projected? The Su-30MKI, Rafale and Jaguar are all reported to have ferry ranges of over 3,000 km without external fuel tanks, while the Mirage 2000 reaches this threshold with tanks. Estimates of any aircraft's combat radius – the maximum distance over which it can travel, perform a given combat mission and safely return – vary greatly, depending as they do on flight profile, weather conditions, loiter time over target, enemy resistance, the nature of air defences, payload and other factors that bear on fuel consumption.[19] Most published estimates of combat radius – such as 1,850 km for the Mirage with two drop tanks[20] – appear to be no more than crude and misleading halvings of range, although even more careful analysis has placed the

---

[15] Benjamin Lambeth, *Airpower at 18,000': The Indian Air Force in the Kargil War* (Washington, DC: Carnegie Endowment for International Peace, September 2012), pp. 20, 31. This is disputed. See also p. 52, footnote 111. See also Anil Chopra, 'Aerial Weapons: Time to Act', *Defence and Security of India*, 2 August 2014.

[16] Adam Entous and Julian E Barnes, 'U.S. Weighs Syria Response', *Wall Street Journal*, 28 April 2013.

[17] Rakesh Krishnan Siha, 'Why the BrahMos Armed Sukhoi is Bad News for India's Enemies', *Russia & India Report*, 20 April 2015.

[18] Tellis suggests India has 'yet to master' avionics development and integration. See Tellis, 'Dogfight! India's Medium Multi-Role Combat Aircraft Competition Decision', p. 63. Lambeth discusses the 'much improved' avionics of the Mirage 2000 in the air-to-ground role. See Lambeth, *Airpower at 18,000'*, p. 28.

[19] Tellis, 'Dogfight! India's Medium Multi-Role Combat Aircraft Competition Decision', p. 55.

[20] Federation of American Scientists (FAS), 'Mirage 2000 (Dassault-Breguet)', 4 April 2000, <http://fas.org/man/dod-101/sys/ac/row/mirage-2000.htm>, accessed 21 October 2015.

Table 3: IAF Present and Projected Force Structure.

Role	2015			2020 (projected)			2030 (projected)		
	Aircraft	Number	Squadrons	Aircraft	Nos.	Sqs.	Aircraft	Nos.	Sqs.
Air superiority	Su-30MKI	144[b]–215[a]	9[a]–10[g]	Su-30MKI	272	13	Su-30MKI	272	12
							FGFA	65[e]–127	3[e]–7
Air combat (medium)	MiG-29	48[b]–55[a]	3[a]	MiG-29	48	3	Rafale	36	2
	Mirage 2000	36[b]–40[a]	3[a]	Rafale	36	2	Rafale/alternative	90	5
				Rafale/alternative	90	5	Advanced medium combat aircraft[f]	?	?
				Mirage 2000	36	3			
Air combat (light)	MiG-21 Bison	96[b]–116[a]	6[b]	Tejas Mark I	40[d]	2[d]	Tejas Mark I	40[d]	2[d]
	MiG-21*bis*	31[b]–48[c]	1[g]–2[b]				Tejas Mark II	80[d]	4[d]
Strike	Jaguar IS	80[b]–81[a]	4[a]–5[b]	Jaguar IS	80	4	Future strike aircraft?	?	?
	Jaguar IM	10[a]	1[a]	Jaguar IM	10	1			
	MiG-27	88[b]–126[a]	5[g]–6[a]						
Total		**533–691**	**32–36**		**~612**	**33**		**~583–645+**	**28–32+**

(Continued)

Table 3: Continued

Notes: *Estimates of aircraft numbers exclude trainers. However, media reports of anticipated procurement probably include trainers in reported numbers. Therefore future squadron numbers, where unsourced, are calculated on the basis of twenty-one aircraft per squadron. Estimates of post-2015 aircraft numbers adopt the lowest bound of 2015 estimates, to reflect attrition, and figures for 2030 assume 2 per cent attrition for Rafale and 5 per cent for the Su–30MKI. This table is modelled on the format used in Ashley J Tellis, 'Dogfight! India's Medium Multi-Role Combat Aircraft Competition Decision', Carnegie Endowment for International Peace, January 2011.*

Sources:

a. IISS, Military Balance.

b. Babrat Rakshak, 'Aircraft Fleet Strength', 31 July 2015, <http://www.bbarat-rakshak.com/IAF/Units/Others/281-Fleet.html>, accessed 21 October 2015.

c. Ajai Shukla, 'Air Force Likely to Get Entire Sukboi-30MKI Fleet by 2019', Business Standard, 22 April 2014.

d. Rajat Pandit, 'For LCA Tejas, it's Now about Months, Not Decades', Times of India, 15 April 2015.

e. Ajai Banerjee, 'IAF Halves its Demand for Russian Fighter Jets', The Tribune, 11 August 2015.

f. Ajai Shukla, 'Top Officials Provide Glimpse of Future Air Force', Business Standard, 20 February 2015.

g. Private information.

Su-30MKI's combat radius over 1,300 km.[21] These highest estimates imply that India could reach as far as Oman and the eastern half of Iran to the west, to most of Central Asia including the southern half of Kazakhstan in the north, and to northern Vietnam and Guangzhou in China – though not quite to Tehran, Astana or Hong Kong. But in practice, these ranges should be tempered by consideration of at least four constraining factors.

First, many such estimates assume that strike aircraft would be unencumbered by other mission-critical aircraft that have shorter legs.[22] Strike aircraft – even if otherwise proficient in air-to-air combat – are likely to require, inter alia, fighter escorts unencumbered by ordnance and electronic-warfare aircraft. Second, the limited number of hardpoints on an aircraft means that there is a trade-off between external fuel tanks, which extend range, and ordnance or other mission-enabling pods.[23] India's strike aircraft have hardpoints numbering from five (on the Jaguar) to twelve (on the Su-30MKI). Third, the maximum payload of aircraft will depend on the altitude from which they take off. Therefore not all points in India – notably, high-altitude northern airbases – will permit the same radius. Fourth, extrapolating from combat radii to potential reach assumes that aircraft take direct routes. In practice, Indian aircraft flying to these points would require right of overflight over neutral or hostile countries. Such overflight privileges are often withheld even among allies, as with the refusal of France, Spain and Italy to allow America's UK-based F-111 bombers to transit their airspace during the 1986 air strikes against Libya.[24] Similarly, any Israeli strike on Iran is complicated by the fact that any reasonable route would have to overfly at least one of Turkey, Iraq or Saudi Arabia; while the most direct route is 1,750 km, the longest, if necessitated by political circumstances, is 2,410 km.[25]

Presumably accounting for some of these limiting factors, Ashley Tellis therefore posits that India's primary strike aircraft have much smaller 'useful operating radii', just 650–1,000 km, meaning that they could barely

---

[21] Carlo Kopp, 'Su-30 vs RAAF Alternatives', *Australian Aviation* (September 2003), p. 36.
[22] Justin Bronk, 'Maximising European Combat Air Power: Unlocking the Eurofighter's Full Potential', *RUSI Whitehall Report* 1–15 (April 2015), p. 15.
[23] Ashley J Tellis, *India's Emerging Nuclear Posture: Between Recessed Deterrent and Ready Arsenal* (Santa Monica, CA: RAND, 2001), p. 535.
[24] Robert E Harkavy, *Bases Abroad: The Global Foreign Military Presence* (Oxford: Oxford University Press, 1989), p. 95.
[25] Whitney Raas and Austin Long, 'Osirak Redux? Assessing Israeli Capabilities to Destroy Iranian Nuclear Facilities', *International Security* (Vol. 31, No. 4, Spring 2007), pp. 23–27.

reach non-Tibetan China, let alone the Arabia Peninsula.[26] These restrictions can be circumvented in one of three ways: in-flight refuelling, the use of aircraft carriers or the use of land- or sea-based missiles. Each is now considered in turn.

Tanker Fleet

India's first option for refuelling is its fleet of six IL-78 Midas tanker aircraft. India's Su-30MKIs, Mirages and Jaguars all have air-to-air refuelling (AAR) capability, while India's MiG-29s are being upgraded to do so.[27] All bar the Jaguar can also refuel one another in-flight in so-called 'buddy' mode, albeit in more limiting ways. One estimate suggests that the Su-30MKI's maximum range with two refuellings is 8,000 km, which would imply a combat radius of somewhere under 4,000 km.[28] If we assume 3,500 km, then this would reach as far as most of Saudi Arabia to the west, Somalia's coast to the southwest, most of China's eastern seaboard to the east (and all of the South China Sea), and to most of Sumatra and the Malacca Strait to the southeast – although the problems of overflight would still arise. Yet tanker aircraft would be especially vulnerable in contested airspace, and they would require additional fighter escorts and therefore an even larger aggregate fuel requirement – perhaps even precluding their use altogether.[29] Tankers are therefore a 'weak link' in any strike package, whose loss would put at risk the survival of a disproportionately large number of supported combat aircraft.[30] India could invest in unmanned refuelling aircraft and longer-legged strike aircraft, but such changes in posture and doctrine can only unfold over many years.

If we adopt more restrictive conditions, and assume that strike aircraft can only be refuelled once (at the edge of Indian airspace), then combat radii would differ only from the unrefuelled estimates given above insofar as the distance between the originating air base and the Indian border

---

[26] Ashley J Tellis, 'Making Waves: Aiding India's Next-Generation Aircraft Carrier', Carnegie Endowment for International Peace, April 2015, pp. 6–7.

[27] Gulshan Luthra, 'IAF Decides for Midair Refueling Capability on All Aircraft', *India Strategic* (December 2012).

[28] Airforce Technology, 'Su-30MKI Multirole Fighter Aircraft, India', n.d., <http://www.airforce-technology.com/projects/su-30mki-multirole-fighter-aircraft-india/>, accessed 21 October 2015. An Indian Air Force (IAF) officer also mentiones an externally refuelled range of 8,000 km, though without mentioning the number of refuellings. See Rahul Bedi, 'India Renovates Airbase for Su-30MKI Build-Up', *IHS Jane's Defence Weekly*, 21 November 2007.

[29] Tellis, *India's Emerging Nuclear Posture*, p. 538.

[30] Greg Knepper and Peter W Singer, 'Short Legs Can't Win Arms Races: Range Issues and New Threats to Aerial Refueling Put US Strategy at Risk', War on the Rocks, 20 May 2015.

could be discounted. If we assume that India's peninsular geography would still allow for refuelling over most of the surrounding ocean, then India's reach would be limited to the north (just southern Afghanistan and, depending on access to the Gulf, much of Iraq, Iran and Saudi Arabia) but more expansive to the south, where forward refuelling could take place more safely.

However, the scope of Indian operations would be limited by tanker numbers.[31] Walter Ladwig extrapolates from American and British air strikes against Iraq to argue that, for conventional strike missions, one medium tanker is required for every four combat aircraft, with the ratio of fighters to tankers falling to two tankers for every five combat aircraft if they are required to loiter for persistent strikes. Ladwig also assumes 85 per cent tanker readiness on the basis of USAF numbers.[32] These ratios suggest that India's present fleet of tankers would yield only five ready refuelling aircraft, in turn sustaining 13–20 combat aircraft – roughly one squadron. These assumptions might be too stringent: a US report notes that the ratio during Operation *Desert Storm* was initially 1:4 for night-time missions, but was later raised and eventually capped at 1:8, as a result of safety concerns over pilot inexperience with night refuelling.[33] This higher ratio would permit up to forty combat aircraft – roughly two squadrons. India also intends to procure six further Airbus Military A330 Multi-Role Tanker Transport (MRTT) aircraft, which would double refuelling capability and sustain between forty and eighty aircraft, or two to four squadrons.

Strike Package Sizing

Putting range aside, how many aircraft are needed for typical air strikes? It varies so greatly that no meaningful assessment can be made without some sense of the mission in question, including the nature of the target, the resources and risk acceptance of the attacker, and the specific capabilities of the aircraft at hand. The following examples give a sense of the variation.

Scholar Gaurav Kampani cites an IAF study from the early 2000s that found 'a typical nuclear task force' could include up to sixty aircraft. This total was reached by assuming two nuclear-armed aircraft, three to four

---

[31] B K Pandey, 'Indian Air Force of the Future', *Indian Defence Review* (Vol. 24, No. 1, January–March 2009). Cited in Walter C Ladwig III, 'India and Military Power Projection: Will the Land of Gandhi Become a Conventional Great Power?', *Asian Survey* (Vol. 50, No. 6, November 2010), p. 1178.

[32] Ladwig III, 'India and Military Power Projection', p. 1178, footnote 58.

[33] US General Accounting Office (GAO), 'Operation Desert Storm: An Assessment of Aerial Refueling Operational Efficiency', GAO/NSIAD-94-68, November 1993, p. 9.

Table 4: Sizes of Selected Historical Strike Packages.

Strike	Aircraft per target in initial strike
Israel/Iraq, 1981	16
Israel/Tunisia, 1985	8
US/Libya, 1986	20
US/Iraq, 1991	41–75
US/Croatia, 1994	30
US/Serbia, 1999	16–36

electronic-warfare escorts, three to four fighter escorts, and further strike aircraft to suppress enemy air defences – together, totalling 15–20 aircraft – plus two to three similar decoy packages.[34] The Israeli strike on Iraq's nuclear reactor at Osirak in 1981 involved sixteen aircraft.[35] Four years later, another Israeli strike on the Palestine Liberation Organization in Tunis used just half that number.[36] During the 1991 Gulf War, the initial strike packages that attacked Basra comprised just forty-one non-stealthy aircraft, including eight bombers, although the average strike package during the war may have been as high as seventy-five.[37] In 1986, US strikes on five Libyan targets involved 100 aircraft, or twenty aircraft per target.[38] In 1994, a strike package of thirty aircraft was required to attack Serbian targets in Croatia as part of Operation *Deny Flight*.[39] On a single day during NATO's 1999 air war against Serbia, a succession of seven strike packages were as varied in number as 36, 32, 30, 16, 28, 24 and 38.[40] These are summarised in Table 4. While not all the strikes discussed in this section involved very long ranges, some – notably Israel's – did.

---

[34] Gaurav Kampani, 'New Delhi's Long Nuclear Journey: How Secrecy and Institutional Roadblocks Delayed India's Weaponization', *International Security* (Vol. 38, No. 4, Spring 2014), p. 101.

[35] Raas and Long, 'Osirak Redux?', p. 11.

[36] Dave Sloggett, *A Century of Air Warfare: The Changing Face of Warfare 1912–2012* (Barnsley: Pen and Sword, 2013), p. 11.

[37] Anthony H Cordesman, *The Iraq War: Strategy, Tactics, and Military Lessons* (Washington, DC: CSIS, 2003), p. 259; Robert W Gaskin, 'A Revolution for the Millenium', in Williamson Murray (ed.), *The Emerging Strategic Environment: Challenges of the Twenty-First Century* (Westport, CT: Greenwood Publishing Group, 1999), p. 143.

[38] William C Martel, *Victory in War: Foundations of Modern Military Policy* (Cambridge: Cambridge University Press, 2006), pp. 156–57.

[39] Steve Davies, *F-15E Strike Eagle Units in Combat 1991–2005* (Oxford: Osprey Publishing, 2005), p. 43.

[40] Benjamin S Lambeth, *NATO's Air War for Kosovo: A Strategic and Operational Assessment* (Santa Monica, CA: RAND, 2001), pp. 49–50.

These examples show that the number of strike aircraft depends greatly on the mission in question. Strike missions are not, of course, merely a function of aircraft numbers plus tankers; they require a host of enabling capabilities. If we set these aside for the moment, India's medium-term tanker fleet will be sufficient, on paper, to support missions involving two to four squadrons of aircraft – assuming, as is likely, that India is acting alone, rather than in a coalition. This is not an insignificant number in the context of the power projection of other nations. It is likely adequate for one-off strike missions against weakly defended targets, such as those India might face as part of any military intervention into weak Indian Ocean island states such as the Maldives or Mauritius – scenarios discussed further in Chapter V. However, India would find it harder to mount a sustained air campaign at reach over a longer period of time, given that maintenance, rest periods and aircraft loss would likely attrite these numbers over time, in addition to other limiting factors like ordnance availability. This assessment is slightly more generous than Ladwig's conclusion that Indian precision air strikes are confined to merely 'symbolic, as opposed to substantive, operations'.[41]

The Air-Defence Environment around India
India's reach is much more limited against targets with advanced air-defence systems or proficient defensive anti-air capabilities. Its reach would depend in part on the specific mission. During the Kargil War, the IAF imposed an altitude floor on operations after two of its aircraft were lost to Pakistani surface-to-air missiles (SAMs). This impeded the IAF's provision of close air support, but it did not prevent successful interdiction missions.[42] A number of other countries lack high-altitude SAMs but have substantial holdings of advanced man-portable air-defence systems (MANPADS). This includes a number of African and Southeast Asian countries that sit within India's declared area of interest. Against such targets, India might be able to destroy a limited number of static targets – such as training camps operated by a terrorist group – but could struggle to provide ongoing close air support to irregular forces. However, the growing proportion of PGMs in the IAF inventory would allow air strikes against high-value targets from higher, safer altitudes. The air-launched BrahMos in particular permits strikes from outside an adversary's air space, especially against the profusion of littoral targets within 300 km of Indian Ocean

---

[41] Ladwig III, 'India and Military Power Projection', p. 1172.
[42] Lambeth, *Airpower at 18,000'*, p. 32.

coastlines (80 per cent of people globally lived within 100 km of the sea in 2012[43]).

The air-defence environment around India – if we take the area roughly within reach of India's strike aircraft – is relatively constraining. A number of states possess advanced air-defence systems: Russia, China, and a cluster of US allies in East Asia and the Gulf. Russia has not yet exported its most advanced platform, the SA-21 (S-400 in Russian designation), although in April 2015 it confirmed it intended to do so to China and, more recently, to India itself.[44] The SA-21 is capable of simultaneously tracking up to 100 targets and engaging twelve, up to 30 km altitude and 400 km range.[45] Even the predecessor system, the SA-10 (S-300), which Russia recently agreed to sell to Iran, and which China and Vietnam both possess, presents a formidable defence that would require a broad and resource-intensive campaign to suppress. This newer generation of Russian air-defence systems is comparable to the US Patriot system.[46] These very advanced systems not only impede Indian force projection into China, they could even hold at risk Indian platforms within Indian airspace.

In addition to SAMs, the regional air-defence environment is also shaped by holdings of combat aircraft. Pakistan and China aside, Malaysia, Singapore, Indonesia and Vietnam all employ small numbers of fourth-generation or better combat aircraft; to India's west, the countries of the GCC employ larger numbers of such aircraft. In practice, Indian security interest in these states is unlikely to be a matter of direct conflict with the governing authority – a state-to-state conflict, as with Pakistan – and therefore the relative air balance is much less relevant than the fact that this airspace is sufficiently contested so as to completely exclude the possibility of India using force as freely as the US has done in theatres like Pakistan or Yemen. The only exception to this may be in the East African littoral, though here India's interests are shallower. One of the most significant non-neighbouring areas of Indian concern – Afghanistan – is

---

[43] David Kilcullen, *Out of the Mountains: The Coming Age of the Urban Guerrilla* (London: Hurst, 2013), p. 80.

[44] Reuben F Johnson, 'Russian Official Confirms S-400 Sale to China', *IHS Jane's Defence Weekly*, 14 April 2015. In October 2015, India expressed its own intention to acquire 'around a dozen' S-400 batteries over several years. See Rajat Pandit, 'India Eyes Safer Skies with Russian S-400 Triumf', *Times of India*, 11 October 2015.

[45] Paul N Schwartz, 'Russia Announces Sale of S-400 to China', Center for Strategic and International Studies (CSIS), rep's blog, 30 June 2014, <http://csis.org/blog/russia-announces-sale-s-400-china>, accessed 21 October 2015.

[46] Carlo Kopp, 'Surface to Air Missile Effectiveness in Past Conflicts', Technical Report APA-TR-2010-1001, Air Power Australia, October 2010, <http://www.ausairpower.net/APA-SAM-Effectiveness.html>, accessed 21 October 2015.

especially inaccessible air space and India's ability to intervene there would depend more on the twin questions of Iran's willingness to grant an air corridor and India's access to bases in Tajikistan (see Chapter IV) than any military calculation. The conclusion is that while India's *reach* is substantial and growing, its *penetration* may be the constraining factor, particularly in those areas – the Middle East, Central Asia and even parts of Southeast Asia – where its interests are deepest.

India's attitude to a campaign of suppression of enemy air defences (SEAD) is an open question, and would likely depend on circumstances. India's ultra-cautious approach to air power in 1999 was largely a function of Pakistan's nuclear status and the risk of escalation. However, Indian political leaders would be wary of a large-scale SEAD campaign – such as that which NATO conducted against Libya in 2011 – for fear of the diplomatic ramifications and the constraint on India's freedom of manoeuvre. Where possible, India would prefer to take a lower-profile approach that relies on the IAF's growing electronic-warfare capabilities and stealth.[47] In terms of targeting adversary radar, India's stocks of anti-radiation missiles (ARMs) – used to target sources of radio transmissions like radars – are unknown, but it reportedly purchased the Russian Kh-31P Krypton for the SU-30MKI in 2001 and, with Russian help, developed the associated SIVA targeting pod in 2009.[48] India also hopes to develop an indigenous ARM by 2017 and acquired around fifty Israeli anti-radiation Harop drones – in effect cruise missiles – in 2012–13.[49]

India's Naval Air Power

An alternative to the use of tankers is the use of aircraft carriers, which serve as mobile, floating airbases that permit aircraft to take off from points closer to their final targets. One major advantage of naval air power over its land-based counterpart is that it can shorten flight times to targets thereby allowing more time 'on station'.[50] India will decommission one of

---

[47] Saurav Jha, 'New "Special Mission" Aircraft for the Indian Air Force', *IBN Live*, 17 January 2014; Airforce Technology, 'India's Tejas Aircraft Receives Advanced Electronic Warfare Suite', *Airforce Technology*, 12 January 2015.

[48] Carlo Kopp, 'Soviet/Russian Tactical Air to Surface Missiles', Technical Report APA-TR-2009-0804, Air Power Australia, April 2012, <http://www.ausairpower.net/APA-Rus-ASM.html>, accessed 21 October 2015.

[49] Y Mallikarjun, 'Anti-Radiation Missile by DRDO to Be Ready in 3–5 Years', *The Hindu*, 26 January 2013; *The Hindu Business Line*, 'India Scaling Up Indigenous Missile Development Programme', 25 August 2014. The Harop deal is recorded in Stockholm International Peace Research Institute (SIPRI), 'Arms Transfers Database', generated 6 October 2015.

[50] Tellis, *Making Waves*, p. 6.

its present carriers, the INS *Viraat*, around February 2016, leaving it with the INS *Vikramaditya*. The smaller INS *Vikrant* is due to be ready around 2017–18, and the larger INS *Vishal* around a decade later.[51] According to some accounts, these carriers are expected to form the core of three task forces centred on the Bay of Bengal, the Indian Ocean and the Arabian Sea.[52] But given that the *Vikramaditya* will be decommissioned somewhere between the mid-2030s and early 2040s, India would also have to start work on a fourth carrier by the early 2020s if it wanted to maintain a fleet of three.[53] Moreover, Western experience suggests that carrier refit and maintenance schedules allow availability 'five years in eight', so a three-carrier fleet would in fact ordinarily sustain, by 2020, only two Indian carriers at sea.[54] British planners assume that a single carrier can have three to four months at sea per year, and even less on station. This can be surged, and it also depends on operational use – for example, the distance typically travelled from home ports – and so India may be able to squeeze more availability on station than, say, France or Britain. Nevertheless, India is unlikely to be able to maintain three concurrently at-sea task forces.

The Indian Navy currently operates one squadron of the maritime-variant MiG-29K Fulcrum for the *Vikramaditya*, with another scheduled for 2015–16 to fly from the *Vikrant*.[55] These replace an older fleet of Sea Harriers, expected to be retired imminently. The *Vikramaditya* will initially host 16–20 MiG-29Ks, along with additional trainer, airborne early warning (AEW) and ASW aircraft.[56] The *Vikrant* can carry both these and

---

[51] Jayanta Gupta, 'Aircraft Carrier INS Vikrant Will Be Delivered to Navy on Time: Cochin Shipyard Chief', *Times of India*, 15 October 2015.

[52] David Brewster, *India's Ocean: The Story of India's Bid for Regional Leadership* (Oxford: Routledge, 2014), p. 14; Ajai Shukla, 'India's Navy: Strong on Aircraft Carriers, Short of Submarines', *Business Standard*, 30 September 2014.

[53] Nivedita Das Kundu, 'Indo-Russian Defence Cooperation: *Admiral Gorshkov* Joins Indian Navy', University of Helsinki, n.d., <http://www.helsinki.fi/aleksanteri/english/news/events/2007/gorshkov21072004.pdf>, accessed 21October 2015.

[54] House of Commons, Defence Committee, *The Strategic Defence and Security Review and the National Security Strategy*, HC 716 (London: The Stationery Office, 2011), p. 46.

[55] International Institute for Strategic Studies, *The Military Balance 2015* (London: Routledge/IISS, 2015), p. 250; Rahul Bedi, 'Indian Navy Chief: Vikramaditya Deployed with MiG-29s Embarked', *IHS Jane's Defence Weekly*, 7 May 2014; Sputnik, 'Russia Ready to Send More MiG-29K Fighters to India', 19 February 2015, <http://sputniknews.com/military/20150219/1018471063.html>, accessed 21 October 2015.

[56] Bedi, 'Indian Navy Chief'. Jane's records the maxium capacity as twenty-four MiG29Ks. See Paul Jackson (ed.), *Jane's: All the World's Aircraft 2009–2010* (McGraw-Hill, 2009), p. 484. The IISS's Military Balance records a present complement of just twelve aircraft. IISS, *The Military Balance 2015*, p. 249.

the navalised Tejas, to a reported total of thirty-six combat aircraft.[57] The *Vishal*, though larger, is currently forecast to accommodate a similar number of strike aircraft, though its catapult take-off and arrested recover system (known as CATOBAR) – or even a more advanced, US-supplied Electromagnetic Aircraft Launch System (EMALS)[58] – could permit the launch of heavier aircraft or the same aircraft with larger payloads.[59]

Measuring Indian Naval Air Power

A given fighter aircraft might ordinarily – without surging – sustain two sorties per twelve-hour flying day, although this naturally depends on the distance of the target and the carrier's overall size, and be available 80 per cent of the time.[60] So the *Vikramaditya*, taking the lower estimate of its aircraft capacity, would have twelve ready aircraft able to sustain twenty-four sorties per day, and the *Vikrant* would have twenty-eight ready aircraft and fifty-six sorties, for a total of eighty sorties per day between the two – assuming a wholly permissive environment, where no aircraft have to be dedicated to air defence (but excluding the effect of flight-deck layout, which could permit sequential launch[61]).

One study describes this as 'modest land bombardment, and only for a modest time'.[62] Indeed, it is less than a single American *Nimitz*-class carrier, which can sustain 120 sorties per day.[63] But this is the wrong point of comparison. Even half of this estimate (forty, rather than eighty) – thus

---

[57] Ajai Shukla, 'While IAF Drags Feet over Tejas, Naval LCA Powers Ahead', Broadsword, 7 February 2015, <http://ajaishukla.blogspot.co.uk/2015/02/while-iaf-drags-feet-over-tejas-naval.html>, accessed 21 October 2015; T Ramavarman, 'India to Launch Aircraft Carrier INS Vikrant Today', *Times of India*, 12 August 2013. For the upper estimate of the *Vikramaditya*'s aircraft capacity, see *IHS*, 'Jane's World Navies: India', 7 May 2015.

[58] Tellis, *Making Waves*, pp. 12–13; H P S Sodhi, 'Electro Magnetic Aircraft Launch System', CAPS In-Focus, Centre for Air Power Studies (CAPS), 5 May 2015.

[59] Tellis, *Making Waves*, p. 9.

[60] galrahn, 'The Monster Myths of the CVL Concept', US Naval Institute blog, August 2009, <http://blog.usni.org/2009/08/27/the-monster-myths-of-the-cvl-concept>, accessed 21 October 2015.

[61] It has been reported that the *Vikrant* will have two take-off runways. See IHS, *Jane's World Navies*, p. 41.

[62] James R Holmes, Andrew C Winner and Toshi Yoshihara, *Indian Naval Strategy in the Twenty-First Century* (Oxford: Routledge, 2009), p. 87; cited in Walter C Ladwig III, 'Indian Military Modernization and Conventional Deterrence in South Asia', *Journal of Strategic Studies* (Vol. 38, No. 4, May 2015), p. 22.

[63] Office of the Director, Operational Test and Evaluation, US Department of Defense, 'CVN-78 *Gerald R. Ford* Class Nuclear Aircraft Carrier', n.d., <http://www.dote.osd.mil/pub/reports/FY2013/pdf/navy/2013cvn78.pdf>, accessed 21 October 2015; see also Mark Gunzinger and John Stillion, 'The Unserious Air War Against ISIS', *Wall Street Journal*, 14 October 2014.

discounting for air-defence duties, lower readiness and other friction – would still be equivalent to the number of combat sorties the IAF was generating daily during the Kargil conflict.[64] It would also exceed the rate of coalition strike sorties against Daesh in Iraq and Syria during 2014–15 (eleven per day) and roughly match the rate against Libya in 2011 (forty-six per day), but would be far below that seen in the opening phases of the air campaigns in Bosnia in 1995, Serbia in 1999, Afghanistan in 2001 and Iraq in 1991 and 2003.[65]

India's Naval Reach

How far can India's naval air power reach? The MiG-29K has a reported combat radius of 850 km, or 1,300 km with external fuel tanks.[66] This would, for instance, theoretically permit strikes on Karachi from within the Gulf of Oman, or on small lengths of China's eastern seaboard from beyond China's so-called 'first island chain'. This would carry serious risks: the Chinese People's Liberation Army Navy (PLAN) is increasingly sending advanced ships beyond the first island chain, and its 'Near Seas Active Defence' strategy requires it to achieve limited sea control in the 'inner and outer rims' of the chain.[67] The naval balance is unlikely to favour India. According to one crude but illustrative calculation, one-tenth of Chinese naval assets could destroy the entire massed fleet of Indian destroyers and frigates.[68] India's land-based tankers could seek to exploit their own long range to refuel carrier-based MiG-29Ks or navalised Tejas closer to their targets, thereby allowing a carrier to position itself even further from shore-based weaponry, but the sheer distance and convoluted flight path (to avoid overflight) would limit the scope of any such operation. In addition, Indian carriers positioned in the Gulf of Oman could allow MiG-29Ks to reach Afghanistan as far as Herat in the west and Kandahar, the site of an infamous Indian hostage crisis in 1999, in the south. Positioned deeper into the Persian Gulf, India could reach as far as an arc stretching from Jordan, to Turkey, through to the Caspian.

---

[64] Lambeth, *Airpower at 18,000'*, p. 21.

[65] Micah Zenko, 'Comparing the Islamic State Air War with History', Politics, Power, and Preventive Action blog, Council on Foreign Relations, 6 July 2015, <http://blogs.cfr.org/zenko/2015/07/06/comparing-the-islamic-state-air-war-with-history/>, accessed 21 October 2015.

[66] Vivek Kapur, 'INS Vikramaditya: A Boost to India's Power Projection Capabilities', In Focus, CAPS, February 2014.

[67] Andrew S Erickson, 'Rising Tide, Dispersing Waves: Opportunities and Challenges for Chinese Seapower Development', *Journal of Strategic Studies* (Vol. 37, No. 3, Summer 2014), pp. 389–90.

[68] Jaganath Sankaran, 'The Tactical Reach and Requirement of the Indian Navy', S Rajaratnam School of International Studies, October 2013, p. 8.

Access in the Maritime Environment
Despite the US's large network of global bases, naval air power has played a pivotal role in American force projection over the past decade. During Operation *Enduring Freedom* against the Taliban and Al-Qa'ida in 2001, carrier-based air power 'substituted almost entirely for land-based theatre air forces', largely because of a paucity of suitable land bases. In the three-week Operation *Iraqi Freedom* in 2003, air wings from six carriers flew around half of all fighter sorties conducted by US Central Command.[69] However, carrier-based aviation also faces restrictions. In these campaigns, sea-based combat aircraft enjoyed a highly permissive environment both around the carrier itself and, in the case of Afghanistan, over enemy territory, thereby freeing up aircraft for ground-attack missions rather than securing air superiority. In the Falklands War of 1982, the British carrier battle group did face a persistent Argentine air threat, resulting in the loss of four frigates and destroyers – though that was without AEW such that India would enjoy in the form of the KA-31 helicopter, albeit with limited range and endurance.[70] In the case of the *Vikramaditya*, its own protective short- and long-range weapons systems will be fitted over the next two years (2015–17).[71] The British example shows that (largely) sea-based air power can play an important role even in non-permissive environments, but also how difficult and costly this can be.

India's carriers will also be supported, by 2020, by a network of other surface ships, including twenty-nine destroyers and frigates (notably the *Kolkata*-class guided-missile destroyer), up to twenty attack submarines, medium- and long-range maritime surveillance aircraft (notably eight, and possibly twelve, Boeing P-8I Neptunes), other ASW aircraft and a dedicated naval communications satellite.[72] Two Italian-procured fleet

---

[69]   Benjamin S Lambeth, *American Carrier Air Power at the Dawn of a New Century*, 1st ed. (Santa Monica, CA: RAND Corporation, 2006), p. iii. Jermy notes, however, that while land-based aircraft flew just 22 per cent of sorties in Operation *Enduring Freedom*, they dropped 75 per cent of the bombs by weight owing to greater B-2 and B-52 capacity. India's trade-off is less steep, given its preference for multi-role aircraft over dedicated bombers.
[70]   Steve Jermy, 'Maritime Air Power', *RUSI Defence Systems* (Vol. 7, No. 2, Autumn 2004), p. 84; on the limits of heliborne airborne early warning (AEW), see Tellis, *Making Waves*, p. 13; on the KA-31's endurance, see *IHS*, 'Jane's World Navies'.
[71]   Bedi, 'Indian Navy Chief: Vikramaditya Deployed with MiG-29s Embarked'; Anil Kumar Singh, 'INS Vikramaditya and India's Naval Security', *Indian Defence Review* (Vol. 29, No. 3, July–September 2014).
[72]   Ashok Sawhney, 'The Navy in India's Socio-Economic Growth and Development', in Rajesh M Basrur, Ajaya Kumar Das, and Manjeet Singh Pardesi (eds), *India's Military Modernization: Challenges and Prospects* (New Delhi: Oxford University Press, 2014), pp. 37–40; on submarine numbers, see Ajai Shukla,

tankers also allow Indian ships to sustain themselves without port access for longer periods.[73]

Each of these supporting assets builds up India's aggregate naval capability, but each also represents a potential weak link in force projection, particularly in highly contested areas. Consider submarines: the American norm has been that two submarines are assigned to protect a single carrier group (although typically with independent tasking in the allocated area, rather than under the carrier group's command) with 'at least four [submarines] needed to maintain one forward'.[74] Two at-sea carriers would therefore require four attached submarines, and in turn a total fleet of sixteen submarines. India's present submarine availability is currently six days in ten, constrained mainly by a lack of spare parts.[75] However, these ratios are not written into stone. Other carrier-operating countries take different approaches. France integrates submarines into carrier groups to a greater extent, because its submarines are less proficient in independent roles such as intelligence collection, while the UK – with only seven working nuclear attack submarines – relies on allies to make up its task groups.

India certainly need not emulate the US Navy, but it would have to accept more gaps in coverage, more time on station, a more permissive naval environment, or simply lesser protection around a carrier and therefore greater risk of losing a highly symbolic asset it possesses in extremely small quantities.[76] What is clear is that large escorts would absorb most of India's dwindling submarine fleet and divert these platforms from intelligence and independent strike roles.

'A Powerful Surface Navy Lacks Submarine Punch', Broadsword, 2 October 2014, <http://ajaishukla.blogspot.co.uk/2014/10/a-powerful-surface-navy-lacks-submarine.html>, accessed 21 October 2015; on the *Kolkata*-class destroyers, see Rahul Bedi, 'India Commissions First-of-Class Destroyer Kolkata', *IHS Jane's Defence Weekly*, 18 August 2014.

[73] Abhijit Singh, 'The Indian Navy's New "Expeditionary" Outlook', ORF Occasional Paper No 37, ORF, October 2012, p. 3.

[74] Norman Friedman, *Seapower as Strategy: Navies and National Interests* (Annapolis, MD: Naval Institute Press, 2001), p. 280; Ivan Eland, *Putting 'Defense' Back Into U.S. Defense Policy: Rethinking U.S. Security in the Post-Cold War World* (Westport, CT: Greenwood Publishing Group, 2001), p. 214; GAO, 'Navy Carrier Battle Groups: The Structure and Affordability of the Future Force', GAO/NSIAD-93–74, February 1993, p. 17. India's Type 209s are assumed to be superior to the originals, though this is likely offset by poorer-quality batteries.

[75] Sudhi Ranjan Sen, 'Why India's Submarine Fleet Is Deployed for Just 6 Out of 10 Days', *NDTV*, 27 August 2015.

[76] Recent accounts suggest that the Indian Navy does indeed plan on the basis of two submarines per carrier. See Sushant Singh, 'Explained: India's Submarine Story in Deep Waters, Long Way to Go', *Indian Express*, 12 November 2015.

India currently operates thirteen diesel-electric submarines, the last of which was acquired in the late 1990s, plus a single nuclear-powered *Akula*-class attack submarine leased from Russia since 2012. Four of the conventional submarines are of the *Shishumar* class and nine of the *Sindhughosh* class, variants of the German Type 209 and Russian *Kilo*-class respectively. Assuming their ranges correspond roughly to these parent classes, that would suggest that both can travel around 740 km submerged and over 10,000 km snorkelling.[77] This would barely allow submerged transit of even something as relatively close as the Malacca Strait.

Under India's Project 75, the first of six *Kalvari*- (*Scorpène*-) class diesel-electric submarines was floated in April 2015 and will be commissioned by summer 2016, with the remaining five to be delivered by 2020.[78] The follow-on Project 75I is intended to produce six indigenous attack submarines with air-independent propulsion, but are only due to arrive after 2030[79] – India has also asked Japan to participate in this tender with its *Soryu*-class submarines.[80] Finally, in February 2015 the Indian government cleared a \$12-billion proposal to build six nuclear-powered attack submarines, with two reportedly allocated for each hypothetical carrier group.[81] Given Western sensitivity around the non-proliferation implications of nuclear propulsion, this would almost certainly require further Russian assistance with reactor design on top of that extended by Moscow to New Delhi's SSBN programme. Even if these programmes proceed on course – highly doubtful – the retirement of older platforms means that the navy would struggle to meet its 1999 target of twenty-four submarines by 2030.[82]

Under these circumstances, India faces difficult trade-offs. Iskander Rehman quotes Ravi Ganesh, a retired vice admiral, as acknowledging that the primary roles of Indian attack submarines will continue to be forward-deployed sea-denial and surveillance – for instance, holding Chinese platforms in the Indian ocean at risk or monitoring Chinese activity in Indian Ocean ports – rather than the defence of SSBNs or

---

[77] Paul E Fontenoy, *Submarines: An Illustrated History of Their Impact* (Santa Barbara, CA: ABC-CLIO, 2007), pp. 330, 358.

[78] Ridzwan Rahmat and Rahul Bedi, 'India Floats out First Scorpene Submarine', *IHS Jane's Defence Weekly*, 7 April 2015.

[79] Iskander Rehman, 'The Indian Navy Has a Big Problem: The Subsurface Dilemma', *National Interest*, 4 November 2014.

[80] Rahul Bedi, 'India Asks Japan to Offer Soryu Subs for Project 75I Requirement Soryu', *IHS Jane's Defence Weekly*, 29 January 2015.

[81] Sandeep Unnithan, 'The Indian Ocean Riposte', *India Today*, 6 April 2015.

[82] *Economic Times*, 'Indian Navy to Soon Invite Tenders for Six Conventional Submarines', 12 July 2015.

carriers, in part because of Indian weakness in sonar and underwater-communications technology.[83] Critics also point to serious gaps in India's deep-water ASW, at a time when technological changes may be making oceans more transparent – if indeed they were ever as opaque as assumed.[84] Indian SSBNs operating in bastion mode, close to India, might be somewhat insulated from adverse technological shifts, given the salinity and thermal layers of the Indian Ocean.[85] But attack submarines would have to operate more widely. Ongoing submarine proliferation in Asia will increase the vulnerability of Indian surface platforms, and could therefore force India to choose between maintaining a given level and assuredness of naval air-power projection capability by assigning submarines to escort and land-attack duties on the one hand, and maintaining capabilities across a broader spectrum of tasks on the other.[86]

In addition to protection from adversary surface ships and aircraft, missiles present a further problem for naval air power. The maturation of anti-ship ballistic missiles (ASBMs), notably China's 1,500-km-range DF-21D, in concert with improving target-acquisition capabilities – collectively known as the 'reconnaissance-strike complex' – has provoked a vigorous debate among American analysts over the threat to surface vessels, and their ability to operate within flying-range of such threats.[87] The range of naval strike aircraft has expanded more slowly than that of newer SAMs, which are also increasingly mobile and therefore harder to locate and

---

[83] Iskander Rehman, 'Murky Waters: Naval Nuclear Dynamics in the Indian Ocean', Carnegie Endowment for International Peace, 2015, p. 11; on the submarines' intelligence capabilities, see Desmond Ball, *Signals Intelligence (SIGINT) in South Asia: India, Pakistan, Sri Lanka (Ceylon)* (Canberra: Australian National University, 1996), p. 24.

[84] Shukla, 'A Powerful Surface Navy Lacks Submarine Punch'; Rehman, 'Murky Waters', p. 46; on US visibility into Soviet SSBN movements, see Austin Long and Brendan Rittenhouse Green, 'Stalking the Secure Second Strike: Intelligence, Counterforce, and Nuclear Strategy', *Journal of Strategic Studies* (Vol. 38, Nos. 1–2, January 2015), pp. 47–51.

[85] Walter C Ladwig III, 'Drivers of Indian Naval Expansion', in Harsh V Pant (ed.), *The Rise of the Indian Navy: Internal Vulnerabilities, External Challenges* (Burlington, VT: Ashgate, 2012), p. 29.

[86] Nuclear Threat Initiative (NTI), 'Submarine Proliferation Resource Collection', 26 September 2014, <http://www.nti.org/analysis/reports/submarine-proliferation-overview/>, accessed 21 October 2015.

[87] Peter Dutton, Andrew S Erickson and Ryan Martinson (eds), *China's Near Seas Combat Capabilities* (Newport, RI: Naval War College Press, 2014), pp. 20–21; Ian Easton, 'China's Evolving Reconnaissance-Strike Capabilities: Implications for the U.S.-Japan Alliance', Japan Institute of International Affairs (JIIA) and Project 2049 Institute, February 2014.

suppress.[88] Indian carriers would also be vulnerable to air-launched cruise missiles, such as the CJ-10 launched from China's H-6 K bomber, the latter possessing a combat radius of 2,400–3,300 km – comfortably exceeding the combat radius of any one of India's naval aircraft – as well as wake-homing torpedoes, if closer to China's near seas.[89]

The emerging threat to American carrier groups and even US bases in East Asia has been one factor behind the development of 'Air-Sea Battle', an ambitious doctrine-*cum*-strategy that seeks to neutralise Chinese reconnaissance and strike assets and thereby restore maritime freedom of manoeuvre.[90] This strategy presumes an initial large-scale Chinese assault on US forces and airbases in the region, and relies for its response on the use of conventional-missile and stealth-bomber capability of the sort that India will not possess in the medium term. Nevertheless, whether as part of a broader war which affects the Indian mainland or a limited war which does not, India, when projecting its power against adversaries with conventional precision-strike capabilities of their own, will be forced to do one or more of the following: defend launching points (for example, hardened bases and better-protected carriers); launch strikes from outside the range of such weaponry (for example, land-based air power and missiles, or longer-legged naval air power); employ platforms that are less vulnerable (for example, stealthy aircraft) or more disposable (for example, unmanned aircraft); or seek to blind or destroy those weapons, whether with conventional or non-conventional (for example, cyber-warfare) capabilities.[91] India is in a similar position to France or Britain, whereby the loss of even one of a small number of carriers could have disproportionate political and strategic consequences, thereby deterring Indian political leaders from authorising their deployment in the first place, except in the most desperate circumstance such as a significant attack on the Andaman and Nicobar Islands.

---

[88] David Barno, Nora Bensahel and M Thomas David, 'The Carrier Air Wing of the Future', White Paper, Center for a New American Security (CNAS), February 2014, p. 10.

[89] Carlo Kopp, 'XAC (Xian) H-6 Badger', Technical Report APA-TR-2007-0705, Air Power Australia, April 2012, <http://www.ausairpower.net/APA-Badger.html>, accessed 21 October 2015; Ronald O'Rourke, 'China Naval Modernization: Implications for U.S. Navy Capabilities – Background and Issues for Congress', RL33153, Congressional Research Service, December 2014, pp. 12, 60. The H-6K was tested several times in 2015 and in October declared capable of 'precision attacks'.

[90] Aaron L Friedberg, *Beyond Air-Sea Battle: The Debate over US Military Strategy in Asia*, Kindle ed. (Oxford: Routledge, 2014).

[91] The author is grateful to Iskander Rehman for suggesting these points.

But an equally important question is how far such anti-access/area-denial technologies are likely to constrain India in the lower-level scenarios it might face when projecting power outside of war with near-peer or superior adversaries. Comparatively few states will possess ASBMs, let alone the means of cueing strikes against moving sea-based targets. Defending carrier resilience, Indian naval officer Gurpreet Khurana argues that 'even if a carrier is hit by one or two missiles, this is unlikely to affect even its fighting efficiency, let alone its ability to come back to harbour or to stay afloat'.[92] In the absence of examples of modern carriers being struck by modern anti-ship missiles, this claim is hard to evaluate. Yet even non-ballistic missiles present serious challenges, particularly if fired in salvos that can overwhelm ship-based defences. In the modern period, 68 per cent of missiles fired at ships 'that had defences but failed to use them properly', as Michael O'Hanlon describes it, struck their targets, and 26 per cent where defences were employed.[93]

The incapacitation of over a quarter of an Indian carrier group could gravely impact its effectiveness or even survival. Even Pakistan, a land-focused, inferior naval power, has sought Chinese assistance in creating an anti-access 'bubble' around the northern Arabian Sea, deploying anti-ship cruise missiles on mobile coastal launch-pads, aboard stealthy fast attack craft, and on its JF-17 fighter aircraft.[94] Other middle naval powers in the Indian Ocean region, such as Indonesia and Myanmar, could pursue similar defensive approaches, given the relatively low cost of anti-ship missiles, while some, like Iran, have already done so.[95] Pakistan's platforms would be within reach of India's land-based air power, and it is likely that the IAF would be tasked with suppression of Pakistani surface vessels and coastal sites in wartime, but this not only requires sound ISR – discussed in Chapter IV – but would also present diplomatic and political difficulties if India were compelled into initiating a conflict before it could allow power-projection platforms to loiter in a forward position.

---

[92] Gurpreet S Khurana, 'Aircraft Carriers and India's Naval Doctrine', *Journal Of Defence Studies* (Vol. 2, No. 1, 2008), p. 104.
[93] Michael E O'Hanlon, *The Science of War: Defense Budgeting, Military Technology, Logistics, and Combat Outcomes* (Princeton, NJ: Princeton University Press, 2009), p. 93.
[94] Iskander Luke Rehman, 'Tomorrow or Yesterday's Fleet? The Indian Navy's Operational Challenges', in Anit Mukherjee and C Raja Mohan (eds), *India's Naval Strategy and Asian Security* (New York, NY: Routledge, 2015).
[95] Terrence K Kelly et al., *Employing Land-Based Anti-Ship Missiles in the Western Pacific* (Santa Monica, CA: RAND Corporation, 2013), p. 16.

India's Missile Forces

An alternative to land-based or naval combat air power would be the use of India's cruise or ballistic missile forces.[96] While combat aircraft have greater persistence and flexibility (for example, in loitering over targets), missiles can be used with no risk to a pilot – potentially an advantage in less-permissive environments – and require a smaller supporting infrastructure than a typical fighter squadron.[97] Of the wide range of operational, deployed or near-operational Indian land-based missile forces, those with the relevant range to be of use for long-range force projection include the 1,250 km-range Agni-I and 3,500 km-range Agni-II ballistic missiles and the 750 km-range Shaurya cruise missile. Relevant sea-launched forces include the 350 km-range Prithvi-variant Dhanush, 750 km-range Sagarika, and 300 km-range naval BrahMos.

The first question is whether India views ballistic missiles as conventional force-projection platforms at all. In April 2015, Defence Minister Manohar Parrikar, responding to a question about whether India would fulfil its complete order of Rafale jets – something that now looks improbable – argued that some of India's ageing MiG variants could 'be replaced by even proper stockpiling of missiles', which 'nowadays … can attack some targets'.[98] Parrikar did not explain what he meant by this, but it could refer to fixed targets such as bases, ports and other infrastructure. However, despite confusing signals sent by the Defence Research and Development Organisation (DRDO), it is overwhelmingly likely that India is prioritising purely nuclear roles for long-range ballistic missiles like the Agni 1 and 2.

The Prithvi family of missiles is the only realistic exception, but its range is too short (350 km for the Prithvi 2) and is very likely prioritised for the nuclear role too. Short legs also hamper the cruise-missile force. Ladwig observes that the 300-km BrahMos, though faster and harder to intercept, has just a fraction of the range of a US Tomahawk (1,700–2,500 km, depending on variant).[99] The BrahMos has been fitted to eight Indian destroyers and frigates across four classes of ship, but delivery to land-based targets would require dangerous proximity to shore. The

---

[96] NTI, 'Design Characteristics of India's Ballistic and Cruise Missiles', November 2014, <http://www.nti.org/media/pdfs/design_characteristics_of_india_ballistic_cruise_missiles.pdf?_=1415821730>, accessed 21 October 2015. Estimates of range vary widely and these numbers below should be taken as indicative.

[97] John R Harvey, 'Regional Ballistic Missiles and Advanced Strike Aircraft: Comparing Military Effectiveness', *International Security* (Vol. 17, No. 2, Fall 1992), p. 45.

[98] Shishir Gupta and Rahul Singh, 'IAF Consulted on Direct Buy of Rafales: Parrikar', *Hindustan Times*, 16 April 2015.

[99] Ladwig III, 'India and Military Power Projection', p. 1176.

submarine-launched BrahMos, tested in March 2013 and intended for the *Scorpène/Kalvari*-class, or the aircraft-delivered variant, would be easier to deliver from a position closer to distant targets, but these would still have extremely shallow inland reach. Force projection will therefore depend on conventional roles being assigned to longer-range ballistic-missile forces, or the maturation of longer-range cruise missiles like the 1,000 km-range Nirbhay. However, the Nirbhay failed three tests between March 2013 and October 2015.[100]

Six other possible issues arise with Indian conventional missile use for power projection. First, missile targeting differs from that of aircraft, with mobile targets presenting greater difficulty for missiles in the absence of sophisticated ISR and guidance.[101] In particular, accuracy typically deteriorates with range.[102] While shorter-range missiles like the 150 km Prahaar are associated with a circular error probable (CEP – a measure of accuracy) of as low as 10 metres, the lowest public estimates for India's longer-range (500 km-plus) missiles, most relevant in the power-projection context, are around 25 metres for the Agni-I and 40 metres for the Shaurya and Agni-III.[103] Ajay Lele and Parveen Bhardwaj have argued that the majority of Indian missiles have a CEP of around 50 metres.[104] These are of obviously limited utility for non-nuclear use. Only the non-ballistic BrahMos is known to have satellite-aided midcourse guidance.[105] By comparison, even unguided bombs dropped from aircraft with advanced aiming systems are estimated to have CEPs of 8–12 metres, and precision munitions as low as 3 metres at stand-off range.[106]

---

[100] *Economic Times*, 'Test Fire: India's Indigenous Cruise Missile Nirbhay Fails Midway', 16 October 2015. The second test was hailed as 'perfect', but the missile failed to maintain a low altitude and Indian officials expressed serious doubts over its flight-control software and resilience. See Hemant Kumar Rout, 'Is Nirbhay Missile Set for Trial with "Shortcomings"?', *New Indian Express*, 15 October 2015.

[101] Harvey, 'Regional Ballistic Missiles and Advanced Strike Aircraft', p. 52; Bharat Karnad, *India's Nuclear Policy* (Westport, CT: Praeger Security International, 2008), p. 101.

[102] Verghese Koithara, *Managing India's Nuclear Forces* (Washington, DC: Brookings Institution Press, 2012), p. 131.

[103] NTI, 'Design Characteristics of India's Ballistic and Cruise Missiles'; for the Agni-III estimate, see Arms Control Association, 'Arms Control and Proliferation Profile: India', February 2015, <http://www.armscontrol.org/print/3197>, accessed 21 October 2015.

[104] Ajay Lele and Parveen Bhardwaj, *India's Nuclear Triad: A Net Assessment* (New Delhi: IDSA, 2013), p. 35.

[105] *Business Standard*, 'HAL Delivers First BrahMos-Integrated Su-30 to IAF', 19 February 2015.

[106] Raas and Long, 'Osirak Redux?', pp. 16–17.

Second, missiles tend to be both less reliable and less exhaustively tested than aircraft. India has also tested its strategic missiles comparatively less than other nuclear-armed states before inducting them.[107]

Third, missiles are scarcer and possibly more expensive than other forms of projecting force. A crude comparison might be made as follows: consider that the unit cost of the Indian Navy's BrahMos missiles is reported to be approximately $2.3 million.[108] The unit cost of a Joint Direct Attack Munition (JDAM), a guidance kit that converts unguided bombs into aircraft-launched PGMs, is around $20,000.[109] Even if adding the cost of the bomb itself (say, $3,100 for a Mark 84) and the highest estimates of flying costs for a modern combat aircraft ($24,000 per flying hour for the F/A-18 Super Hornet, totalling $203,000 for a ten-hour mission) we still arrive at an estimate less than one-quarter of the BrahMos's cost.[110] Others argue that the larger payload per sortie and re-usability makes aircraft cheaper by a factor of two, to the point where it would take 9 per cent loss rates for missiles to become as cost-effective.[111] In India's case, limited production of conventional missiles means that it could be a long time before missiles unit costs fall significantly.

Fourth, the use of missiles, particularly ballistic missiles, may be deemed especially escalatory within a conflict, to a greater degree than the use of air power.[112] Conventional ballistic missiles have been used in relatively few inter-state conflicts, and usually confined to smaller, less capable Scud-type missiles. Cruise missiles have only ever been put to wartime use by the US, the UK, France, Italy and Russia, all of which have been largely invulnerable to reciprocal strikes from the targeted states or groups, such as Libya.[113] It might be argued that the US and the UK have, through repeated use, weakened any taboo on conventional missile use for routine military tasks, including

---

[107] Koithara, *Managing India's Nuclear Forces*, pp. 131–32.

[108] Roughly $110 million, or £70 million, for forty-nine missiles.

[109] US Navy, 'Joint Direct Attack Munition (JDAM)', fact file, 20 February 2009, <http://www.navy.mil/navydata/fact_display.asp?cid=2100&tid=400&ct=2>, accessed 21 October 2015.

[110] FAS, 'GBU-15', 18 February 2015, <http://fas.org/man/dod-101/sys/smart/gbu-15.htm>, accessed 21 October 2015; Edward Hunt, 'Fast Jet Operating Costs: Cost Per Flight Hour Study Of Selected Aircraft', White Paper, IHS Jane's, March 2012, p. 9.

[111] Harvey, 'Regional Ballistic Missiles and Advanced Strike Aircraft', p. 50.

[112] George Perkovich and Toby Dalton, 'Modi's Strategic Choice: How to Respond to Terrorism from Pakistan', *Washington Quarterly* (Vol. 8, No. 1, Spring 2015), p. 32.

[113] Russia fired the Kalibr sea-launched cruise missile (SLCM) from the Caspian Sea at targets 1,500 km away in Syria in October 2015.

use against strategic targets. But this is not how Indian decision-makers are likely to see it when presented with the option by military leaders.

Fifth, the use of missiles is less deniable than that of air-delivered munitions. Outside of civil conflicts, the use of ballistic missiles has rarely gone unattributed; by contrast, air strikes have frequently been conducted semi-anonymously, to varying degrees of plausibility: consider Israel's 2007 strike on Syria's Al-Kibar reactor;[114] Egyptian and Emirati strikes on Libya in 2014;[115] and Israel's numerous strikes on Syrian territory from 2013 to 2015.[116]

Sixth, and finally, the dual uses of Indian missiles might lead to confusion over whether the payload of a particular strike is nuclear or conventional.[117] However, this is only likely to be a serious concern against other nuclear-armed adversaries. Moreover, as Christopher Clary notes, the widespread expectation of mutual conventional missile use in wartime has a perversely positive side effect: it makes launch-on-warning postures impossible, because each side will have to cope with a higher probability that any given ambiguous missile is conventional rather than nuclear.[118]

India has given relatively little indication of how it views the role of missile forces in power projection. In part, this is understandable: whereas some long-range capabilities can be couched in benign terms – air lift as integral to humanitarian missions, warships to anti-piracy and even combat aircraft can be viewed as an integral part of India's air defences – missiles afford no such rhetorical cloak. Moreover, they are associated primarily with India's nuclear arsenal, an association that can hinder rather than facilitate India's efforts to seek respectability and influence on the national stage. However, India has invested substantial amounts into the development of cruise missiles in recent years. Although their currently limited range constrains how these can be used, they could – for some missions where targets are hardened or overflight presents political difficulties – represent a superior alternative to air strikes.

---

[114] George W Bush, *Decision Points* (London: Random House, 2010), pp. 420–23; David Makovsky, 'The Silent Strike', *New Yorker*, 17 September 2012.
[115] David D Kirkpatrick and Eric Schmitt, 'Arab Nations Strike in Libya, Surprising U.S.', *New York Times*, 25 August 2014.
[116] *BBC News*, 'Syria Profile – Timeline', 22 May 2015.
[117] Christopher Clary, 'Command and Control Trends and Choices for the Next Decade in South Asia', in Feroz Hassan Khan, Ryan Jacobs and Emily Burke (eds), 'Nuclear Learning in South Asia: The Next Decade', Naval Postgraduate School, June 2014, p. 98.
[118] *Ibid.*, p. 98.

Air Power Trade-Offs

It is important to note that these platforms will be deployed and used in line with national priorities and government decisions at the time. As explained in the previous chapter, while power projection is increasingly salient in Indian military doctrines and national strategy, India's overarching defence posture remains dominated by local concerns and power projection is as much about generating new ways to use or threaten force against Pakistan and, to a larger extent, China. India's hoped-for Airbus tankers, for instance, would be based at Panagarh in West Bengal, the base of the China-focused mountain strike corps.[119] Expeditionary air power will be a *by-product*, not the central aim, of Indian procurement. Similarly, the air force has shown comparably little interest – though more so than in previous decades – in training for special long-range missions, as Israel did over the Mediterranean in 2008 in order to signal interest and prepare for a possible attack on Iranian nuclear facilities.[120] And although India's air force is growing into one of the most offensively capable forces in Asia, it nevertheless lacks depth: if India were to devote several squadrons of the Su-30MKI to conduct air strikes in the Middle East or in Afghanistan, for instance, it might be seen to have an appreciable effect on the immediate air balance *vis-à-vis* Pakistan – particularly if it were as part of a longer deployment, such as participation in a multinational coalition with open-ended aims.

Conclusion

This chapter has shown that India's land-based and naval aircraft are growing into a substantial force, capable of producing and sustaining sizeable packages of combat aircraft, armed with PGMs and cruise missiles, over 1,000 km from Indian soil. While India lacks a strategic bomber and shows no interest in acquiring one, the primary combat aircraft in its fleet – the Su-30MKI, Mirage 2000, Jaguar and potentially Rafale – are all proficient in the strike role and benefit from a rapidly growing tanker fleet. India has created a strong base for air-power projection, but it will take decades for this capability to mature. India's ability to use long-range combat-air power against adversaries with advanced air-defence systems, large air forces that could overwhelm strike packages and threaten vulnerable platforms like tankers, or hold at risk carriers with mobile anti-access weapons is still fairly limited – and more

---

[119] Jayanta Gupta, 'IAF Bolsters its Capabilities in the Eastern Sector, Lands Super Hercules at Panagarh', *Times of India*, 4 August 2015.
[120] Michael R Gordon and Eric Schmitt, 'U.S. Says Israeli Exercise Seemed Directed at Iran', *New York Times*, 20 June 2008.

so when we consider prolonged campaigns, that could require a sustained forward presence and persistent strikes. This is an important constraint, but it is not an overwhelming one. Most applications of air power by NATO states in recent years have been against relatively weaker adversaries, often, like Iraq or Afghanistan, with virtually no air force or air-defence system at all. More capable air-defence systems have required considerable risk-acceptance, as in the Balkans, larger initial strike campaigns, as in Libya, or tacit agreements with the local governments, as in Syria or (in relation to drones) Pakistan.

The specific scenario in question, discussed in Chapter V, would therefore set the context. Were India participating in strikes against terrorist groups where the risk of escalation was low and international sympathy was high, it might have access to local bases, perhaps even as part of a coalition. It could be on its own if, by contrast, the target was a government on an Indian Ocean island pursuing policies that New Delhi opposed. Given the number of unknowns, uncertainty around Indian capabilities could by itself generate bargaining power for New Delhi, as long as adversaries believed there was some prospect of force being used. Naval air power offers unique advantages and drawbacks, being especially useful for signalling through forward deployment, but also particularly vulnerable in a shifting anti-access/area-denial environment. The military challenge for India is now less about possession of more combat platforms, but about the enablers necessary to generate air power as a whole: special forces capable of gathering intelligence and cueing strikes, the ability to convey information from sensors to combat aircraft, search-and-rescue aircraft capable of recovering downed pilots, and so on.

III. LAND-POWER PROJECTION

Power projection is about delivering kinetic attacks at a considerable distance from one's homeland. These attacks can be delivered from the air by aircraft or missiles. But they can also be delivered by ground forces, transported to the target by air, land or sea, and kept there for a matter of minutes or years. While the term 'expeditionary warfare' has been used to describe forces forward deployed for long periods, it would be unusual to apply this term to short, sharp operations – such as the Israeli raid at Entebbe in 1976 – so, instead, I use the broader term of land-power projection.

In the West, land power faces a period of reassessment. Large-scale counter-insurgency campaigns in Iraq and Afghanistan have come to be viewed as inconclusive at best and disastrous at worst. Air power, meanwhile, furnishes a quicker, cheaper, more politically palatable – indeed, as with American air strikes in Afghanistan through 2015, often domestically invisible – national response. Yet limited interventions, with and without air power, continue to demand important ground components. The pan-Arab intervention in Yemen in 2015 involves, at the time of writing, 2,800 Emirati and Saudi Arabian troops, including an armoured brigade.[1] Russia's intervention in Ukraine over 2014–15 involved over 12,000 troops.[2] Campaigns where ground forces are largely absent – as with the coalition against Daesh formed in 2014 – struggle to seize and hold territory, except when third-party forces are present and able to co-ordinate with intervening powers (such as the Kurds and other rebel groups in Syria).

India does have experience of projecting land forces over long distance. As noted earlier, three of its four experiences in overseas power projection – peacekeeping, the Maldives and Sri Lanka – have involved integral contributions from the Indian Army. Yet even fighting in adjacent territory has involved projecting power over long distances, albeit from

---

[1]   Michael Knights and Alexandre Mello, 'The Saudi-UAE War Effort in Yemen (Part 1): Operation Golden Arrow in Aden', Policywatch 2464, Washington Institute for Near East Policy, 10 August 2015..

[2]   Mark Urban, 'How Many Russians Are Fighting in Ukraine?', *BBC News*, 10 March 2015.

home bases. One reason for this is that India has unusually long interior lines of communication: one of India's three strike corps, XXI Corps, is based roughly 900–1,200 km from the Pakistani border. India has no dedicated military railway track and the armed forces are accorded low priority to the congested civilian track in peacetime, which limits the co-operation necessary for rapid wartime mobilisation.[3] Railway lines identified as military priorities have received minimal attention, with work begun on just two out of fourteen such lines. Indian roads are relatively poor, with only fifteen out of seventy-three key project roads near the Sino–Indian border completed, despite a 2012 deadline. India's interior lines of communication are therefore not just long, but also weak. Another reason is that India's neighbours are also large. India penetrated over 300 km into East Pakistan (Bangladesh) in the 1971 war. In some ways, India's embryonic mountain strike corps is intended precisely as an instrument of local power projection, allowing theatre-level offensive operations into China over exceptionally adverse terrain. Large-scale airlift was crucial to India in its first war as an independent country over Kashmir in 1947, and would be important in any ground conflict with China. The transport aspect of land-power projection is, therefore, familiar to India. Other aspects are less so, particularly complex joint operations in more contested environments.

Types of Land-Power Projection

Land-power projection might be divided into two categories: first, the forces that do the fighting; and, second, the forces that transport them to the targets and sustain them afterwards.

In the first category, we would include traditional ground forces, namely infantry and armour, as well as three more specialised types of units – air-assault forces, airborne-assault forces and amphibious forces – that deserve greater attention (special forces are taken up in Chapter IV, given their enabling role in other operations). Air assault refers to the insertion of usually light infantry by rotary-wing aircraft in contested conditions, while airborne assault, more uncommon in contemporary warfare, refers to larger-scale drops of paratroopers on the battlefield.[4]

---

[3] This section draws on Sushant K Singh, 'Optimising India's Strategic Infrastructure', unpublished manuscript, 2015.

[4] Department of the Army and US Marine Corps, 'Operational Terms and Graphics', Field Manual, FM 1-02/MCRP 5-12A, September 2004, p. 5. For the Soviet/Russian terminology of equivalent concepts, see David M Glantz, *A History of Soviet Airborne Forces* (London: Taylor and Francis, 1994), p. xvi.

Amphibious operations involve naval and landing forces launched from the sea against a hostile, or potentially hostile, shore.[5]

In the second category, transport forces, we would include ground transport, airlift and sealift. Although ground transport is important to power projection, as NATO's experience in Afghanistan with the Northern Distribution Network and Pakistani routes has shown, it is the latter two considered in detail here. Airlift and sealift are important not only to the three specialised forms of land-power projection outlined a moment ago, but also to so-called 'red-carpet operations', in which forces are delivered into a distant theatre under *non-contested* conditions.[6]

It should be noted that these are operational categories: they refer to the manner of inserting forces. Various strategic missions – such as long-term counter-insurgency or a short, punitive strike – could then be pursued with the projected forces, although there are obvious limits to, for instance, pursuing broad territorial objectives with a small force of commandos. Moreover, these are not mutually exclusive alternatives: air-assault teams might secure a staging area, allowing airlift or sealift under more permissive conditions. Finally, while I have avoided use of the term sea power in this study, the navy naturally plays a crucial – and sometimes predominant – role in each of these areas. However, its ultimate effect is delivered through aircraft, missiles or ground forces.

Air-Assault Capabilities

Air-assault capabilities are built around rotary-wing aircraft, which allow take-off and landing in limited space and the rapid disembarkation of forces. This typically means both attack and transport helicopters, depending on the mission. Air-assault operations can form one part of a broader operation, such as the six-day joint US–Iraqi Operation *Swarmer* in 2006 against insurgents,[7] or serve as strategic operations in their own right, such as Operation *Neptune Spear* in 2011 in which Osama bin Laden was killed. The mobility and flexibility of air assault makes it 'particularly well suited for operations in the restrictive terrain of mountains, urban areas, jungles, and the arctic'.[8]

---

[5] British Maritime Doctrine, quoted in Julian Thompson, 'Force Projection and the Falklands Conflict', in Stephen Badsey, Rob Havers and Mark Grove (eds), *The Falklands Conflict Twenty Years On: Lessons for the Future* (London: Frank Cass, 2005), p. 82.

[6] *Ibid.*, p. 82.

[7] Jim Muir, 'How US Assault Grabbed Global Attention', *BBC News*, 17 March 2006.

[8] US Department of the Army, 'Infantry, Airborne, and Air Assault Brigade Operations', Field Manual FM 7–30, 1981, pp. 8–7.

Helicopter Numbers

India's helicopter and transport fleet are both in a period of transition. India possesses two squadrons of Mi-25/35 attack helicopters, twenty in all, which have been criticised as obsolete, and four of which may shortly be gifted to Afghanistan.[9] In terms of transport helicopters, India operates three Mi-26s for heavy lift; ninety Mi-8s, eighty Mi-17-1Vs and 121 newer Mi-17-V5s for medium lift; and forty Dhruv, sixty Cheetahs, and forty Chetaks at the lower end.[10] A significant proportion of this fleet has been described as unreliable and verging on obsolete.[11]

At present, India's helicopter fleet compares relatively unfavourably with other large military powers globally and within Asia. It has roughly the same number of attack helicopters as Singapore, fewer than half as many as France and fewer than a third as many as Britain. Although India's overall fleet of transport and multi-role helicopters is larger than any state bar China, Russia and the US, India is severely deficient in heavy lift, with just three frequently grounded Mi-26s that were procured in the mid-1980s.[12] Only one is typically available at any given time, with limitations in high altitudes and narrow valleys.[13] And while India has provided more attack and multi-role helicopters to UN peacekeeping missions than any other contributing state, it was forced to withdraw some from the Democratic Republic of the Congo in 2011 because of an overall shortage.[14]

The Indian fleet will, however, expand in coming years. India hopes to beef up its medium-lift capability with forty-eight Mi-17V-5s to add to its current 121, but these are replacements for ageing Mi-8s and some will be

---

[9] International Institute for Strategic Studies (IISS), *The Military Balance 2015* (London: Routledge/IISS, 2015), p. 251; B S Pawar, 'Growing Needs: The Highs and Lows of Indian Military Helicopters', *Force*, June 2012.
[10] IISS, *The Military Balance 2015*, p. 251. The IISS's Mi-26 estimate has been discounted to account for a crash five years ago and the Mi-17V-V5 estimate supplemented in line with newer sources. Mi-17 variants have been classified here as medium lift, although the *Military Balance 2015* labels these as multi-role.
[11] Pranay S Ahluwalia, 'Army Aviation: Does the Army Need its Own Air Force?', ORF Issue Brief No. 81, Observer Research Foundation, November 2014, p. 6.
[12] A K Sachdev, 'Helicopter Fleet for the IAF', *Indian Defence Review* (Vol. 28, No. 2, April–June 2013).
[13] Shiv Aroor, 'Chinook In IAF Colours: 5 Big Reasons the IAF Is Smiling', Livefistdefence.com, 28 September 2015, <http://www.livefistdefence.com/2015/09/chinook-in-iaf-colours-5-big-reasons.html>, accessed 22 October 2015.
[14] Sushant K Singh and Richard Gowan, 'India and UN Peacekeeping : The Weight of History and a Lack of Strategy', in Waheguru Pal Singh Sidhu, Pratap Bhanu Mehta and Bruce Jones (eds), *Shaping the Emerging World: India and the Multilateral Order* (Washington, DC: Brookings Institution Press, 2013), p. 183.

Figure 8: Attack, Transport and Multi-Role Helicopter Holdings of Major States.

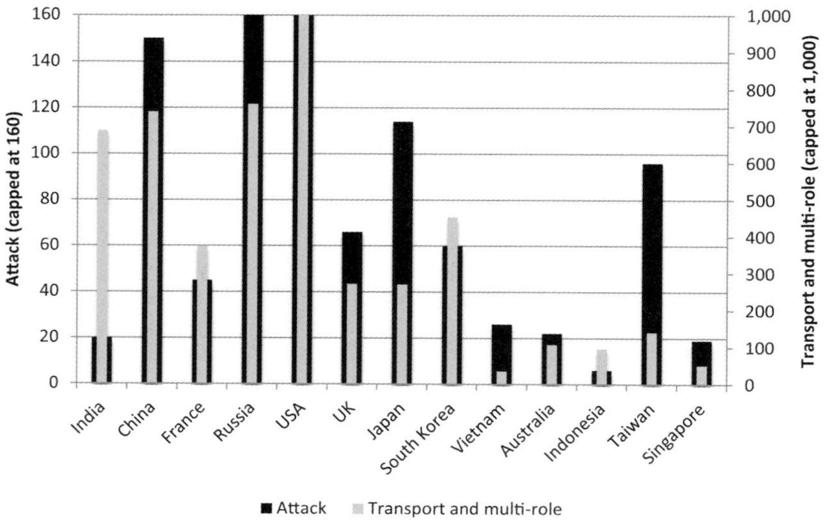

■ Attack   ▨ Transport and multi-role

Source: *IISS Military Balance 2015.*
Note: *Mi-17 variants have been classified here as medium lift, although* The Military Balance *2015 labels these as multi-role.*

diverted for VIP duties.[15] India has also ordered twenty-two AH-64E Apache attack helicopters and fifteen CH-47F Chinook heavy-lift helicopters from the US for $2.5 billion, with an option for eleven more Apaches and seven more Chinooks.[16] The Army Aviation Corps is pursuing a separate requirement for thirty-nine Apaches. The IAF has expressed an interest in the tilt-rotor V-22 Osprey, but there is no indication that this will be pursued.[17] The Apache and Chinook deals represent an important moment in the broader Indian tilt towards high-end American platforms, outlined in Chapter I. However, the result

---

[15] Sputnik, 'Russia Delivered 121 Mi-17V-5 Helicopters to India, Ready to Send More', 18 February 2015, <http://sputniknews.com/science/20150218/1018442073. html#ixzz3nm8RRUsD>, accessed 22 October 2015; Manu Pubby, 'IAF Moves Proposal to Acquire 48 Mi 17 Choppers from Russia to Strengthen Transport Fleet', *Economic Times*, 20 July 2015.
[16] Rahul Bedi, 'India Moves to Sign off on Apache, Chinook Deals', *IHS Jane's Defence Weekly*, 28 May 2015; Airforce Technology, 'Boeing Receives Apache and Chinook Order from India', 2 October 2015, <http://www.airforce-technology. com/news/newsboeing-receives-apache-and-chinook-order-from-india-4683367>, accessed 22 October 2015.
[17] Sachdev, 'Helicopter Fleet for the IAF'.

would still be a relatively small attack-helicopter capability compared with that which sustains other air-assault units such as the UK's 16 Air Assault Brigade (which has sixty-six Apaches).

In addition to numbers, India faces two other issues with helicopters. First, Indian helicopters are endowed with more limited quantities of electronic and physical protection and stealth than their American counterparts.[18] This is especially problematic for specialised missions in less-permissive conditions. Second, a large proportion of this fleet will be absorbed by existing requirements – notably border security, counter-insurgency and VIP transport.[19] The new Chinooks, for example, will have a number of claims on their use, including demands by the Border Roads Organisation (BRO) to facilitate projects in remote northeastern areas that require heavy airlift through narrow valleys.[20]

Capabilities

India's air-assault capabilities were given limited attention in the late 1980s, when then army chief General Sundarji re-labelled the Hyderabad-based 54 Infantry Division as an air-assault division and set out an ambitious plan to raise two such divisions by 2000.[21] These plans were grandiose and were reversed for a variety of reasons, one of which was that helicopters were simply too expensive to procure in sufficient numbers.[22] More recently, defence analyst Gurmeet Kanwal has argued that an air-assault brigade could be built around Mi-17s, three specially trained battalions, and 'two to three flights of attack and reconnaissance helicopters'. He estimates that this would cost 'the equivalent of a light armoured division to raise and maintain'.[23] Walter Ladwig suggests that

---

[18] A K Sachdev, 'Helicopters in Special Operations', *Indian Defence Review* (Vol. 27, No. 4, October–December 2012), p. 16.

[19] B S Pawar, 'Army Aviation 2030: Bright Future', *CLAWS Journal* (Winter 2011), pp. 48–49; Sachdev, 'Helicopter Fleet for the IAF'.

[20] Manu Pubby, 'Here is Why Apache and Chinook Helicopters are Game Changers for India', *Economic Times*, 23 September 2015.

[21] Amit Gupta, *Building an Arsenal: The Evolution of Regional Power Force Structures* (Westport, CT: Praeger, 1997), p. 58; Ali Ahmed, *India's Doctrine Puzzle: Limiting War in South Asia* (New Delhi: Routledge, 2014), p. 44; Ken Conboy and Paul Hannon, *Elite Forces of India and Pakistan* (Oxford: Osprey Publishing, 2012), p. 15.

[22] Gupta, *Building an Arsenal*, p. 60.

[23] Gurmeet Kanwal, 'India: Need for an Air Assault Brigade and Rapid Reaction Force', Institute of Peace and Conflict Studies, 1 August 2006, <http://www.ipcs. org/article/military/india-need-for-an-air-assault-brigade-and-rapid-reaction-2084. html>, accessed 22 October 2015; Gurmeet Kanwal, *Indian Army: Vision 2020* (New Delhi: HarperCollins Publishers/India Today Group, 2008), p. 247.

the Agra-based 50 (Independent) Parachute Brigade could form its nucleus.[24]

Air-assault capabilities also have a strong dual-use aspect: they could be employed at distance whether independently or as part of other types of Indian power projection, but they could also reinforce India's China-focused mountain strike corps by enabling India to conduct offensive operations over otherwise semi-impassable terrain. Numerous Indian analysts emphasise the importance of an air-assault component to an effective mountain strike corps.[25] Yet given that the mountain strike corps was pruned for budgetary reasons in May 2015, and given other capital commitments, it is highly unlikely that any large, independent air-assault unit will be seen as affordable in the near-term.[26]

Airborne Assault

While air-assault forces can use their organic attack and transport helicopters to 'manoeuvre on the battlefield', the reliance on helicopters also constrains their overall size.[27] Airborne assaults, which drop paratroopers, can deliver larger groups of infantry into areas where airfields are unavailable or limited.

India has such a capability in the form of the aforementioned 50 Parachute Brigade.[28] The brigade has been extensively deployed both in India's local wars and expeditionary campaigns. The most celebrated use of Indian paratroopers was during the 1971 war, when India's 2 Parachute Battalion was paradropped 200 km into East Pakistan to capture a key bridge and cut off retreating Pakistani forces.[29] Later, India would deploy

---

[24] Walter C Ladwig III, 'India and Military Power Projection: Will the Land of Gandhi Become a Conventional Great Power?', *Asian Survey* (Vol. 50, No. 6, November 2010), p. 1180.

[25] Gautam Banerjee, 'Mountain Strike Corps along Indo-Tibet Border and Strategic Advantage', Vivekananda International Foundation (VIF), 19 September 2014, <http://www.vifindia.org/article/2014/september/19/mountain-strike-corps-along-indo-tibet-border-and-strategic-advantage>, accessed 22 October 2015; Gurmeet Kanwal, 'Deterring the Dragon', *Vayu Aerospace and Defence Review* (No. 1, January–February 2013), p. 55; G D Bakshi, 'Restructuring the Indian Armed Forces', *Journal Of Defence Studies* (Vol. 5, No. 2, April 2011), p. 30.

[26] Surya Gangadharan, 'What Raising a New Mountain Strike Corps Means for India', *IBN Live*, 18 July 2013; Shantanu K Bansal, 'Army Aviation Corps: On the Wings of Transformation', *Indian Defence Review* (Vol. 30, No. 1, January–March 2015).

[27] See Department of the Army, 'Tactics', Field Manual FM 3–90, July 2001, Appendix C.

[28] Ladwig III, 'India and Military Power Projection', p. 1180.

[29] J F R Jacob, *Surrender at Dacca: Birth of a Nation* (New Delhi: Manohar Publishers & Distributors, 1997), p. 77.

five battalions of 50 Parachute Brigade in Operation *Pawan* (Sri Lanka) and one of its units as the vanguard force for Operation *Cactus* (the Maldives), though never conducting paradrops.[30] During the large-scale Exercise Sanghe Shakti in 2006, the brigade practised airdropping a battalion and supporting equipment, including artillery, drawing on fifteen An-32 and two Il-76 transporters.[31]

At root, airborne forces rest on the quality and quantity of airlift capacity. This capacity is discussed below. However, the very rationale of conventional airborne operations has also been called into question. Major General Sukhwant Singh, in his history of Indian wars, argues that 'parachute formations have no future in the context of the type of wars India is required to fight on the subcontinent and should be done away with in the foreseeable future. India would never have the capability of achieving a favourable air situation against Pakistan or China to allow paratrooping in any depth'.[32] More broadly, there have been very few examples of airborne warfare in any recent conflict. These include airdrops by the US in Afghanistan in 2001 and Iraq in 2003, Britain in Afghanistan in 2010 and France in Mali in 2013.[33] However, others note that China – with an airborne assault of Taiwan in mind – has developed its own three-division XV Airborne Corps, directly under the control of the People's Liberation Army Air Force Headquarters, expanding it in 1993 and later adding external roles to its previously internal-focused duties, such that it now serves as 'China's primary national-level [rapid-response unit]'.[34] India continues to train for airborne operations,

[30] Parachute Regiment Training Centre, 'History', n.d., <http://www.indianparachuteregiment.kar.nic.in/history.htm>, accessed 22 October 2015; Salute, 'The Prickly Tale of Operation Cactus', 5 March 2012, <http://salute.co.in/the-prickly-tale-of-operation-cactus/>, accessed 22 October 2015.

[31] Oneindia, 'Pak Informed of "Sanghe Shakti": Lt Gen Daljeet Singh', 18 May 2006, <http://www.oneindia.com/2006/05/18/pak-informed-of-sanghe-shakti-lt-gen-daljeet-singh-1147946942.html>, accessed 22 October 2015.

[32] Sukhwant Singh, *India's Wars Since Independence: The Liberation of Bangladesh* (New Delhi: Vikas, 1980).

[33] Mir Bahmanyar, *Shadow Warriors: A History of the US Army Rangers* (Westminster, MD: Osprey Publishing, 2012), pp. 178–87; Michael R Gordon and Bernard E Trainor, *Cobra II: The Inside Story of the Invasion and Occupation of Iraq* (New York, NY: Pantheon Books, 2006), p. 340; Michael Smith, 'Paras Make First Jump since Suez', *Sunday Times*, 26 December 2010; Leigh Neville, *Special Operations Forces in Afghanistan* (Westminster, MD: Osprey Publishing, 2012), pp. 13, 25–27; Michael Shurkin, 'France's War in Mali: Lessons for an Expeditionary Army', RAND Corporation, 2014, p. 21.

[34] Kenneth W Allen, 'The Organizational Structure of the PLAAF', in Richard P Hallion, Roger Cliff and Phillip C Saunders (eds), 'The Chinese Air Force: Evolving Concepts, Roles, and Capabilities: Evolving Concepts, Roles, and Capabilities', Center for the Study of Chinese Military Affairs, 2012, p. 96; Dennis J Blasko, *The*

notably practising high-altitude airdrops near its contested border with China.[35]

Airlift

Inserting forces into a theatre of combat – whether dropping them into a combat zone or delivering them to a secure staging point – depends on adequate airlift. This can often be the weak link in power projection. France, for instance, needed American and British help with transporting its forces to fight Al-Qa'ida in the Islamic Maghreb in Mali in 2013, while the UK faced several issues with the reliability of its air bridge to both Afghanistan and Iraq.

On paper, the Indian airlift fleet is a strong aspect of its power-projection capabilities. It has over 200 transport aircraft in all, about twice as many as France and four times as many as Britain (though at least 5 per cent are for VIP transport). While China has more transporters overall, India has about twice as many in the heavy-lift category. The most important Indian transporters are eight C-17As, 24 Il-76MDs (both heavy lift), five C-130J-30 (medium lift), and over 100 lighter transporters that include old and modernised An-32s. India has ordered six further C-130s, will shortly receive two more C-17s and may yet order six more.[36] These will replace the older An-32 and Il-76, which will be phased out in a decade or so.[37] The ongoing acquisition of C-17s – which India used for evacuation and humanitarian missions in Yemen and Nepal in 2015[38] – is increasing India's ability to access countries and areas with lower-quality airstrips, which are common in the region. Both the C-17 and C-130 can land at 'austere' airfields, enabling access to less-developed areas without engineering teams first having to upgrade runways.[39] A study by the USAF in 2009 found that the C-17 could take off and land on 65 per cent of the world's soil.[40]

Chinese Army Today: Tradition and Transformation for the 21st Century (Oxford: Routledge, 2013), p. 104.

[35] Rajat Pandit, 'Paradrop Training along LAC to Check China', *Times of India*, 10 September 2012.

[36] Gareth Jennings, 'India Exercises Option for Six More Hercules Transport Aircraft', *IHS Jane's Defence Weekly*, 24 July 2014.

[37] Ashok Goel, 'Indian Air Force and its Transport Fleet', *India Strategic*, October 2008.

[38] Jatinder Kaur Tur, 'Silver Lining: C-17 Globemaster III Gives Major Boost to Rescue Ops', *Times of India*, 31 July 2015.

[39] William G T Tuttle Jr, *Defense Logistics for the 21st Century* (Annapolis, MD: Naval Institute Press, 2005), p. 80.

[40] Rachel Martinez, 'Austere Runway Ops Validate C-17 Combat Capability', Air Mobility Command, US Air Force (USAF), 12 April 2013, <http://www.amc.af.mil/news/story.asp?id=123344265>, accessed 22 October 2015.

The readiness rate for these aircraft varies. France, for example, could only draw on six to seven out of its fourteen C-130Hs during Mali operations in 2013, though these were older models than India's C-130J-30s.[41] Between 2009 and 2013, readiness rates for the American C-17A fleet ranged from 85 to 87 per cent, and those for the C-130J variants 78 to 82 per cent.[42] The average readiness rate of India's transport fleet is even lower, however, at around 65 per cent.[43] Even with an optimistic assumption that this would rise to the US level as the average age of the Indian fleet falls, this would imply that ten C-17s and eleven C-130s are likely to produce between eight and nine ready aircraft of each type at any given time. Unlike other countries, such as France in Mali, India is less likely to be able to call upon emergency support from partners.

Stephen P Cohen of the Brookings Institution suggested in 2005 that if India drew on its military and civilian airlift capacity, it could 'soon be able to move a brigade or more of troops to a hotspot in the Indian Ocean region or Central Asia'.[44] I test this assertion by estimating the aggregate capacity of India's fleet. The C-17A, developed as a strategic airlifter for 'long-range forcible-entry operations',[45] can carry 77,500 kg, which is the equivalent of one of the following loads: 102 paratroopers (with equipment); 134 troops; thirteen Land Rover-sized vehicles; a Chinook; two to three Apaches; three light helicopters; one of any one of India's main battle tanks; or approximately three lighter armoured vehicles.[46] The C-17A's unrefuelled one-way range is 6,480 km, allowing India to reach Japan to the east, Germany or Libya to the west, and Mauritius or most of

---

[41] Philippe Gross, 'Libya and Mali Operations: Transatlantic Lessons Learned', Foreign Policy Papers, German Marshall Fund, July 2014.

[42] Brian Everstine, 'Readiness Declines in Aging, Overworked Fleet', *Military Times*, 2 October 2013.

[43] Rahul Bedi and James Hardy, 'Internal IAF Report Criticises Serviceability Rate for Fighter Fleet', *IHS Jane's Defence Weekly*, 23 October 2014.

[44] Stephen P Cohen, 'The Bad, the Ugly, and the Good: South Asian Security and the United States', testimony given before the House of Representatives, Committee on Armed Services Defense Review Threat Panel, Washington, DC, 26 September 2005, p. 8; cited in Ladwig III, 'India and Military Power Projection', p. 1179.

[45] Tuttle Jr, *Defense Logistics for the 21ˢᵗ Century*, p. 98.

[46] *Force*, 'Backbone of the World: C-17 Provides Unmatched Airlift Capability', February 2013; RAF, 'C-17A Globemaster', n.d., <http://www.raf.mod.uk/ equipment/c17aglobemaster.cfm>, accessed 22 October 2015; USAF, 'C-17 Globemaster III', fact sheet, May 2014, <http://www.af.mil/AboutUs/FactSheets/ Display/tabid/224/Article/104523/c-17-globemaster-iii.aspx>, accessed 22 October 2015. Others have questioned whether the Arjun can be carried. See Atul Chandra, 'India's Arjun Mk.2 Tank Revealed', Livefistdefence.com, 10 August 2012, <http:// www.livefistdefence.com/2012/08/indias-arjun-mk2-tank-revealed.html>, accessed 22 October 2015.

Indonesia to the south – assuming, conservatively, that it operates from a central Indian airbase.[47] Its out-and-back radius is 3,700 km, which still reaches Hong Kong to the east, Iraq or Saudi Arabia to the west and Diego Garcia to the south. The C-130J-30 is smaller. Designed for tactical rather than strategic airlift, its range is shorter, at 3,150 km at maximum normal payload, and it can carry ninety-two paratroopers or 128 troops, but only 15,400 kg.[48] Even with this shorter range, it could reach the South China Sea or Malacca Strait to the east, the eastern half of Saudi Arabia to the west, or even large parts of Afghanistan (assuming routing over Iran). Air-to-air refuelling, discussed in Chapter I, could extend the range of both these aircraft.

On the basis of the readiness rates discussed above, eight C-130s and eight C-17s could therefore transport around 1,000 troops, fifty-two off-road utility vehicles and twelve lighter armoured vehicles to virtually any location, subject only to the availability of tanker aircraft. This is closer to a large battalion than a brigade. Factoring in the IL-76 fleet would allow for another 1,700–2,000 troops (the lower end of a brigade) or 700 tonnes,[49] and adding the AN-32s, a further 2,300 troops or 370 tonnes of load.[50] Taken together, and in theory, an upper estimate of India's airlift capacity using only its American aircraft would therefore be over 5,000 troops, approximately two brigades.

In practice, however, these forces would also have logistical requirements (such as ammunition), and the rate of transport would be constrained by loading/unloading times, airfield throughput and operational friction. It is worth taking a moment to explain why the airlift of combat forces requires more time and capacity than would seem apparent on paper. Political scientist Peter Krause estimates that it would take sixteen to thirty-three C-17-equivalents between two and three days to transport a single battalion of the US 82nd Airborne Division – just 800 troops, but 770

---

[47] For range estimates, see Air Mobility Command, USAF, 'Global En Route Strategy White Paper', July 2014.

[48] USAF, 'C-130 Hercules', fact sheet, September 2003, <http://www.af.mil/AboutUs/FactSheets/Display/tabid/224/Article/104517/c-130-hercules.aspx>, accessed 22 October 2015.

[49] Assuming 60 per cent readiness, a capacity of 120 infantry, 140 paratroops; see *Aerospaceweb.org*, 'IL-76', <http://www.aerospaceweb.org/aircraft/transport-m/il76/>.

[50] Assuming 60 per cent readiness, and a capacity of 6.08 tonnes or thirty-nine troops. India's upgraded AN-32s will see their capacity rise to 6.8 tonnes. See Vivek Raghuvanshi, 'Ukraine Conflict Stalls Indian AF Upgrade', *Defense News*, <http://www.defensenews.com/story/defense/air-space/support/2015/03/28/india-ukraine-transport-fleet-upgrade-antonov-avro-air-force/70441446/>, accessed 28 March 2015.

tonnes of equipment.[51] A study by another scholar, Alan Kuperman, further suggests that wartime conditions can reduce aircraft payload limits by up to 30 per cent, or 544 tonnes (roughly seven C-17 loads); that, therefore, the maximum realistic 'load-out' rate from a single US airborne division from one base is 544 tonnes (roughly seven C-17 loads); that smaller airfields[52] have maximum daily loads of 363 tonnes (four to five C-17 loads); and that the supply of refuelling aircraft – analysed in Chapter II – turns out to be a major constraint.[53]

As a result of these various factors, during Operation *Desert Shield* the 82nd Airborne Division took seven days to transport 2,300 personnel and around 4,000 tonnes in 165 sorties. It took the 101st Air Assault Division five days merely to prepare for loading, and then three weeks to transport 2,742 personnel and around 3,600 tonnes of cargo, including 117 helicopters.[54] More recent operations confirm these longer timelines. In January 2013, it reportedly took 'several weeks' for five American C-17s to airlift a French mechanised-infantry battalion, with relatively light armour, from France to Mali – despite support from six further C-17s from Canada, Sweden, the UAE, the UK and various other airlifters, as well as significant sealift.[55] There is no reason to suppose that India could exceed these timelines. Finally, it should be remembered that a single airborne brigade in combat requires around 270 tonnes per day in food, water, fuel and ammunition – in other words, at least four C-17 sorties.[56] Therefore sustaining any intervention by air would be almost as difficult as initiating it.

Sealift and Amphibious Operations

Sea-based platforms enjoy two key advantages in projecting force: mobility and persistence.[57] The latter is especially useful in providing decision-makers with flexible options. While aircraft face human, fuel and threat limitations on endurance above a target, naval platforms can remain

---

[51] Peter John Paul Krause, 'The Last Good Chance: A Reassessment of US Operations at Tora Bora', *Security Studies* (Vol. 17, No. 4, December 2008), p. 661.

[52] Kuperman cites Mombasa and Entebbe.

[53] Alan J Kuperman, *The Limits of Humanitarian Intervention: Genocide in Rwanda* (Washington, DC: Brookings Institution Press, 2004), pp. 57–62.

[54] *Ibid.*, p. 59.

[55] US Africa Command, 'U.S. Airlift of French Forces to Mali', news release, 24 January 2013, <http://www.africom.mil/Newsroom/Article/10206/us-airlift-of-french-forces-to-mali>, accessed 22 October 2015; Shurkin, 'France's War in Mali', p. 35.

[56] Michael E O'Hanlon, *The Science of War: Defense Budgeting, Military Technology, Logistics, and Combat Outcomes* (Princeton, NJ: Princeton University Press, 2009), p. 145.

[57] Peter Roberts, 'The Future of Amphibious Forces', *RUSI Journal* (Vol. 160, No. 2, April/May 2015), p. 46.

forward deployed for extended periods of time. Amphibious platforms, in particular, allow a state to project land power ashore, and therefore achieve direct territorial control in a way air power cannot.[58]

Amphibious Capacity
India significantly grew its holdings of amphibious ships in the 1980s, and made a major statement when it acquired the large American landing platform dock (LPD) USS *Trenton*, re-naming it the INS *Jalashwa*, in 2007. The *Jalashwa* can transport six landing craft, mechanised, and either forty tanks or around a thousand troops and six medium helicopters (with four operating from the deck at once). India also possesses nine other landing ships: four landing ships, medium (LSMs) of the *Kumbhir* class, which carry 160 troops and five tanks; and five landing ships, tank, of which two of the *Magar* class carry fifteen tanks and 500 troops, and three in the modified *Magar* class carry eleven tanks and 500 troops. Finally, India has thirty-two landing craft, twenty-four of which form part of the *Jalashwas* and *Magars*, and eight landing craft, utility (LCUs), each capable of taking two armoured personnel carriers and 120–60 troops.[59]

Assuming full availability, this produces a carrying capacity of around 123 tanks or a little over 4,000 troops: smaller than a US Marine Corps 15,000-strong Marine Expeditionary Brigade, but comfortably equivalent to a 1,900-strong Marine Expeditionary Unit with its associated platforms – and not far off the size of the initial British assault force for the Falkland Islands in 1982 (about 5,500 men).[60] If we assume 80 per cent availability, this falls to ninety-two tanks or just under 3,000 troops.[61] As with other aspects of its power-projection capabilities, India has considerable ambitions for expansion. In this case it is planning to acquire a further four LPDs and eleven LCUs.[62] If

---

[58] Colin S Gray and Roger W Barnett (eds), *Seapower and Strategy* (Annapolis, MD: Naval Institute Press, 1989), p. 41.
[59] Publicly available estimates of capacity differ. See IISS, *The Military Balance 2015*, p. 250; Press Information Bureau, Government of India, 'INS Jalashwa Joins the Eastern Fleet', media release, 13 September 2007, <http://pib.nic.in/newsite/erelease.aspx?relid=31220>, accessed 22 October 2015; Abhijit Singh, 'The Indian Navy's "New" Expeditionary Outlook', ORF Occasional Paper No. 37, Observer Research Foundation, October 2012, pp. 7–8.
[60] Congressional Budget Office (CBO), 'Moving the Marine Corps by Sea in the 1990s', October 1989, p. 15; Douglas C Lovelace Jr, *Terrorism: Commentary on Security Documents. Volume 121–140* (New York, NY: Oxford University Press, 2014), p. 212; Lawrence Freedman, *The Official History of the Falklands Campaign. Vol. 2: War and Diplomacy* (London: Routledge, 2005), p. 175.
[61] This rough figure is derived from discounting the availability rates of American amphibious ships. See CBO, 'An Analysis of the Navy's Amphibious Warfare Ships for Deploying Marines Overseas', No. 4172, November 2011, p. 9.
[62] Singh, 'The Indian Navy's "New" Expeditionary Outlook', pp. 3–4.

these were of comparable size to India's existing vessels, they would increase capacity at full availability by over 5,000 troops, bringing the total to over 9,000. Recent reports suggest that the new LPDs will be larger, at 35,000–40,000 tonnes, compared with the *Jalashwa*'s 17,000.[63] If this proportionately generates double the capacity, then total capacity could rise to just under 15,000 troops. In 2012, Vice Admiral Satish Soni, then commander-in-chief of the Southern Naval Command, claimed that by 2022 India would possess a 'brigade-lift capability'.[64] The calculations here suggest that this would be at the very edge of India's capability. It would depend on construction procurement proceeding implausibly smoothly and swiftly, and assume unrealistically high availability rates.

These calculations show India's theoretical carrying capacity. But amphibious landings hinge on whether an attacker can resupply its landing force faster than an adversary can concentrate defensive forces.[65] A single brigade-size force, with little in reserve, would be effective only against a numerically limited or immobile adversary, though it should be noted that Argentine defenders outnumbered the successful British attackers more than two to one in 1982.[66] Reinforcement would also prove difficult. Indian Director of Naval Operations Rahul Parmar writes that medium LPDs have endurance of around 15,000 km at 20 knots.[67] It would therefore take around three to four days to sail from, say, Mumbai (home of the Indian Navy's Western Naval Command) to the Gulf of Aden; four to five days from Kochi (home of Southern Naval Command) to Madagascar; and just over three days from Vizag (home of Eastern Naval Command) to Malacca. These are not overly long timelines, but in the context of a fast-moving crisis they could complicate Indian decision-making.

As former naval officer Peter Roberts notes, even the US Marine Corps, the most capable amphibious force in the world, would undertake high-

[63] Ajay Banerjee, 'India to Ramp Up Amphibious Capabilities with Four Warships', *The Tribune*, 11 January 2015.

[64] Pranav Kulkarni, 'Navy Will Reach "Brigade-Lift" Capability by 2022, Says Vice-Admiral Soni', *Indian Express*, 30 November 2012.

[65] O'Hanlon, *The Science of War*, p. 86; Allan R Millett, 'Assault from the Sea: The Development of Amphibious Warfare between the Wars – The American, British, and Japanese Experiences', in Williamson R Murray and Allan R Millett (eds), *Military Innovation in the Interwar Period* (Cambridge: Cambridge University Press, 1998), p. 89.

[66] David A Welch, *Painful Choices: A Theory of Foreign Policy Change* (Princeton, NJ: Princeton University Press, 2005), p. 82.

[67] Rahul Parmar, 'HADR in the IOR & the Indian Navy', Integrated Headquarters of Ministry of Defence, n.d., <http://goo.gl/CKEtEi> (cached version), accessed 20 October 2015.

intensity amphibious operations (for example, 'the full militarised assault of a beach defended by a near peer rival') only in extreme circumstances; this downgrade in risk and casualty acceptance represents a 'major shift' in its approach.[68] When compared with other medium-to-large military powers, India's evolving amphibious capability is closer to Australia's large and flexible force structure, designed for a variety of regional scenarios, than to Japan's smaller, focused capability tailored to particular targets, notably disputed island chains.[69]

Other Amphibious Challenges

India is making gradual progress in developing and exercising its amphibious capability. However, this could be constrained by the slow military development of the Andaman and Nicobar Islands and questions around adequate air support for amphibious operations.

India's 340 (Independent) Infantry Brigade was previously tasked with 'island protection duties' and trained for amphibious warfare, which it employed during the initial stages of intervention in Sri Lanka.[70] In 2009, it was reported that India was re-raising the 91 Infantry Brigade as an amphibious formation based in Thiruvananthapuram, with a reported strength of 3,000 personnel and anticipated to rise to 5,000.[71] This would be a Reorganised Amphibious Formation, comprising an amphibious brigade, air-mobile brigade and one reserve infantry brigade.

In 2008, the navy established its Advanced Amphibious Warfare School and Fleet Support complex on the east coast, to assist in raising three naval infantry battalions.[72] That same year, the Integrated Defence Staff also released a joint doctrine for amphibious warfare.[73] Starting in 2009, India has conducted large-scale, tri-service amphibious exercises (known as *Tropex*), involving thousands of troops and both active carriers.[74] Many of India's amphibious capabilities are attached to the joint

[68]   Roberts, 'The Future of Amphibious Forces', p. 44.

[69]   *Ibid.*, p. 44.

[70]   Shankar Bhaduri and Afsir Karim, *The Sri Lankan Crisis* (New Delhi: Lancer Publishers, 1990), p. 113.

[71]   Globalsecurity.org, '91 Infantry Brigade', n.d., <http://www.globalsecurity.org/military/world/india/91-bde.htm>, accessed 22 October 2015. One Indian naval source suggests that this unit is now a division rather than a brigade.

[72]   Prasun K Sengupta, 'Vertical Envelopment', *Force*, September 2012.

[73]   Rajat Pandit, 'Forces Ready with Joint Amphibious Warfare Doctrine', *Times of India*, 7 September 2008.

[74]   Press Information Bureau, Government of India, 'Amphibious Landing Exercise off Gujarat Coast', media release, 9 February 2009, <http://pib.nic.in/newsite/erelease.

Andaman and Nicobar Command, which was created in 2001, but which scholar Anit Mukherjee has called a 'grand failure'. He notes that the navy sees its creation as a mistake, each service has denied the command control of its own assets and there are no plans for permanent aircraft deployments. Morale on the islands was also devastated by the 2004 tsunami.[75] The Modi government has announced a significant expansion of the Andaman and Nicobar Command, promising new jetties and runways, a naval air station at Campbell Bay and the eventual deployment of a division-sized force, a fighter squadron and multiple warships.[76] If these projects come to fruition in a reasonable time-frame, they would represent not only a significant basis for India's amphibious infrastructure but they would also increase India's ability to project power into Southeast Asia, notably the Malacca Straits, and even into East Asia.

Basing and infrastructure aside, the commander who oversaw 91 Infantry Brigade's conversion to the amphibious role has also noted two major operational challenges to India's amphibious capability. One is the lack of fire support in the initial phases of a landing, given the limited number of naval guns aboard Indian warships. A second is the difficulty of landing artillery and engineering stores given the poor 'fording capabilities' of the larger landing ships used on the final stretch.[77]

Finally, virtually all successful amphibious landings under contested conditions – such as that at San Carlos in the Falklands War – have required significant air cover.[78] Indeed, the Falklands campaign is atypical as a successful amphibious landing with air cover, but without air superiority.[79] Air superiority – 'sufficient control of the air to make air attacks on the enemy without serious opposition'[80] – has usually been considered as a prerequisite for successful amphibious landing.[81]

Successful Indian power projection against adversaries with credible air power would therefore require any landing to be within range of land-based aircraft or, more likely, within range of supporting carrier-based

aspx?relid=47351>, accessed 22 October 2015; *Business Standard*, 'Indian Navy Concludes Annual TROPEX Exercise', *Business Standard India*, 27 February 2015.
[75] Anit Mukherjee, 'India's Joint Andaman and Nicobar Command is a Failed Experiment', Asia Pacific Bulletin No. 289, East-West Center, November 2014, pp. 1–2.
[76] Rajat Pandit, 'India to Slowly but Steadily Boost Military Presence in Andaman and Nicobar Islands', *Times of India*, 7 May 2015.
[77] Danvir Singh, 'Indian Army: Reminiscences of a Soldier', *Indian Defence Review* (Vol. 29, No. 1, January–March 2014).
[78] Freedman, *The Official History of the Falklands Campaign: Vol. 2*, pp. 399–401.
[79] O'Hanlon, *The Science of War*, p. 86.
[80] John Warden III, *The Air Campaign: Planning for Combat* (Washington, DC: National Defense University Press, 1988), ch. 1.
[81] Theodore L Gatchel, *At the Water's Edge: Defending Against the Modern Amphibious Assault* (Annapolis, MD: Naval Institute Press, 2013), ch. 13.

aircraft.[82] This would depend on the target's distance from India, the local air balance and the quality, quantity and mobility of anti-access capabilities that the defender could bring to bear. The latter two factors could in turn be influenced by the scope and success of prior power projection, such as Indian cruise-missile strikes against the defender's shore-based missiles. These calculations could be affected by the potential willingness of India's regional adversaries – in effect, Pakistan or China – to transfer anti-ship or surface-to-air missiles to weaker powers or non-state actors facing an Indian assault. This would not prevent Indian intervention, but it could raise the costs sufficiently to deter New Delhi.

Sustainability

Logistics

Projecting land power is not just about conveying combat forces over long distances. It is also about keeping them there – whether the forces in question are landing ships or carriers waiting offshore or armies enmeshed in long-distance counter-insurgency. One part of this sustainability challenge is about the sheer capacity of airlift and sealift to carry supplies to the forward operating environment. This problem is especially severe for large armies in the field. The effort to supply and later withdraw the NATO-led International Security Assistance Force (ISAF) in Afghanistan at its peak involved multiple sea and air routes into Middle Eastern and Pakistani ports, and multiple further ground routes into Afghanistan via Pakistan and Central Asia.[83] These required complex diplomatic negotiation with non-allied nations – above all Russia – resulting in caveats on the types of equipment that could be conveyed by particular routes and therefore reliance on expensive airlift for the most sensitive items.

India is not without experience in such sustainment. During India's intervention in Sri Lanka, for instance, the IAF ferried over 274,000 troops and 18,000 tonnes of load in over 42,500 sorties,[84] while the Indian Navy transported 200,000 troops, 100,000 tonnes, and 8,000 vehicles[85] – a

---

[82] Walter C Ladwig III, 'Drivers of Indian Naval Expansion', in Harsh V Pant (ed.), *The Rise of the Indian Navy: Internal Vulnerabilities, External Challenges* (Burlington, VT: Ashgate, 2012), p. 32.

[83] Francois Van Loven, 'The Logistical Challenges Confronting the Afghanistan Drawdown', Civil-Military Fusion Center, NATO, June 2013.

[84] Calculated from figures in A K Tiwary, 'Helicopter Operations in Sri Lanka', *Indian Defence Review* (Vol. 27, No. 3, July–September 2012).

[85] Jyotirmoy Banerjee, 'Seaward Security: Modernizing the Indian Navy', Anjali Ghosh et al. (eds), *India's Foreign Policy* (New Delhi: Pearson, 2009), p. 83.

combined average rate of 15,800 troops and 4,000 tonnes per month over the three-year campaign. They were helped by India's merchant fleet and the state-owned Indian Airlines respectively.[86] But the relatively short distance involved and India's dominant position in the air and maritime space along the route made this a relatively straightforward task. For over a decade, India has also kept a little-noticed deployment of paramilitary Indo-Tibetan Border Police (ITBP) in Afghanistan, growing from forty in 2005, to 400 in 2008, and up to 800 in 2015.[87] This force, which protects Indian interests after a series of targeted attacks, exceeds the size of all but three NATO-member contributions to Afghanistan as part of the Alliance's post-2014 *Resolute Support* mission. However, its logistical arrangements are unknown.

In some ways, India's experience of supplying forces *domestically* replicates some of the difficult logistical conditions of land-power projection. Snowfall periodically closes some ground routes, such as those into Kashmir, and the extreme altitude and climatic conditions of some outposts, such as those on the Siachen glacier, make re-supply exceptionally hard.[88] The experience, skills and technology necessary to sustaining forces in adverse circumstances at home may have positive spillover effects on India's ability to manage land-power projection. This may in part be the rationale behind India's decision to jointly explore co-development and co-production of the US Marine Corps's Mobile Electric Hybrid Power Sources, technology that could assist expeditionary forces or those in isolated locales.[89]

Endurance

Resources also shape the sustainability of land forces. In light of the nuclear environment, the risks of escalation and likely international pressure, Indian military planners have come to expect and prepare for short wars, measured

---

[86] Pradeep P Barua, *The State at War in South Asia* (Lincoln, NE: University of Nebraska Press, 2005), p. 247.

[87] George Iype, 'Indians in Aghanistan: Fear is the Key', Rediff, 1 December 2005, <http://www.rediff.com/news/2005/dec/01spec1.htm; PTI>, accessed 22 October 2015; Rediff, 'India to Send More ITBP Troops to Afghanistan', 23 September 2008; Abhishek Bhalla, 'Why Indian Missions in Afghanistan are Soft Terror Targets', *India Today*, 15 May 2015.

[88] John H Gill, 'Military Operations in the Kargil Conflict', Peter R Lavoy (ed.), *Asymmetric Warfare in South Asia: The Causes and Consequences of the Kargil Conflict* (Cambridge: Cambridge University Press, 2009), pp. 112–13.

[89] Ashley J Tellis, 'Beyond Buyer-Seller', *Force*, August 2015, p. 8.

in weeks rather than months or years.[90] One consequence of this is on ammunition holdings. India's CAG, a constitutionally mandated oversight body, notes that the Indian Army – which blames budgetary constraints and low production capacity – has allowed ammunition to dwindle well below the forty-day War Wastage Reserve requirements: as mentioned in Chapter I, half of Indian ammunition types would not last for ten days under Indian planning assumptions and just under three-quarters would not last for twenty days.[91] Half of all types of Indian ammunition, including a significant proportion of large-calibre artillery and armoured-fighting-vehicle ammunition, fall into the category of under ten days' availability.[92] These shortages are in part the result of deliberate policy, aimed at minimising peacetime wastage of ammunition with a short shelf life. However, they could have an impact on the early phases of an open-ended Indian expeditionary force, at least until the Ordnance Factory Boards ramp up production.

Numbers

Finally, the relatively large size of the Indian Army should not be taken to imply the presence of surplus manpower for secondary power-projection tasks to be conducted simultaneously with local, higher-priority wars. As scholars Paul Kapur, Christopher Clary and Walter Ladwig all note in separate studies, a combination of deeper unit locations and slower mobilisation times give India 'parity at best, if not actual disadvantages, in the number of troops it could bring to bear in the early days of a conflict' with Pakistan, in contrast with the conventional wisdom that it possesses crushing superiority over its smaller neighbour.[93] As explained in Chapter I, India's defence posture is firmly built around threats from Pakistan and China. Power projection is likely to remain below these in priority. In the event that discretionary power-projection tasks clash with local contingencies, the latter would likely divert resources, manpower and mission-critical platforms such as transporters.

---

[90] Walter C Ladwig III, 'Indian Military Modernization and Conventional Deterrence in South Asia', *Journal of Strategic Studies* (Vol. 38, No. 4, May 2015), p. 23.

[91] Union Government, Defence Services, 'Report of the Comptroller and Auditor General of India on Ammunition Management in Army (for the Year Ended March 2013)', PA 19, May 2015, p. 8.

[92] *Ibid.*, p. 10.

[93] Ladwig III, 'Indian Military Modernization and Conventional Deterrence in South Asia', p. 34; Christopher Clary, 'What Might an India-Pakistan War Look Like?', *précis*, Spring 2012; S P Kapur, 'India and Pakistan's Unstable Peace: Why Nuclear South Asia is Not Like Cold War Europe', *International Security* (Vol. 30, No. 2, Fall 2005), pp. 138–40.

Conclusion

This chapter has looked at India's land-power-projection capabilities: its ability to deploy ground forces through short, sharp air-assault operations; large-scale airborne-assault and amphibious operations; as well as to transport forces by air and sea in less-demanding conditions. While some operations, like airborne assault, are decreasingly common in modern wars, others, like airlift, are crucial to a wide range of both soft- and hard-power-projection missions, and others still, like amphibious assaults, are especially important in the maritime environment of the Indo-Pacific. India is making strides in all these areas. Within the next decade, India is likely to be able to move more than a brigade's worth of troops long distances in a short space of time and conduct amphibious operations with brigade-sized forces. India is increasingly testing these capabilities in tri-service exercises and limited operational contexts, largely involving disaster relief and evacuation.

India would, however, struggle against peer or near-peer opponents, which would not find it very difficult to muster greater defensive numbers than the viable size of an Indian amphibious force. The growing anti-access challenge exacerbates this problem, particularly if India is projecting power beyond the range of its land-based aircraft. In addition, India is especially weak in specific platforms, such as attack helicopters. India will be reluctant to deploy such scarce platforms abroad for long periods, given the important role they play in local contingencies against Pakistan or China. This underscores the broader point that India's growing power-projection capability may be greater on paper than in practice, because of the way in which new capabilities will have important allocated roles on local fronts rather than still-hypothetical distant ones. Finally, one of the biggest obstacles to Indian land-power projection is the poor state of integration and co-ordination between India's service arms. The question of jointness, and its importance to complex power-projection operations that bring together multiple services and even multiple nations, is considered in Chapter IV as part of the broader question of enablers.

IV. ENABLERS: THE SINEWS OF POWER PROJECTION

This Whitehall Paper has surveyed Indian power projection largely in terms of a relatively small number of core platforms: strike aircraft; aircraft carriers; refuelling tankers; missiles; helicopters; transport aircraft; and amphibious vessels. These platforms are at the heart of India's growing ability to reach ever farther from its shores with air power and land power. But platforms by themselves do not constitute a capability. They do so only in concert with a variety of institutional and material enablers that allow the assets of different services to operate together, information to be acquired and distributed, weapons to be targeted and logistical hurdles surmounted. These capabilities are rarely as prominent as large platforms, but they represent the sinews of power projection.

Entire power-projection campaigns have hinged on these enabling capabilities. During the anti-Daesh air campaign that began in 2014, the absence of search-and-rescue aircraft led the UAE to suspend its participation entirely.[1] France's war in Mali in 2013 depended on foreign assistance not just with airlift, as outlined in Chapter III, but also with intelligence, surveillance and reconnaissance (ISR) assets and communications.[2] A previous RUSI Whitehall Paper, *The Defence Industrial Triptych,* shows how Britain's decade-long combat operations in Afghanistan depended on the support of 5,000 private contractors whose cost ran to 60 per cent of spending on the campaign in 2010, and who were themselves the product of a strong defence-industrial base.[3]

---

[1] Helene Cooper, 'United Arab Emirates, Key U.S. Ally in ISIS Effort, Disengaged in December', *New York Times*, 3 February 2015.
[2] Philippe Gross, 'Libya and Mali Operations: Transatlantic Lessons Learned', Foreign Policy Papers, German Marshall Fund, July 2014, p. 11.
[3] Henrik Heidenkamp, John Louth and Trevor Taylor, *The Defence Industrial Triptych: Government as Customer, Sponsor and Regulator of Defence Industry*, RUSI Whitehall Paper 81 (London: Taylor and Francis, 2013), p. 3.

The campaign against Libya in 2011 relied on Qatari special forces not only giving weeks of training to Libyan rebels, but directly participating in the final assault on Tripoli.[4]

For India, the situation is even more challenging because, unlike the cases here, it is neither a member of an alliance nor accustomed to participating in coalitions with larger and better-endowed military partners. Even if future Indian power projection does come in the context of a multinational operation – something discussed in Chapter V – India may still face much greater issues of interoperability and political sensitivity about asset-sharing when compared with the European and Arab power projectors discussed throughout this study. As one example, India has refused to sign key documents that the US has agreed with other close defence partners. The two most important of these are the Communications and Information Security Memorandum of Agreement (CISMOA), which would allow communications interoperability between US and Indian platforms, and the Logistics Support Agreement (LSA), which allows each country to request (though not guarantee) logistics, services and even base access from the other.[5] And so, while India's security partnerships are more diverse and substantial than those of China, which is relatively isolated, New Delhi is still likely to have to generate more of its own enablers than many of the other countries that routinely project power. If India hopes to translate its new and future acquisitions into a coherent force, it will have to invest – politically, economically and diplomatically – in the capabilities outlined in this chapter.

The remainder of this chapter discusses institutional and material enablers: jointness; command, control, communications, computers, intelligence, surveillance, and reconnaissance (C4ISR); special forces; basing; and finally defence industry. In large part, the enablers discussed in this chapter are being procured or developed for local conflicts, with only incidental or secondary applications for power projection. This should be remembered when considering how India might allocate resources towards addressing the various weaknesses outlined below.

---

[4]   Bruce R Nardulli, 'The Arab States' Experiences', in Karl P Mueller (ed.), *Precision and Purpose: Airpower in the Libyan Civil War* (Santa Monica, CA: RAND Corporation, 2015), pp. 365–67.

[5]   Sujan Dutta, 'Revived: Plan to Give Access to Bases', *The Telegraph* [India], 22 January 2015; Saroj Bishoyi, 'Logistics Support Agreement : A Closer Look at the Impact on India-US Strategic Relationship', *Journal of Defence Studies* (Vol. 7, No. 1, January–March 2013), p. 154. India is not alone. Many US partners – like Indonesia, Brazil and Egypt – have held out from signing a CISMOA, for instance.

Jointness

Modern warfare places an increasing premium on jointness: the close integration of all service arms in the preparation and prosecution of war.[6] This premium is greater still for power projection, for reasons explained by British scholars Andrew Dorman, Lawrence Smith and Matthew Uttley:[7]

> During the Cold War 'a distinction between the institutional and operational arrangements for the armed forces made some sense' because of the functional roles of each service within NATO's overall force posture ... The primary focus of the alliance's land assets and supporting air elements was the Central Front in West Germany whilst maritime forces concentrated on anti-submarine warfare in the North Atlantic. The consequence was that operational integration was primarily combined between the maritime, land and air forces of the different alliance members rather than with the other armed services of a particular state. Since the Cold War, however, the requirement to project military power has created an imperative for the systematic integration of national forces and planning, or as the current terminology has it, 'jointery': planning for 'military operations in which elements of more than one service participate'. The primary drivers for jointery, or 'jointness', are the requirement for the projection of power from littoral areas of the sea by naval forces and the deployment of expeditionary forces which are supported by air elements, as a means to meet contingencies on a global scale.

Traditional expeditionary powers have therefore only forged joint institutions in the heat of power projection, learning by doing over the past three decades. The British case is instructive. During the Falklands War, improvised command structures produced 'a lack of lateral understanding between the [British] commanders ... exacerbated by their ambiguous inter-relationship and limited communications'.[8] 'It is quite clear now', wrote a naval officer much later, 'that what was needed was an overall joint force commander in theatre to share the load with the joint commander back in the United Kingdom', adding that 'it is clear that the development of what we

---

[6] Keith Hartley, 'Jointery – Just Another Panacea? An Economist's View', *Defense Analysis* (Vol. 14, No. 1, April 1998); Jeremy Black, *War since 1945* (London: Reaktion Books, 2005), pp. 164–65.

[7] Andrew Dorman, Mike Lawrence Smith and Matthew Uttley, 'Jointery and Combined Operations in an Expeditionary Era: Defining the Issues', *Defense Analysis* (Vol. 14, No. 1, April 1998), p. 3.

[8] Stephen Prince, 'British Command and Control in the Falklands Campaign', *Defense and Security Analysis* (Vol. 18, No. 4, December 2002), pp. 345–46.

now recognise as modern joint doctrine started following the Falklands Conflict'.[9]

Although British institutions evolved over the subsequent decade, during the First Gulf War it still took Britain seven weeks to establish a joint-force commander.[10] In 1994, both these experiences – as well as a drive for cost reductions[11] – led the UK to establish a three-star Permanent Joint Headquarters (PJHQ) that absorbed the command roles of each service.[12] This was initially viewed as a 'radical and dangerous solution', particularly in the army and air force.[13] But PJHQ has since underpinned British force projection: in Afghanistan, for instance, the national command chain ran 'from Helmand to Northwood [PJHQ's headquarters]', bypassing the British deputy commander of the NATO-led coalition entirely.[14] Summarising this institutional shift, Theo Farrell describes Britain's trajectory as a 'move from the large-formation force structure of the Cold War to joint modular expeditionary force packaging'.[15] This trend is not confined to the UK. France similarly created several joint institutions after its experience in the First Gulf War, establishing joint planning and operational centres, which were updated further in 2002.[16] Italian jointness was driven by its experience in the Balkans in the 1990s.[17] Indeed, in most European countries, the coalition power-projection operations of the 2000s have catalysed reforms in the direction of jointness.[18]

How has India fared? Its defence structures were briefly examined in Chapter I and found wanting in several respects. It is clear that Indian institutions remain very far from the inter-service integration seen in other

---

[9] Jonathan Band, 'British High Command During and After the Falklands Campaign', in Stephen Badsey, Rob Havers and Mark Grove (eds), *The Falklands Conflict Twenty Years on: Lessons for the Future* (London: Frank Cass, 2005), pp. 34–35.

[10] Prince, 'British Command and Control in the Falklands Campaign', p. 346.

[11] Martin Edmonds, 'Defense Management and the Impact of Jointery', *Defense Analysis* (Vol. 14, No. 1, April 1998), pp. 22–24.

[12] Prince, 'British Command and Control in the Falklands Campaign', p. 346.

[13] Band, 'British High Command During and After the Falklands Campaign', p. 37.

[14] Hew Strachan, 'One War, Joint Warfare', *RUSI Journal* (Vol. 154, No. 4, August 2009), p. 23.

[15] Theo Farrell, 'The Dynamics of British Military Transformation', *International Affairs* (Vol. 84, No. 4, July 2008), p. 777.

[16] Sten Rynning, 'From Bottom-Up to Top-Down Transformation: Military Change in France', Terry Terriff, Frans Osinga and Theo Farrell (eds), *A Transformation Gap? American Innovations and European Military Change* (Stanford, CA: Stanford University Press, 2010), pp. 71–72.

[17] Piero Ignazi, Giampiero Giacomello and Fabrizio Coticchia, *Italian Military Operations Abroad: Just Don't Call it War* (Basingstoke: Palgrave Macmillan, 2012), p. 108.

[18] Gordon Adams and Guy Ben-Ari, *Transforming European Militaries: Coalition Operations and the Technology Gap* (Oxford: Routledge, 2006), ch. 2.

power-projecting states. In a nod to the global trend towards jointness, India established an Integrated Defence Staff (IDS) in October 2001, as a staff for the relatively weak Chairman of the Chiefs of Staff Committee.[19] A joint doctrine was released in 2006, with a further two, on air-land operations and psychological warfare, four years later.[20] While its officers would resist such a characterisation, it is widely recognised that the IDS 'has little impact on how India formulates and implements its military policies'.[21] A former Indian officer concludes, with diplomatic phrasing, that 'a review of HQ IDS's endeavours since 2001 would indicate difficulties being experienced in forging jointness and integration in planning processes and structures'.[22] Another, a retired general, argues that the 'headless' IDS 'serves little purpose', largely because 'all issues of any consequence are dealt with by the civil officials of MoD'.[23] In any case, these reforms concern staff rather than command functions – and would therefore have relatively little impact on the actual conduct of power projection.

One of the major debates in Indian defence revolves around the possible creation of a Chief of the Defence Staff (CDS) post with command responsibility. Such a post has been proposed by a series of official committees stretching back decades.[24] Indian bureaucrats and politicians – from all parties – have remained wary of acting on this recommendation, in part because of fear of the political salience and influence a CDS might come to acquire, as well as periodic opposition from the air force. In March 2015, Defence Minister Manohar Parrikar acknowledged that 'integration of the three forces [services] does not exist in the existing structure', and merely requested that he be given more time to 'work it out'.[25]

---

[19] A K Lal, *Transformation of the Indian Armed Forces 2025: Enhancing India's Defence* (New Delhi: Vij Books, 2012), p. 110.
[20] Ali Ahmed, *India's Doctrine Puzzle: Limiting War in South Asia* (Routledge, 25 September 2014), p. 166.
[21] Stephen P Cohen and Sunil Dasgupta, *Arming without Aiming: India's Military Modernization* (Washington, DC: Brookings Institution Press, 2010), p. 44.
[22] Vinod Anand, 'Integrating the Indian Military: Retrospect and Prospect', *Journal of Defence Studies* (Vol. 2, No. 2, Winter 2008).
[23] S K Sinha, 'The Chief of Defence Staff', *Journal of Defence Studies* (Vol. 1, No. 1, August 2007), p. 135.
[24] Anit Mukherjee, *Failing to Deliver: Post-Crises Defence Reforms in India, 1998–2010* (New Delhi: IDSA, 2011), pp. 28–30; Steven I Wilkinson, *Army and Nation: The Military and Indian Democracy since Independence* (Cambridge, MA: Harvard University Press, 2015), p. 219; Anit Mukherjee, 'Closing the Military Loop', *Indian Express*, 1 April 2015.
[25] 'Defence Minister Parrikar Says Nation Needs Chief of Defence Staff', *India Today*, 14 March 2015, <http://indiatoday.intoday.in/story/manohar-parrikar-gen-bikram-singh-defence-ministry-chief-of-defence-staff-india-today-conclave/1/423782.html>.

India has established a few tri-service bodies, such as the Defence Intelligence Agency, as well as entirely new joint commands, notably the Andaman and Nicobar Theatre Command (created 2001), discussed in Chapter III, and the nuclear-tasked Strategic Forces Command (2003). Yet these, like the IDS itself, 'own' no military assets, and are therefore institutionally weak in relation to the individual services.[26] In the absence of a CDS or, at least, powerful theatre commands on the US model, senior Indian military officers agree that Indian weakness with jointness is likely to remain. General Sundararajan Padmanabhan, army chief 2000–02, described the IDS *sans* CDS as 'an exercise in futility'.[27] General J J Singh, army chief 2005–07, has said Indian jointness is still 'in a state of transition from single-service entities', with 'a long way to go on the road to further integration'.[28]

In short, India stands approximately where Britain was in the 1980s, albeit with greater constraints on reform. Complex or sustained force-projection operations involving close co-ordination between different service arms – such as an amphibious landing supported by both land and naval air power – would place extreme stress on embryonic, weak and potentially hollow institutions.[29] This has also been evident in India's past force projection. A remarkable example of inter-service dissonance was seen during Indian preparations for an aborted amphibious intervention against Mauritius in 1983. A lack of co-ordination between the army and navy resulted in troops attempting to force themselves onto a docked warship, both services quarrelled over the question of overall command and the vice chief of the army may have leaked the entire operation to the US Embassy in New Delhi as a consequence.[30] Despite this fiasco, Indian forces in Sri Lanka, several years later, were still lacking a joint headquarters, although events then ran more smoothly.[31]

---

[26] Mukherjee, *Failing to Deliver*, p. 38; Vipin Narang, *Nuclear Strategy in the Modern Era: Regional Powers and International Conflict: Regional Powers and International Conflict* (Princeton, NJ: Princeton University Press, 2014), p. 101.

[27] Verghese Koithara, *Managing India's Nuclear Forces* (Washington, DC: Brookings Institution Press, 2012), p. 189.

[28] J J Singh, *A Soldier's General: An Autobiography* (New Delhi: HarperCollins Publishers, 2012).

[29] Vinod Anand, 'Achieving Synergies in Defence', Institute for Defence Studies and Analysis (IDSA), January 1994, <http://www.idsa-india.org/an-jan9-4.html>, accessed 22 October 2015.

[30] David Brewster and Ranjit Rai, 'Operation Lal Dora: India's Aborted Military Intervention in Mauritius', *Asian Security* (Vol. 9, No. 1, March 2013), pp. 67–69.

[31] John H Gill and David W Lamm, 'The Indian Peace Keeping Force Experience and U.S. Stability Operations in the Twenty-First Century', Sumit Ganguly and David P Fidler (eds), *India and Counterinsurgency: Lessons Learned* (London: Routledge, 2009), p. 177.

Such institutional weakness places unquantifiable but serious limitations on the capabilities outlined in previous chapters. Some Indians concede this point but dismiss its relevance. As one recent study observes, many officers and bureaucrats argue that joint operational commands are *only* useful for power projection, and therefore unsuited to India's local wars.[32] Such arguments are at odds with history, as the 1983 debacle shows, and also with the service's own stated aspirations to power projection outlined earlier in this study. Like the owl of Minerva, Indian institutions may only adapt to the demands of power projection after their weaknesses become more apparent in practice.

The inter-service question is closely related to a slightly distinct issue, concerning the relationship not between Indian services but between the military as a whole and the civilian leadership. While this issue is too complex to address here at length, it is worth bearing in mind that India's peculiar system of civil-military relations – strong civilian control through a powerful layer of bureaucrats, but with significant military autonomy in select areas – may have its deleterious effects on power projection.[33] In particular, it could hinder the integration of political and military strategy, especially important in particular types of expeditionary warfare.[34] 'Most officers from the armed forces', writes former army chief V P Malik, 'continue to have doubts over India's higher defence control organization and its functioning in in any future out-of-area contingencies'.[35]

C4ISR

Like jointness, C4ISR is increasingly important to modern warfare, particularly in relation to precision-strike weaponry and the related concepts of a Revolution in Military Affairs and the so-called

---

[32] Patrick Bratton, 'The Creation of Indian Integrated Commands: Organisational Learning and the Andaman and Nicobar Command', *Strategic Analysis* (Vol. 36, No. 3, May 2012), p. 445.

[33] Anit Mukherjee, 'The Absent Dialogue', Seminar, July 2009, <http://www.india-seminar.com/2009/599/599_anit_mukherjee.htm>, accessed 20 October 2015; Shashank Joshi, 'The Coup-Proofing of India', *Survival* (Vol. 57, No. 2, March 2015), pp. 199–200.

[34] Eliot A Cohen, *Supreme Command: Soldiers, Statesmen, and Leadership in Wartime*, 1st ed. (New York, NY: Anchor Books, 2003), pp. 209–24; Hew Strachan, 'Making Strategy: Civil–Military Relations after Iraq', *Survival* (Vol. 48, No. 3, August 2006); Robert Egnell, 'Explaining US and British Performance in Complex Expeditionary Operations: The Civil-Military Dimension', *Journal of Strategic Studies* (Vol. 29, No. 6, December 2006).

[35] V P Malik, *India's Military Conflicts and Diplomacy: An Inside View of Decision Making* (Noida, Uttar Pradesh: HarperCollins Publishers India, 2013), p. 52.

reconnaissance-strike complex touched on in Chapter II.[36] C4ISR assumes particular significance in power projection, because states are typically operating in unfamiliar environments, with less pre-existing intelligence on targets, and without the benefit of their fixed domestic-communications infrastructure. Key C4ISR capabilities include the collection of information through human and technical means – from human agents and special forces, to satellites and aircraft – and communication of that information to those who need it, such as aircraft cueing strikes or the political leadership at home. A comprehensive assessment of Indian capabilities is beyond this study, but this section briefly surveys some of the most important areas.

Aerial ISR

Aerial ISR can be a particular constraint where power projection is largely undertaken through air power, but it can also be important to ground operations. France, for instance, possesses both advanced reconnaissance satellites and reconnaissance pods on aircraft, but its lack of 'persistent' ISR – that is able to loiter above the battlefield for extended periods – meant that the French intervention in Mali required extensive assistance from the UK and US.[37] The same problem occurred earlier, in Libya during 2011, where the US conducted roughly three-quarters of all ISR, and US personnel played a major role in cueing air strikes conducted by allies and conducting battle-damage assessment.[38] And during anti-Daesh operations in 2014, US officials found themselves hampered by the fact that they enjoyed six to ten times less ISR than was available in Afghanistan and Iraq, resulting in a surfeit of aircraft but dearth of targets to strike.[39] For operations where precise air power is less important, or a higher level of risk is acceptable, states can operate with less: the African-led international mission in Mali, for instance, had nowhere near the level of ISR that the French enjoyed.[40]

---

[36] Andrew F Krepinevich, 'Cavalry to Computer: The Pattern of Military Revolutions', *National Interest* (No. 37, Fall 1994), p. 30; Michael Horowitz and Stephen Rosen, 'Evolution or Revolution?', *Journal of Strategic Studies* (Vol. 28, No. 3, June 2005).

[37] Gross, 'Libya and Mali Operations', p. 11.

[38] *Ibid.*, pp. 5–6.

[39] Scott Vickery, 'Operation Inherent Resolve: An Interim Assessment', Policywatch 2354, Washington Institute for Near East Policy, January 2015.

[40] Peter Hille, 'West African Forces Begin Mali Mission', *Deutsche Welle*, 18 January 2013; Soufan Group, 'TSG IntelBrief: UN Mission and ISR Support in Africa: A New Paradigm', 4 December 2013, <http://soufangroup.com/tsg-intelbrief-un-mission-and-isr-support-in-africa-a-new-paradigm/>, accessed 22 October 2015.

India's own aerial ISR capabilities are growing rapidly.[41] Although the IAF retired the MiG-25 Foxbat in 2006 and the Canberra in 2007 – its two traditional reconnaissance platforms – it now fields three Gulfstream IV SRA-4s and five squadrons of the IAI Searcher II reconnaissance drone. The IAF is considering the creation of a separate cadre for drone operators.[42] It is also building up its fleet of airborne early warning and control (AEWC) aircraft. Between 2009 and 2010, the IAF received three Israeli Phalcon radars fitted on IL-76TD transport aircraft – technology that the US had previously prevented Israel from transferring to China[43] – with two to three possible further orders in progress. In addition, India's DRDO fitted an indigenous radar onto two Embraer ERJ-145 business jets, and plans to do the same with Airbus A330s.[44] While such AEWC radars are configured for detecting other aircraft, they can also perform electronic intelligence (ELINT) missions.[45] These platforms can also convey collected intelligence to those analysing and using it – something scholars have identified as an Indian weakness.[46]

In addition to these dedicated platforms, the IAF can also use a variety of ISR pods on its combat aircraft. India is reported to have fit the Israeli-made Litening pod to the Mirage 2000 and Jaguar during the Kargil War in 1999, and at least one account suggests that the IAF used it during the campaign to acquire the target for its first-ever use of laser-guided bombs.[47] SIPRI data

---

[41]   For overviews, see Joseph Noronha, 'Flying High: The Bright Future of India's Military UAVs', *Indian Defence Review* (Vol. 29, No. 4, October–December 2014); Tekendra Parmar, 'Drones in India', Need to Know, Center for the Advanced Study of India, University of Pennsylvania, 4 December 2014, <http://dronecenter.bard.edu/drones-in-india/>, accessed 22 October 2015; Guilem Monsonis, 'UAVs Gaining Currency with Indian Armed Forces', *Indian Defence Review* (March/April 2012).

[42]   Chethan Kumar, 'Indian Air Force Plans for Wars of Future with a Separate UAV Cadre', *Times of India*, 12 September 2015.

[43]   Jeremy Pressman, *Warring Friends: Alliance Restraint in International Politics* (Ithaca, NY: Cornell University Press, 2012), pp. 114–16.

[44]   Neelam Mathews, 'Indian Official Describes Latest AEW&C Plans', *Aviation International News*, 27 March 2015, <http://www.ainonline.com/aviation-news/defense/2015-03-27/indian-official-describes-latest-aewc-plans>, accessed 22 October 2015.

[45]   SP's Aviation, 'India Chooses Litening G4 for Combat Aircraft Fleet', 10 February 2014, <http://www.spsmai.com/exclusive/?id=406&q=India-chooses-Litening-G4-for-combat-aircraft-fleet>, accessed 22 October 2015.

[46]   George Perkovich and Toby Dalton, 'Modi's Strategic Choice: How to Respond to Terrorism from Pakistan', *Washington Quarterly* (Vol. 38, No. 1, Spring 2015), pp. 39–40.

[47]   Benjamin Lambeth, *Airpower at 18,000': The Indian Air Force in the Kargil War* (Washington, DC: Carnegie Endowment for International Peace, September 2012), pp. 19–20.

Table 5: ISR-Relevant Indian UAVs by Type, Number and Capabilities.

	No.	Ceiling (m)	Endurance (hours)
Searcher Mk I	36	4,575	14
Searcher Mk II	71	7,000	20
Heron	65	9,100	36
Nishant	14	3,600	4.5

Sources: *Estimates of holdings calculated from SIPRI, 'SIPRI Arms Transfers Database 1950–2014'; adjusted as per reported crashes as recorded in Drone Wars UK, 'Drone Crash Database', n.d., <http://dronewars.net/drone-crash-database/>, accessed 22 October 2015; specifications collated from* Technology in Focus, *'Unmanned Aircraft Systems and Technologies' (Vol. 8, No. 6, December 2010); Dale W Van Cleave, 'Trends and Technologies for Unmanned Aerial Vehicles', in Tariq Samad and Gary Balas (eds),* Software-Enabled Control: Information Technology for Dynamical Systems *(Hoboken, NJ: John Wiley & Sons, 2003), p. 11;* UPI, *'Indian Army Gets its First Nishant UAVs', 10 February 2011, <http://www.upi.com/Business_News/Security-Industry/2011/02/10/Indian-army-gets-its-first-Nishant-UAVs/82741297336680/>, accessed 22 October 2015;* Press Information Bureau, Government of India, *'DRDO Conducts 5th Successful Flight of UAV Rustom – 1', media release, 11 November 2011, <http://pib.nic.in/newsite/erelease.aspx?relid=77118>, accessed 22 October 2015; Vivek Raghuvanshi, 'India to Rely on Domestic Firms for Combat Drone',* Defense News, *2 January 2015, <http://www.defensenews.com/story/defense/air-space/strike/2014/12/31/india-combat-uav-rustom/21114745/>, accessed 22 October 2015; Ajai Shukla, 'Rustom-1 Drone to Monitor Maritime Boundary with Lanka',* Business Standard, *26 June 2015; Airforce Technology, 'Rustom Unmanned Aerial Vehicle (UAV), India', n.d., <http://www.airforce-technology.com/projects/rustom-uav/>, accessed 22 October 2015.*

show that Israel transferred at least 172 Litening pods, including the Litening-3, for almost all of India's combat fleet between 2007 and 2013.[48]

Separately to the IAF, the navy operates two squadrons of maritime patrol aircraft, including the long-range Tu-142M Bear and the Dornier Do-228, both used during Kargil, and a single squadron of unmanned reconnaissance aircraft including the Searcher and the larger Heron (with an endurance of 52 hours, against the Heron's 18). It is also acquiring eight Boeing P-8I Neptune maritime patrol aircraft, with six having arrived by late 2014.[49] Although these are likely to be prioritised in the ASW role, they can also be adapted for land-power projection. For instance, the UK's Nimrod

---

[48] Stockholm International Peace Research Institute (SIPRI), 'SIPRI Arms Transfers Database 1950–2014', n.d., <http://www.sipri.org/databases/armstransfers>, accessed 20 October 2015; see also SP's Aviation, 'India Chooses Litening G4 for Combat Aircraft Fleet'; Neelam Mathews, 'Indian Air Force Mirage 2000 Upgrade Progresses Despite Groundings', *Aviation International News*, 19 September 2014, <http://www.ainonline.com/aviation-news/defense/2014-09-19/indian-air-force-mirage-2000-upgrade-progresses-despite-groundings>, accessed 22 October 2015.

[49] Ridzwan Rahmat, 'Boeing Delivers Sixth P-8I Aircraft to Indian Navy', *IHS Jane's Defence Weekly*, 26 November 2014.

maritime patrol aircraft collected ELINT over Libya in 2011 and supplied real-time imagery to British troops in Afghanistan and Iraq.[50] Finally, the Indian Army has a fleet of small, low-endurance Nishant drones, as well as a dozen Searcher variants of its own. It also hopes to co-develop 600 mini-drones, probably with an American or Israeli company.[51]

Overall, India possesses a large, diverse and rapidly growing fleet of aerial ISR assets, although its holdings of unmanned aircraft – perhaps the most politically feasible to deploy in contested airspace – remain relatively small compared with the extent of its border-security commitments. One further aspect of ISR, satellite capability, is discussed further below.

Human Intelligence

Air power also frequently depends on a continued flow of high-quality human intelligence, particularly against high-value targets that cannot be identified by aerial imagery alone. Accordingly, and contrary to the popular view that armed drones obviate a human footprint, the US's longstanding air strikes in Pakistan depend on human intelligence partly generated by an extensive intelligence network within Pakistan and collected from forward bases in eastern Afghanistan.[52]

Indian intelligence capabilities are shrouded in uncertainty and mythology.[53] However, public accounts present severe weaknesses. Analyst Dhruva Jaishankar concludes one study by noting that 'India's intelligence agencies are not just ineffective, they lack influence. Certainly their covert action capabilities have been uneven, their resources remain inadequate, and their bureaucratic standing has been tempered by the

---

[50] Dave Sloggett, *A Century of Air Warfare: The Changing Face of Warfare 1912–2012* (Barnsley: Pen and Sword, 2013), p. 42; Michael Napier, *Blue Diamonds: The Exploits of 14 Squadron RAF 1945–2015* (Barnsley: Pen and Sword, 2015), p. 276.
[51] Ankit Panda, 'The Indian Army Wants 600 Mini Drones', *The Diplomat*, 26 August 2015.
[52] On the intelligence burden of similar operations in Somalia and Yemen, see *The Intercept*, 'The Drone Papers', 15 October 2015, <https://theintercept.com/drone-papers/>, accessed 22 October 2015; Declan Walsh, 'Drone War Spurs Militants to Deadly Reprisals', *New York Times*, 29 December 2012.
[53] A useful summary can be found in Rudra Chaudhuri, 'India', in Robert Dover, Michael S Goodman and Claudia Hillebrand (eds), *Routledge Companion to Intelligence Studies* (Oxford: Routledge, 2013); other accounts include Asoka Raina, *Inside R.A.W.: The Story of India's Secret Service* (New Delhi: Vikas, 1981); Bruce Vaughn, 'The Use and Abuse of Intelligence Services in India', *Intelligence and National Security* (Vol. 8, No. 1, January 1993); Maloy Krishna Dhar, *Open Secrets: India's Intelligence Unveiled* (New Delhi: Manas Publications, 2005); V K Singh, *India's External Intelligence: Secrets of Research and Analysis Wing (RAW)* (New Delhi: Manas Publications, 2007); B Raman, *The Kaoboys of R&AW: Down Memory Lane* (New Delhi: Lancer Publishers, 2008).

creation of ever more agencies'.[54] The veteran national-security journalist Praveen Swami paints a similar picture in his account of challenges facing the Research and Analysis Wing (R&AW), India's foreign intelligence agency:[55]

> R&AW, estimated to have some 5,000 personnel ... is short of some 130 management-level staff, the sources said, particularly cutting-edge under-secretaries and deputy secretaries. R&AW is also short of personnel with specialist language and area knowledge, particularly Arabic, Chinese and minor Pakistani languages.
>
> R&AW's technological capabilities have also fallen behind, leaving it blind to the digital world. Its economic analysis desk is headed by a police officer on deputation from a north-eastern state with no training in the discipline; its scientific division, again, by a police officer with no postgraduate qualification in science.
>
> The most critical deficiencies, however, are in critical technology positions – the core of modern espionage. R&AW, the sources said, is now approximately a third short of its sanctioned strength of cryptanalysts, who are charged with breaking enemy codes and ciphers.

Whether or not these assessments from public sources are a true representation of R&AW capabilities, it is clear that India's ability to respond to events has been constrained by intelligence. For example, India had seemingly limited insight into the kidnapping and subsequent murder of Indian nationals in Mosul, Iraq, in June 2014.[56]

Even closer to home, in India's core area of interest and likeliest theatre of war, this appears to be a problem. Although the apparent absence of Indian covert action against Pakistan appears to be a deliberate policy choice – dating to the late 1990s[57] – rather than solely a function of poor intelligence, analysts George Perkovich and Toby Dalton quote a former Indian intelligence officer who acknowledges that 'we might have acquired precision munitions, but the data we have on the [terrorist] camps and infrastructure [in Pakistan] is not so accurate'.[58] In Sri Lanka in the 1980s, Indian officers complained that their intelligence agencies 'failed to provide objective assessments or accurate information ... when the operations were being planned or conducted',

---

[54] Dhruva Jaishankar, 'Spies Who Remained in the Cold: India's External Intelligence Agencies', unpublished manuscript, April 2015, p. 12.

[55] Praveen Swami, 'India's Spy Agencies More Toothless than Ever', *Indian Express*, 1 December 2014.

[56] Charu Sudan Kasturi, 'Twin Versions on Mosul Puzzle Delhi', *The Telegraph* [India], 23 June 2014.

[57] Raman, *The Kaoboys of R&AW*, ch. 15.

[58] Perkovich and Dalton, 'Modi's Strategic Choice', p. 28.

despite R&AW's own long history in working with insurgents there.[59] If India has found it difficult to acquire accurate information for high-priority targets in neighbouring territory, despite ample supply of those who speak the same language and belong to the same ethnic group as the targets, it would be reasonable to surmise that intelligence in the extended neighbourhood would present even greater difficulty.

Satellites

Satellites play important roles in both ISR and communications. They generate intelligence, and they play a crucial role in allowing the flow of that intelligence – as well as other data – between tactical, operational and strategic levels. For instance, an Indian drone might collect real-time imagery of targets on a battlefield and convey it to infantry on the ground, strike aircraft or an operations centre in India. This process is, naturally, data intensive and typically requires datalinks that are also redundant and secure. India's growing domestic array of *domestic* military communication channels, including an expanding fibre-optic network, cannot service Indian forces outside the country.[60]

The greatest demands are on military satellite communications (MILSATCOM). Expeditionary operations can be increasingly bandwidth intensive: during the 1991 Gulf War, peak demand was 100 megabits per second (mbps) for half a million troops, but by 2003 fewer than 150,000 troops needed 2,400 mbps;[61] just one Global Hawk drone, for instance, requires 500 mbps.[62] Coverage can also be an issue. France, to draw on the Mali example once more, would have been unable to operate its Heron-derived Harfang drones were it not for US assistance with satellite communications, as its own civilian satellites did not cover the Sahel area.[63] Moreover, even allied capability may not be available in circumstances where a nation is operating away from the areas of interest

---

[59] Malik, *India's Military Conflicts and Diplomacy*, p. 42.

[60] Manan Kakkar, 'India Investing $3.1 Billion in Defense Network, to Build Cyber Defense System', *ZDNet*, 11 May 2012, <http://www.zdnet.com/article/india-investing-3-1-billion-in-defense-network-to-build-cyber-defense-system/>, accessed 22 October 2015; Indian Army, 'The Corps of Signals', n.d., <http://indianarmy.nic.in/Site/FormTemplete/frmTemp2PMR7C.aspx?MnId=7P5GMzTXCQb3×1oia4w6rw==&ParentID=Pxdk70d4YithuiJiR2LsFw==>, accessed 22 October 2015.

[61] Todd Harrison, 'The Future of MILSATCOM', Center for Strategic and Budgetary Assessments, 2013.

[62] Jeremiah Gertler, 'U.S. Unmanned Aerial Systems', Congressional Research Service, R42136, January 2012, p. 17.

[63] Gross, 'Libya and Mali Operations', p. 11.

Table 6: Selected Military and Dual-Purpose Indian Satellites.

Series	Role	Launched
RISAT-1	Earth observation	2012
RISAT-2	Earth observation	2009
CARTOSAT-2A	Earth observation	2008
CARTOSAT-2B	Earth observation	2010
OCEANSAT-2	Oceanographic (incl. ASW)	2009
GSAT-7	Communication (Navy)	2013
IRNSS series	Navigation	2013–

Source: *Rajeswari Pillai Rajagopalan, 'Synergies in Space: The Case for an Indian Aerospace Command', ORF Issue Brief No. 59, Observer Research Foundation, October 2013.*

of its allies. During the Falklands War, Britain received no satellite imagery from the US.[64]

India's drone fleet, outlined above, relies largely on radio datalinks and therefore line-of-sight operation, which in turn limits its versatility.[65] Greater satellite-communications capacity would allow Indian platforms to operate over longer distances away from ground stations or relay aircraft. One senior IAF officer notes that, with the MiG-25 retired, 'the onus of providing accurate intelligence for strategic targeting has shifted to space-based sensors'.[66] In both these areas, communications and observation satellites, New Delhi has made great strides in recent years. An Integrated Space Cell was created under the IDS in 2008.[67] India operates several dual-purpose or military satellites, with over twenty others allocated to social or development roles, and has significant plans for expansion.[68]

Three types of satellites with defence functions are worth considering. First, imaging: although India had previously launched multiple remote-sensing optical satellites before, its first two radar-imaging – and therefore all-weather – satellites, RISAT-2 and RISAT-1, were launched in 2009 and 2012 respectively. Although Indian officials have played down the military

---

[64] Alastair Finlan, 'British Special Forces and the Falklands Conflict: Twenty Years on', *Defense and Security Analysis* (Vol. 18, No. 4, December 2002), p. 322.

[65] Pramod K Mehra, 'The Indian Air Force of Tomorrow', in Rajesh Basrur, Ajaya Kumar Das, and Manjeet Singh Pardesi (eds), *India's Military Modernization: Challenges and Prospects* (New Delhi: Oxford University Press, 2014), p. 74.

[66] Arjun Subramaniam, 'The Strategic Role of Airpower: An Indian Perspective on How We Need to Think, Train, and Fight in the Coming Years', *Air and Space Power Journal* (Vol. 22, No. 3, Fall 2008).

[67] Press Information Bureau, Government of India, 'Special Cell Set Up to Counter Growing Threat to Space Assets', media release, 10 June 2008, <http://pib.nic.in/newsite/erelease.aspx?relid=39503>, accessed 22 October 2015.

[68] Dilip Kumar Mekala, 'Eyes in the Sky', *Force*, February 2015.

role of the latter, both appear to have resolutions as low as one metre.[69] RISAT-2 has a 'revisit period' – the time between observations of the same point on earth – of three or four days, which is why it is more useful for strategic reconnaissance, such as for infrastructure or gradual military preparations, rather than for fast-changing operational intelligence.[70]

Second, communications: India was long reliant on the multipurpose Indian National Satellite (INSAT) system for MILSATCOM, but the first dedicated military satellite, the GSAT-7 for the navy, was launched in 2013.[71] The IAF is likely to receive its own satellite by the end of 2015 (GSAT-7A) and the army thereafter.[72] GSAT-7 networks the navy's ships to one another, to headquarters ashore and to drones, while GSAT-7A will connect radar stations, airbases and AEW&C aircraft.[73] This and the other satellites will be especially important as the communications burden grows in line with the size of India's drone fleet and the data demands of modern sensors.[74] In practice, India can also draw on civilian satellite communications capacity for military purposes, much as the US does.

Third, navigation: in January 2015 India launched the fourth of seven Indian Regional Navigation Satellite System (IRNSS) navigational satellites. Like GSAT-7, these are geostationary – remaining above the same point on the earth throughout their orbit. They will form a navigation and positioning system extending up to 1,500 km from Indian borders, accurate to 10 metres over the Indian landmass and to 20 metres over the Indian Ocean, with a restricted encrypted service for military users.[75] Although this provides excellent coverage of India's immediate maritime surroundings, and therefore helps New Delhi to monitor China's growing presence there, it includes very little of the broader Indian Ocean

---

[69] Ajay Lele, 'India Launches Radar Satellite', Comment, IDSA, 27 April 2012, <http://www.idsa.in/idsacomments/IndiaLaunchesRadarSatellite_alele_270412.html>, accessed 22 October 2015.

[70] eoPortal, 'RISAT-2 (Radar Imaging Satellite-2)', n.d., <https://directory.eoportal.org/web/eoportal/satellite-missions/r/risat-2>, accessed 22 October 2015.

[71] *The Hindu*, 'GSAT-7: India's First Military Satellite Launched Successfully', 30 August 2013; Arianespace, 'A Satellite Launch for Telecommuications in the Middle East, North Africa, Central Asia and India', n.d., <http://www.arianespace.com/images/launch-kits/launch-kit-pdf-eng/VA215-Eutelsat25B-EShail1-GSAT7-GB.pdf>, accessed 22 October 2015.

[72] *The Hindu*, 'Space, Cyber Joint Command Taking Shape: IAF Chief', 30 November 2014.

[73] Ranjit Rai, 'Indian Navy: A C4ISR Nuclear Force', *India Strategic*, August 2010.

[74] Saurav Jha, 'India's Armed Drone Fleet', *The Diplomat*, 25 June 2015.

[75] *The Hindu*, 'ISRO Gears Up to Launch IRNSS 1D', 6 January 2015; Vijainder K Thakur, 'Space: The New Battle Zone', *Indian Defence Review* (Vol. 30, No. 2, April–June 2015).

littoral – something that could be especially limiting for missile targeting, as described in Chapter II.

The interface between space and military authorities is not fully known. In 2010, a former Indian director of Naval Operations wrote that India's primary space agency, the Indian Space Research Organisation, and National Technical Research Organisation, the principal technical intelligence agency, 'can control the satellites in coordination with the Armed Forces tasking and specially cater to the Navy's requests'.[76] One long-term issue for Indian space policy is the possible creation of an Aerospace Command, mooted as part of three new joint commands along with an army-controlled special-forces command (see below) and, mystifyingly, a navy-controlled Cyber Command.[77] Indian politicians have so far held back from approving these measures, although there are some indications they might be introduced in 2016.[78]

Special Forces

Special forces can provide strategic force projection in their own right – as the 2011 US operation that killed Osama bin Laden demonstrated – particularly when used as a specialised type of air-assault unit.[79] But they can also function as enablers for other forms of power projection, including both air-power and land-power projection. These roles include deep reconnaissance; forward air control (FAC) for guiding air strikes to concealed or mobile targets; smaller-scale amphibious or air assault operations in support of a broader offensive, such as seizing an airstrip; or direct support for local counter-insurgents. Reconnaissance tasks can be especially important in power projection, where a country is likely to be operating in areas farther away from its periphery, and therefore areas where it has less experience of warfare and the associated human and physical terrain.

Lieutenant General P C Katoch, a retired special-forces officer, and journalist Saikat Datta claim that India has over 20,000 special forces, but – in an echo of its intelligence shortcomings – 'one tenth' of US capabilities, as a result of inadequate officer numbers, training, intelligence, language skills, air support and lack of a centralised

---

[76] Rai, 'Indian Navy'.
[77] Rajeswari Pillai Rajagopalan, 'The Growing Case for an Indian Space Policy', Brookings India Impact Series, Brookings Institution, May 2015.
[78] Rajat Pandit, 'Modi Government Gets Cracking on Three New Tri-Service Commands', *Economic Times*, 20 August 2015.
[79] Nicholas Schmidle, 'Getting Bin Laden', *New Yorker*, 8 August 2011.

command.[80] One study notes that Indian special forces do have 'niche specialization' in assault and night-landing in mountainous or jungle terrain, honed over years of practice.[81] But George Perkovich and Toby Dalton cite the views of Indian expert interviewees that 'India does not now have the capability to combine special operations in Pakistan with precision air support'.[82] This would imply an even more limited capability for operations further afield than Pakistan. In mid-2014, the army announced the creation of two new parachute (special forces) battalions to add to the existing eight.[83] However, it is unclear whether these new forces will be genuine special forces, or merely repurposed paratroopers without the appropriate level of training and equipment.

One recent episode is worth considering in a little more detail. In June 2015, Indian special forces conducted a cross-border raid into Myanmar to attack rebel camps in response to an earlier ambush of Indian soldiers. While this was not the first such special-forces raid, it received a high level of attention because of the ostensible non-involvement of Myanmar's forces (as on previous joint raids), the assertive and occasionally lurid rhetoric of the government (one government minister portrayed it as a message to Pakistan and China), and the perception that India was surmounting a perceived reluctance to use force to pursue its interests. In fact, the raid is not an especially useful guide to Indian capabilities or future conduct. India is almost certain to have consulted and received prior permission from Myanmar, which in any case had little control of that segment of the border.[84] India did not therefore face resistance from a conventional military power. Moreover, subsequent accounts suggest that India did not attack the perpetrators of the ambush itself but merely an associated faction.[85] Nor, according to some reports, did it see 'a single target of value killed or captured'.[86] This seems likelier to have been a function of poor intelligence rather than the intrinsic weakness of special

[80] P C Katoch and Saikat Datta, *India's Special Forces: History and Future of Indian Special Forces* (New Delhi: Vij Books/United Service Institution, 2013), ch. 6.
[81] Jonah Blank, Jennifer D. P. Moroney, Angel Rabasa, and Bonny Lin, *Look East, Cross Black Waters: India's Interest in Southeast Asia* (Santa Monica, CA: RAND Corporation, 2015), p. 20.
[82] Perkovich and Dalton, 'Modi's Strategic Choice', p. 42.
[83] Rajat Pandit, 'Para-Special Forces Get Two New Battalions', *Times of India*, 17 August 2014.
[84] Praveen Swami, 'How MEA Helped Army Set Stage for Strike in Myanmar', *Indian Express*, 11 June 2015.
[85] Praveen Swami, 'Myanmar Strike: Seven Dead Bodies Recovered, Less than a Dozen Injured, Say Official Sources', *Indian Express*, 12 June 2015.
[86] Praveen Swami, 'A New Toolkit: For Talks to Succeed, India Needs to Tackle Pak's Covert War', *Indian Express*, 14 August 2015.

forces, but it points to the challenges that these forces would face when operating at greater distance, in environments where the intelligence picture may be even more limited.

Basing

Most recent Western expeditionary operations have relied on allied assistance of various kinds. One of the most important parts of this assistance is the use of local airbases as launching points for air strikes, ISR sorties or logistical hubs. The British air bridge to Afghanistan, for instance, was reliant on use of an airbase in the UAE. ISAF as a whole relied on facilities in over a dozen countries.[87] France used a network of North African bases for operations in Mali. The anti-Daesh coalition is reliant on Gulf bases (and the UK on Cyprus) for operations in Iraq and Syria. Turkey's decision to allow armed aircraft to operate from Incirlik Air Base in August 2015 meant that flight times to Daesh strongholds in northern and eastern Syria could be cut significantly, allowing more time on station.

Traditional expeditionary powers like the US, Britain, France and even the historically land-centric Russia have typically operated networks of permanent foreign military bases. However, over the past decade US military thinking, prompted by the anti-access/area-denial developments outlined in Chapter II, has shifted towards a strategy of 'places, not bases': more flexible diplomatic agreements securing access to facilities and logistics, with little of the permanent infrastructure associated with traditional bases.[88] China's development of overseas naval infrastructure – widely noted and debated within India – is seen as one example of this approach.[89]

India is far behind both traditional expeditionary powers and China. Traditionally, New Delhi has had an ambivalent view of foreign military basing, associating it with Cold War military alliances. Since the 1990s, India's most prominent foreign facilities have been in Tajikistan. These have included a field hospital at Farkhor airbase near the border with Afghanistan, where the fatally wounded Northern Alliance leader Ahmed Shah Massoud was treated in September 2001 and, from 2002 onwards,

---

[87] Robert E Harkavy, *Strategic Basing and the Great Powers, 1200–2000* (London: Routledge, 2007), p. 1.

[88] Ely Ratner et al., 'More Willing and Able: Charting China's International Security Activism', Center for a New American Security, May 2015, pp. 59–60, 65.

[89] Daniel J Kostecka, 'Places and Bases: The Chinese Navy's Emerging Support Network in the Indian Ocean', *Naval War College Review* (Vol. 64, No. 1, Winter 2011), p. 60.

Ayni Air Base near the capital Dushanbe.[90] Farkhor was reportedly 'revived' in 2012 and reported to have seventy personnel, although most of these were likely to have been construction-related personnel and there is little evidence of any ongoing presence.[91] Ayni was refurbished in the mid-2000s at the cost of $70 million, with aircraft rotationally deployed for short periods and a 'small crew', reportedly over 100 personnel, maintained there, although this too is likely to have been transient construction-related personnel rather than combat-capable forces.[92] Although some reports indicated that India planned to base MiG-29 Fulcrums at Ayni, this has not yet occurred – by some accounts, because of Russian pressure.[93] In general, the size and significance of these facilities – let alone any Indian presence – has been exaggerated. However, India's familiarity with these sites would allow New Delhi to introduce and ramp up a military presence quickly if circumstances arose. Ayni would have obvious utility for future Indian power projection into Afghanistan, although this would require Russian acquiescence.

In addition to these Tajik facilities, India has access to a number of other places:[94]

- A radar monitoring station in Madagascar since 2007
- Berthing rights in Oman since 2008
- Use of an old British airbase in the Maldives, on Gan island, for reconnaissance flights since 2009

---

[90] Rahul Bedi, 'India and Central Asia', *Frontline* (Vol. 19, No. 19, September 2002); Matthieu Aikins, 'India in Afghanistan', *The Caravan*, 1 October 2010.

[91] Jyoti Malhotra, 'Second Chance in Asia's Cockpit', *The Hindu*, 20 July 2012; Evirupa Mitra, 'Eye on China, PM Cosies Up to Tajikistan', *New Indian Express*, 28 June 2015.

[92] Joshua Kucera, 'The White Elephant in Tajikistan', *The Caravan*, 1 November 2010; *Economic Times*, 'IAF Rejects "Extravagant" HAL Basic Trainer Aircraft Project', 4 October 2013; Vijay Shukla, 'Antony Non-Committal on Ayni Air Base in Tajikistan', *Outlook*, 5 October 2011; Press Trust of India, 'India, Tajikistan to Step up Counter-Terrorism Cooperation', *Business Standard*, 11 September 2014.

[93] Shiv Aroor, 'India's Base at Ayni, Tajikistan', Livefistdefence.com, 21 July 2007, <http://www.livefistdefence.com/2007/07/indias-base-at-ayni-tajikistan.html>, accessed 22 October 2015; Sandeep Unnithan, 'PM Modi to Ask Tajikistan for Lease of Ex-Soviet Airbase', *India Today*, 12 July 2015.

[94] David Scott, 'India's Aspirations and Strategy for the Indian Ocean – Securing the Waves?', *Journal of Strategic Studies* (Vol. 36, No. 4, February 2013), p. 11; Oscar Nkala, 'India Developing Network of Coastal Radars', *Defense News*, 10 March 2015, <http://www.defensenews.com/story/defense/naval/2015/03/20/india-seychelles-coastal-radar-china-modi-indian-ocean/25084237/>, accessed 22 October 2015. Political changes in Sri Lanka and the Maldives have complicated the progress of the coastal surveillance radar in those places.

- A network of coastal surveillance radar stations in the Seychelles and Mauritius beginning in 2015.

Facilities and agreements for which there is less public evidence include:

- Berthing rights at Vietnam's Nha Trang port since 2013, which an Indian official framed as giving India 'the key to sustainable presence in the South China Sea'[95]
- Use of Oman's US-operated Thumrait airbase by the IAF[96]
- A security agreement with Qatar, described – certainly exaggeratedly – by one Indian official as 'just short of stationing troops' and by another as implying that 'we will go to the rescue of Qatar if Qatar requires it, in whatever form it takes'.[97]

Finally, India's logistical reach could also expand if it signs the LSA with the US, discussed at the beginning of this chapter.[98] US facilities in the Persian Gulf and in East Asia, where India's presence is much lighter, could be especially useful, although New Delhi would be wary of the reciprocal obligations that such use might bring.

Defence-Industrial Base

Western experience of persistent land-power projection since the 1990s – long-term troop deployments, typically as part of asymmetric wars – suggests that overseas deployment can place severe demands on a country's defence-industrial base. This is true in at last two ways: dependence on contractors to support military operations; and a flexible flow of military equipment that can respond as lessons are learnt in the field.[99] Some of the dissonance between the needs of long-term deployments and India's current preparation for short wars, notably with regard to ammunition, has already been discussed.

It should be noted that India is no stranger to long-term land-power deployments. Although paramilitary forces have taken the greatest counter-insurgency burden in recent years, a dozen out of seventeen major Indian Army campaigns between 1947 and 1995 were within India's

---

[95] V Balachandran, 'Presence in South China Sea will be a Misadventure', *Sunday Guardian*, 24 July 2011.
[96] David Brewster, *India's Ocean: The Story of India's Bid for Regional Leadership* (London: Routledge, 2014), p. 112.
[97] David Brewster, 'An Indian Sphere of Influence in the Indian Ocean?', *Security Challenges* (Vol. 6, No. 3, Spring 2010), p. 11.
[98] Dutta, 'Revived: Plan to Give Access to Bases'.
[99] Heidenkamp, Louth and Taylor, *The Defence Industrial Triptych*, pp. 153–54.

borders, and the army was deployed to assist the civilian authorities no less than 721 times between 1982 and 1989 alone.[100] By one account, 'the Indian Army has had more experience in counter-insurgency than almost any other army in the world'.[101] These campaigns have involved learning and adaption over time – albeit less so over the past 25–30 years, and largely in the realm of doctrine and strategy rather than hardware.[102]

Yet despite this experience, India's defence-industrial base falls short on operations. On numerous occasions, inappropriate, inadequate or insufficient equipment, and a non-responsive procurement process, has affected counter-insurgency and counter-terrorism operations. In Sri Lanka, for instance, the army found that standard-issue footwear rotted in the jungle, helmets were too heavy and radio sets failed in built-up areas.[103] Its standard rifle was inferior to that of the insurgents, and it lacked body armour, night-vision devices and sniper rifles.[104] Within India, counter-insurgent forces have also found themselves short of radio sets, night-vision devices and surveillance devices, although the situation has been improving since 2002.[105]

More broadly, India's defence-industrial base is weak. As of 2010, Indian industry received only a fifth – just under $2 billion – of the country's annual procurement budget, and it has been dominated by inefficient public-sector entities that routinely produce sub-par equipment well behind schedule.[106] 'The self-reliance in defence production', wrote Sushant Singh in October 2015, 'is still estimated to be less than 35 per cent'.[107]

---

[100] Sunil Dasgupta, 'India: The New Militaries', in Muthiah Alagappa (ed.), *Coercion and Governance: The Declining Political Role of the Military in Asia* (Stanford, CA: Stanford University Press, 2001), pp. 96–97.

[101] Rajesh Rajagopalan, '"Restoring Normalcy": The Evolution of the Indian Army's Counterinsurgency Doctrine', *Small Wars and Insurgencies* (Vol. 11, No. 1, 2000), p. 44.

[102] *Ibid.*, pp. 58–65.

[103] Rajesh Kadian, *India's Sri Lanka Fiasco: Peace Keepers at War* (New Dehli/Bombay: Vision Books, 1990), p. 130.

[104] Ashok K Mehta, 'India's Counterinsurgency Campaign in Sri Lanka', in Sumit Ganguly and David P Fidler (eds), *India and Counterinsurgency: Lessons Learned* (London: Routledge, 2009), p. 170.

[105] Anit Mukherjee, 'India's Experiences with Insurgency and Counterinsurgency', in Sumit Ganguly, Andrew Scobell and Joseph Chinyong Liow (eds), *Handbook of Asian Security Studies* (Oxford: Routledge, 2009), pp. 146–47.

[106] *The Military Balance 2013*, 'Reforming India's Defence Industries' (Vol. 110, No. 1, February 2010), pp. 473–75.

[107] Sushant Singh, 'Indigenous Production: Self-Reliance, the Best Defence', *Indian Express*, 13 October 2015.

Although in August 2014 the Modi government raised the cap on foreign direct investment (FDI) in the defence sector to 49 per cent stakes of companies, foreign defence companies will still be deterred from significant investments in India without a majority controlling stake that would protect key technology and ensure overall control.[108] And despite the number of industrial licenses issued to the domestic private sector growing substantially from 2014 to 2015, Defence Minister Manohar Parrikar has acknowledged that it remains at a 'nascent stage'.[109] The result is continued dependence on imports, particularly in moments of crisis: during the Kargil War, for instance, India turned to companies from Israel, Sweden and South Africa for ammunition and technology.[110] The structural conditions for this dependence have not drastically changed since 1999 and would be manifest during any sustained power-projection effort.

Indian reliance on private military companies has been relatively slight, compared to the growing and massive dependence on these contractors by a number of Western forces. In Afghanistan, for instance, the paramilitary ITBP, rather than Indian contractors, have played the primary role in protecting Indian interests. Indian discussions of military contractors have portrayed the issue as a foreign phenomenon and a potential challenge to Indian military recruitment, rather than a practice to emulate.[111] This reflects both a different attitude towards the private sector's role in defence, as well as larger armed forces and India's lower average labour costs. It is unlikely that contractors will play a major role in Indian operations over the medium term.

Conclusion

Even more so than regards to specific air and land capabilities, the capabilities discussed here – with the possible exception of foreign basing – are crucial to India's military power in both local and broader contexts. Jointness, communications, intelligence, special forces and defence-industrial responsiveness will shape India's ability to meet the challenges set out in Chapter I, including the demands of prosecuting and controlling

---

[108] Ashley J Tellis, 'Beyond Buyer-Seller', *Force*, August 2015, p. 10.

[109] Jon Grevatt, 'India Reports Increase in Private Sector Defence Licences', *IHS Jane's Defence Weekly*, 5 July 2015; *Economic Times*, 'Manohar Parrikar: Private Defence Sector at a Nascent Stage; Welcome Foreign Companies to "Make in India"', 21 May 2015.

[110] Jerome M Conley, *Indo-Russian Military and Nuclear Cooperation: Lessons and Options for U.S. Policy in South Asia* (Oxford: Lexington Books, 2001), p. 75.

[111] Shantanu Chakrabarti, 'Growth and Implications of Private Military Corporations', *Journal Of Defence Studies* (Vol. 2, No. 1, Summer 2008).

a limited war against Pakistan, and developing India's offensive capabilities along the long, underdeveloped Sino-Indian border. These military enablers aid power projection, but their primary rationale is in local wars.

India is showing more progress in some areas than others. C4ISR is developing quickly. Although India has lost its dedicated strategic reconnaissance aircraft, space-based sensors are on the path to taking up the slack. India's UAV fleet is growing, although it remains unclear whether indigenous aircraft will have the quality to substitute for large-scale imports of Israeli platforms. The ISR capabilities of India's combat aircraft also seem to be growing. India's emphasis on border and coastal security, the prospect of counter-terrorism or retaliatory precision-strike missions against Pakistan and the armed force's general embrace of network-centric warfare will all generate strong momentum towards continued focus on and investment in C4ISR. These will continue to be optimised for local operations – as we see with Indian navigational satellites' coverage – with longer-range applications a secondary concern.

Other areas, however, are less promising. India's human-intelligence reach appears to remain limited and its special forces are large in number but lack unified command and adequate specialist supporting platforms. In these areas, institutional reform and gradual investment is likely to improve capabilities, but over a long period of time. Above all, however, India's inter-service and civil-military structures are, in effect, stuck in the 1950s. This is a fundamentally political problem. Only when the system shows its flaws in an armed conflict is an Indian government likely to begin to tackle it.

Others areas still, such as foreign basing, are bound up with much larger strategic and diplomatic shifts, rather than merely technical choices about defence policy or even political ones about the civil-military balance. If Pakistan and China consume virtually all of India's defence attention in the decades to come, and power projection continues to be associated at the political level with neo-colonial interventionism and breaches of international law, then it is unlikely that future Indian governments will see much need to develop international basing beyond partnerships with small island nations. If, on the other hand, the spread of Indian interests drives a continued rhetorical and military interest in power projection, then Indian choices could be quite different. The next chapter delves into these questions, asking how, why and where India might project power.

V. THE FUTURE OF INDIAN POWER PROJECTION

Why is India acquiring the capabilities outlined in this study? In discussions of power projection, many Indians will repeat the popular mantra that India has never invaded another country in several thousand years of existence.[1] When asked about India's spate of interventions in the 1980s, these Indians will demur that India, unlike the West, has only used force with the imprimatur of a UN Resolution or the consent of the host government. When queried about India's build-up of offensive platforms, such as amphibious ships, they will point to the defence of the Andaman and Nicobar Islands. Indians, even those responsible for procuring and operating many of the military platforms discussed here, will emphatically disclaim power projection.[2] Others – Chinese and Pakistanis, but also many of India's smaller neighbours – will argue that there has always been a yawning chasm between India's quietist rhetoric and hegemonic practice.[3]

But the more pertinent point is that Indians' ambivalence towards power projection – the various urges to re-define, renounce or warily reaffirm it – cloud our understanding of what it means in practice: why, and therefore how and where, might India actually use the military forces that are, slowly and unevenly, coming into being? How, moreover, will other states in the region and beyond respond to a widening Indian military footprint? Will they view it in terms of what then US Secretary of State Condoleezza Rice famously called a 'balance of power that favours

---

[1] Compare with Itty Abraham (ed.), *South Asian Cultures of the Bomb: Atomic Publics and the State in India and Pakistan* (Bloomington: Indiana University Press, 2009), p. 165.

[2] Walter C Ladwig III, 'India and Military Power Projection: Will the Land of Gandhi Become a Conventional Great Power?', *Asian Survey* (Vol. 50, No. 6, November 2010), pp. 1162–64.

[3] For an excellent elucidation of Chinese views of Indian 'hegemonism', see John W Garver, *Protracted Contest: Sino-Indian Rivalry in the Twentieth Century* (Seattle, WA: University of Washington Press, 2001), pp. 15–19, 30–31.

freedom', or a threatening impingement on their own freedom of manoeuvre?[4] This concluding chapter surveys this Whitehall Paper's broad findings, while looking at how Indian power projection might unfold in practice.

Power projection is assuming greater importance in India's military thinking and preparation. Like virtually all rising powers in history, the parallel growth of India's economy, interests and strategic vision has, collectively, given New Delhi both the resource base and incentives to be tempted to influence events increasingly far from its immediate periphery. Following a gradual but historic alignment between the US and India from 2005 onward, strongly renewed by Prime Minister Narendra Modi and President Barack Obama during 2014–15, Washington has embraced these Indian aspirations, welcoming India's role as a 'net provider of security in the Indian Ocean and beyond', language that Indian leaders have themselves appropriated. While no other states have embraced this idea as fulsomely, India's deepening network of strategic ties with Australia, Japan and Vietnam, including growing defence engagement, suggests that some of Asia's most significant powers are relatively positive about the growth of Indian power.

Chapters II, III and IV outline the military platforms that give India the ability to project air power and land power over increasingly long distances. They show how India's reach grew especially quickly in the 2000s, with the acquisition of new strike, tanker, transport and AEWC aircraft, a major amphibious ship and a refurbished aircraft carrier with a growing complement of naval strike aircraft. However, these platforms have been little tested together in operational conditions, and they remain limited in quantity. India, for instance, possesses fewer attack helicopters, transporters, tankers and AEWC aircraft than any one of the permanent five members of the UN Security Council, and in many cases fewer than other Asian powers like Australia, Japan, South Korea and Taiwan. The aggregate capability they produce – such as the maximum average daily sortie rate of Indian carrier-based aircraft, or the maximum size of an amphibious force – remains modest by the standards of typical recent power-projection missions, and therefore most useful against much weaker adversaries rather than peers or near-peers.

Even where adversaries are conventionally weak – as they have been in wars in Afghanistan, Iraq, Libya, Syria and Yemen – the problem of quantity still arises. Middle powers with aspirations to power projection – including Britain, France and Saudi Arabia – struggle to generate sufficient

---

4   Condoleezza Rice, 'A Balance of Power that Favors Freedom', Wriston Lecture given at the Manhattan Institute for Policy Research, 1 October 2002.

numbers of forces to prosecute and sustain these campaigns without extensive American involvement. Chapter IV shows that Indian capabilities also remain limited in both the quantity of key platforms, such as tankers, and in the strength of key enablers, such as jointness, intelligence and basing. All these limitations are testament to India's local priorities, its still-limited resources (for example, lower defence spending than any permanent members of the UN Security Council) and, above all, the uniquely high demands of independent power projection. Put simply, power projection is hard.

But many of these assessments depend greatly on why – and therefore where and against whom – India is likely to be projecting military power. A campaign against Chinese supply lines in Tibet presents radically different demands to a stabilisation mission in part of Afghanistan. The remainder of this chapter considers how Indian interests and future power projection may be connected, the role that coalitions might or might not play in this, and how these factors might shape others' responses to Indian actions.

Interests and Power Projection

The Introduction outlines five types of interests that have been growing in importance to India. These include: the regional balance of power, transnational terrorism, economic security, diaspora status and security, and the global commons. Such interests have been the primary historical drivers of power projection. For instance, American and European forward basing and recurrent intervention in the Persian Gulf have been closely linked to its energy resources.[5] Similarly, Russian interventions in Georgia and Ukraine have been shaped by the presence of Russian-speaking and ethnic Russian minorities.[6] To these five interests, we might add a sixth: humanitarian intervention and the associated Responsibility to Protect (R2P), which grew out of Western interventions in the Balkans in the 1990s and was connected to intervention in Libya in 2011. This is excluded from the list because, despite the obvious humanitarian aspects to India's 1971 intervention in Bangladesh, Indian attitudes towards R2P

---

[5] Joshua Rovner and Caitlin Talmadge, 'Hegemony, Force Posture, and the Provision of Public Goods: The Once and Future Role of Outside Powers in Securing Persian Gulf Oil', *Security Studies* (Vol. 23, No. 3, July 2014), p. 556; Fred Halliday, *The Middle East in International Relations: Power, Politics and Ideology* (Cambridge: Cambridge University Press, 2005), p. 142.

[6] Roy Allison, 'Russia Resurgent? Moscow's Campaign to "Coerce Georgia to Peace"', *International Affairs* (Vol. 84, No. 6, November 2008), p. 1167; Roy Allison, 'Russian "Deniable" Intervention in Ukraine: How and Why Russia Broke the Rules', *International Affairs* (Vol. 90, No. 6, November 2014), pp. 1282–89.

are ambivalent at best and hostile at worst.[7] It should be stressed that the discussion that follows is not intended as a list of probable Indian interventions likely to arise in the next several years. Indeed, most scenarios discussed here have relatively small probabilities of occurring. Rather, these are intended to show the geographic spread and nature of various possible challenges to Indian interests, and the type of power projection that such challenges might demand.

Regional Balance of Power

What do these interests mean in practice? The balance of power is the most straightforward. From independence onwards, and especially so at the turn of the 1940s/50s, the early 1960s and again in the 1980s, India has sought a pre-eminent position within South Asia, defined at first as the exclusion of great powers from the region, and later as a high degree of influence over strategic developments.[8] But despite being the single-largest state, India has rarely if ever reached this level of superiority. Over the past fifteen years, India has seen particular threats to its security in the inter-related challenge of growing Chinese influence in South Asia and political changes within smaller regional powers – such as Sri Lanka – that weaken New Delhi's sway and enhance that of Beijing.[9] Today, pre-eminence really means a favourable balance of power. Indian concerns over this balance have driven a variety of diplomatic, economic, intelligence and military-led policies in areas where Sino–Indian rivalry is especially acute. Recent examples, both from 2015, include the alleged use of R&AW to sway Sri Lanka's elections in January and an alleged informal blockade of Nepal to influence its constitution-writing process in October.[10] While India's role is these cases is contested, it has used both covert action and economic coercion as instruments of statecraft in the past.

Throughout the 1980s, the high-water mark of Indian gunboat diplomacy, such concerns drove overt power projection, of which several examples are given below. More recently, New Delhi has shied away from direct military intervention to halt or reverse adverse political shifts. It

---

[7] Ian Hall, 'Tilting at Windmills? The Indian Debate over the Responsibility to Protect after UNSC Resolution 1973', *Global Responsibility to Protect* (Vol. 5, No. 1, 2013).

[8] Garver, *Protracted Contest*, p. 18; Devin T Hagerty, 'India's Regional Security Doctrine', *Asian Survey* (Vol. 31, No. 4, April 1991), pp. 362–63.

[9] C Raja Mohan, 'Samudra Manthan: Sino-Indian Rivalry in the Indo-Pacific', Brief, Carnegie Endowment for International Peace, 2012, chs. 7–9.

[10] John Chalmers and Sanjeev Miglani, 'Indian Spy's Role Alleged in Sri Lankan President's Election Defeat', *Reuters*, 18 January 2015; Krishna Pokharel and Niharika Mandhana, 'Three-Week Bridge Blockade Hurts Nepal Economy', *Wall Street Journal*, 15 October 2015.

showed restraint during a crisis in Sri Lanka in 2000 and in the Maldives during 2012–15, opting to use its intelligence capabilities to influence or change regimes in lieu of heavier-handed means.[11] It would be difficult to imagine India overtly intervening militarily in most free and fair elections, unless these brought violently anti-Indian groups to power. But extra-constitutional changes of power that go against New Delhi, such as coups, are a different matter. Many of the relevant states – Sri Lanka, Maldives, Seychelles and Mauritius – would offer little to moderate conventional military resistance. Others – Bangladesh, Myanmar, Nepal and Bhutan – are more complicated cases, and India would likely rely on traditional diplomatic and intelligence channels to influence events.

A second dimension of the regional balance of power is less to do with competition for influence, and more to do with direct conflict. India is not only worried about Pakistani and Chinese power in the region, but also the ways in which that power could change the nature of a military conflict – even one that begins in a traditional border clash. Many of the power-projection capabilities outlined in this study have important uses in conventional conflicts that take on a regional dimension. This includes both defensive and offensive operations. Ashley Tellis suggests that 'the prospect of a major Chinese naval presence in the Indian Ocean challenges Indian security in novel ways, transforming a hitherto secure rear into a springboard from which coercive power can be brought to bear in new directions against the Indian landmass'.[12] Several Indian civilian analysts and military officers have raised the possibility that 'some inimical power does a Falkland' on India's island possessions.[13] 'The only place where the Chinese can strike without facing any real opposition', claimed one Indian officer in September 2015, 'is the Andamans'.[14] While these fears may appear exaggerated, they reflect a sense of disorientation over the speed with which Chinese influence has grown.

In terms of offensive uses, power-projection capabilities also offer India a range of options. They enable New Delhi to hold at risk the Pakistani littoral, previously inaccessible parts of Tibet, Chinese sea-lanes

---

[11] Neil Devotta, 'Is India Over-Extended? When Domestic Disorder Precludes Regional Intervention', *Contemporary South Asia* (Vol. 12, No. 3, September 2003); Sachin Parashar, 'Nasheed's Party Wants India to Intervene', *Times of India*, 15 March 2015.

[12] Ashley J Tellis, 'Making Waves: Aiding India's Next-Generation Aircraft Carrier', Carnegie Endowment for International Peace, April 2015, p. 5.

[13] Abhijit Singh, 'The Indian Navy's "New" Expeditionary Outlook', ORF Occasional Paper No. 37, Observer Research Foundation, October 2012, p. 10.

[14] Jayanta Gupta, 'Chinese Naval Ships Detected near Andamans', *Times of India*, 4 September 2015.

and any future Chinese military presence in the Indian Ocean, such as ports. Power projection is therefore part of India's defence posture towards its traditional rivals, not merely a substitute for 'local' military capabilities.

Reducing Transnational Terrorism

The four other types of interest pull India in less familiar directions. Terrorism is India's most emotive and directly felt national security concern.[15] Years after the Mumbai attacks of 2008, India's principal terrorism threat continues to emanate from within Pakistan, largely from groups supported and partly controlled by Pakistan's intelligence services. However, India also perceives threats from groups in a variety of other places: in Afghanistan, where Pakistan-based groups have often found sanctuary; from Daesh, headquartered in Syria but with a burgeoning presence beyond, including in Afghanistan; from the extensive networks of Pakistan-based groups in the Persian Gulf, including networks within the Indian diaspora (more on which below); and from ethno-nationalist groups, such as Sikh extremists, based as far afield as Europe and North America. Pakistan is the epicentre of these threats, but they have a regional and even global dimension.

After Pakistan, the foremost Indian concern is Afghanistan: its future after the withdrawal of foreign troops, and the consequences for India of either a Pakistan-brokered peace settlement or deterioration of security.[16] India fears that either scenario could provide opportunities to groups hostile to India, including the Haqqani Network, whose leader, Sirajuddin Haqqani, was appointed deputy to Taliban leader Mullah Mansour in August 2015, as well as the Pakistan-headquartered Lashkar-e-Taiba, which was responsible for the Mumbai attacks and is particularly close to Pakistani intelligence.[17] India's views of Afghanistan are especially strongly shaped by its experience of a Pakistan-supported hijacking of an Indian aircraft in 1999, the Taliban's role in the resulting standoff in Kandahar, and the traumatic prisoner release that followed.[18] Some Indian analysts have recommended that India send troops to

---

[15] Prem Mahadevan, *The Politics of Counterterrorism in India: Strategic Intelligence and National Security in South Asia* (London: I.B.Tauris, 2011), pp. 1–25.

[16] Shashank Joshi, 'India's Role in a Changing Afghanistan', *Washington Quarterly* (Vol. 37, No. 2, Summer 2014).

[17] C Christine Fair, *Fighting to the End: The Pakistan Army's Way of War* (Oxford: Oxford University Press, 2014), pp. 226–60.

[18] A S Dulat and Aditya Sinha, *Kashmir: The Vajpayee Years* (Noida: Uttar Pradesh: HarperCollins India, 2015), ch. 6.

Afghanistan.[19] This remains a fringe position and successive governments have shied away even from providing heavy arms to Kabul.

However, further major attacks on Indian interests – either within Afghanistan or attributed to groups there – could provoke an Indian military response in the future. Yet the use of air power would not be simple. It would depend on securing overflight or transit rights from Iran, de-confliction with Washington and Kabul (both of which operate military aircraft in Afghan airspace) and – depending on whether Tajikistan was used as a staging ground – the acquiescence of Dushanbe and Moscow. Even so, Indian strikes on Afghanistan could, paradoxically, be easier and considerably less escalatory than strikes on what India views as the root of the problem, Pakistan. While such scenarios should be considered low-probability, their large regional impact makes them worthy of careful consideration. Separately, the Afghan government might itself request Indian military assistance if security conditions deteriorated and the US or other Western countries showed little inclination to step in. Such assistance could involve training and advisory teams, the use of Indian air power to augment Afghanistan's meagre close-air-support capability, or, considerably less likely, the deployment of combat troops. India has previously considered such steps unduly provocative, but its attitudes could be swayed by serious backsliding in Afghanistan and concern for the impact of a security vacuum on the stability of Kashmir and other parts of India.

Beyond the medium term, it is also possible that broader currents of Islamic extremism begin to attract greater Indian attention. Although India has rejected participation in the US-led anti-Daesh coalition, New Delhi has been concerned by Indians travelling to Syria and Iraq to fight with Daesh, Daesh-inspired terrorism within India and Daesh's actions against Indian interests in the Middle East, such as the kidnapping and murder of Indian nationals in Mosul in 2014.[20] Over the coming decades, anti-Indian groups might also find sanctuary or common cause with groups in South and Southeast Asia, as well as the Middle East, North Africa and East Africa. India is already concerned about a nexus between Pakistani intelligence and Islamist networks in Bangladesh, Sri Lanka and the

---

[19] Sushant K Singh, 'A Bigger Military Presence Is Essential', *Pragati: The Indian National Interest Review* (No. 17, August 2008); Nitin Pai and Rohit Pradhan, 'Why India Must Send Troops to Afghanistan', *Pragati: The Indian National Interest Review*, 1 January 2010.

[20] Vicky Nanjappa, 'How India and 70 Other Countries Will Fight the ISIS', One India, 5 October 2015, <http://www.oneindia.com/india/how-india-70-other-countries-will-fight-the-isis-1889530.html>, accessed 22 October 2015; *Economic Times*, 'Rapid Increase of ISIS Activities in India's Neighbourhood', 29 September 2015.

Maldives, and the leadership of the Indian Mujahideen terrorist group moves between Pakistan, the UAE and Saudi Arabia.[21] Such concerns could plausibly grow in scope.

India's primary response to terrorism is likely to remain dominated by diplomacy and intelligence, rather than military instruments. Despite serious concern about the lax attitudes of the Gulf monarchies towards terrorist suspects, for instance, India has preferred to deepen its relationship with Riyadh and Abu Dhabi in the hope of co-operation, rather than rely on pressure or coercion.[22] Similarly, in response to the threat from Daesh, India has moved to secure Kurdish support by offering material assistance to the Kurdistan Regional Government in Erbil.[23] But over the longer term, future Indian governments might opt for more militarised approaches. This is especially true in those circumstances where states are either unwilling or unable to offer co-operation, and particularly where, by virtue of a military imbalance, the risks of resistance and escalation are relatively low. Indians' obvious admiration for what they see as a distinctive Israeli mode of military counter-terrorism offers an indication of this possible direction of travel.[24] It is notable that the two states where global disapproval rates for US drone strikes are the very lowest – even more so than within the US itself – are India and Israel.[25]

Preserving Economic Security
The same process that has enabled Indian investment in power-projection capabilities over the last twenty-five years has also resulted in a significant expansion of India's overseas economic interests and increased their importance to India's economy. This has three aspects: first, the status and security of Indian capital overseas; second, the preservation of particular flows of important resources, especially energy; and, third, India's general interest in the stability of areas important to its economy.

---

[21] Stephen Tankel, *Jihadist Violence: The Indian Threat* (Washington, DC: Wilson Center, 2013), p. 8.
[22] Stephen Tankel, 'Pakistan's Sticky Wicket: The India-Saudi Link', *Foreign Policy*, 30 July 2012; *The Wire*, 'Diplomacy Decoded: Terrorism in the India-UAE Joint Statement', 18 August 2015.
[23] Saikat Datta, 'In ISIS Wake, India May Tweak West Asia Policy', *Hindustan Times*, 10 September 2014.
[24] Shashi Tharoor, 'India's Israel Envy', *Project Syndicate*, 12 January 2009; Stephen P Cohen and Sunil Dasgupta, *Arming without Aiming: India's Military Modernization* (Washington, DC: Brookings Institution Press, 2010), p. 184; George Perkovich and Toby Dalton, 'Modi's Strategic Choice: How to Respond to Terrorism from Pakistan', *Washington Quarterly* (Vol. 38, No. 1, Spring 2015), p. 41.
[25] Pew Research Center, 'Global Opposition to U.S. Surveillance and Drones, but Limited Harm to America's Image', July 2014, p. 5.

In terms of capital, although India remains a net FDI recipient, its share of Asian outbound FDI grew from 0.4 to 4.3 per cent from 2001 to 2011.[26] From January 2003 to August 2012, the top destinations for Indian investments in terms of number of projects – comprising a third of the total – were the US, UK and UAE, though the largest capital expenditure was in Indonesia, with the UAE, China, Iran, Nigeria and Oman following behind.[27] Over the 2000s, the combined share of Indian investment going to Africa and the Asia-Pacific jumped from a tenth to over one-half.[28] On top of this, we should note Indian investments with a strategic character and in especially sensitive areas. These include planned or realised investments in the Iranian port of Chabahar, close to Pakistan in the Gulf of Oman; the Hajigak iron ore mines in Afghanistan; and oil exploration in the South China Sea.[29] They also include upstream energy investments in volatile areas: in April 2013, a state-owned energy company lost joint investments in the Deir Ezzor Governate of Syria when an oil field was overrun by rebels.[30] Future Indian power projection could be directed at protecting such investments from seizure.

In terms of broader energy security, India's net oil-import dependency jumped from 43 per cent in 1990 to over 70 per cent by 2012.[31] India also imported a substantial amount of its primary energy source, coal, despite large domestic reserves.[32] The sources of Indian oil imports have fluctuated considerably month-to-month in recent years, in part owing to nuclear-related sanctions on Iran; but as of late 2015, its largest sources were Nigeria and Saudi Arabia, with supplies from Africa and the Middle East comprising, respectively, 26 per cent and 54 per cent of Indian imports.[33]

It is also worth noting that India seeks not just reliable flows, but also cheap ones. The Indian government heavily subsidises both public-sector

[26] Export-Import Bank of India, 'Outward Direct Investment from India: Trends, Objectives, and Policy Perspectives', Occasional Paper No. 165, May 2014, p. 13.
[27] *Ibid.*, p. 15.
[28] *Ibid*, p. 42.
[29] Pranab Dhal Samanta, 'Three Months after Nitin Gadkari's Iran Visit, Chabahar Port Project Runs into Trouble', *Economic Times*, 17 August 2015; Michelle FlorCruz, 'Vietnam and India Sign Oil, Naval Agreement amid South China Sea Disputes, Angering Beijing', *International Business Times*, 29 October 2014.
[30] Kabir Taneja, 'A Survey of India's Energy Prospects in the Middle East Region', discussion document, Takshashila Institution, November 2014, p. 15.
[31] Energy Information Administration, 'India is Increasingly Dependent on Imported Fossil Fuels as Demand Continues to Rise', 14 August 2014, <http://www.eia.gov/todayinenergy/detail.cfm?id=17551#>, accessed 22 October 2015.
[32] *Reuters*, 'Coal Imports Could Slide 3 Percent in 2015/16 – Government', 23 July 2015.
[33] Nidhi Verma, 'Saudi Arabia Loses Spot as Top Crude Supplier to India, China', *Reuters*, 24 June 2015.

domestic oil companies and consumer oil products, and is therefore heavily exposed to adverse shifts in price – particularly if the rupee falls relative to the dollar. To understand the fiscal burden that this can impose, consider that India spent a sizeable 1.75 per cent of GDP on compensation for oil marketing companies in the fiscal year 2012/13 and 1.4 per cent of GDP on overall fuel subsidies since 2008.[34] Although petroleum subsidies were slashed by half in 2015, they were still expected to amount to around $4.5 billion – equivalent to roughly a tenth of the defence budget.[35]

Preserving Diaspora Status and Security

India's relationship with its large diaspora has changed over time. In the years after independence, India effectively told its diaspora to integrate locally and fend for itself.[36] Even when Ugandan dictator Idi Amin expelled tens of thousands of ethnic Indians in 1972, India did little to push back.[37] But, 'by the early 1980s', write scholar David Brewster and India's former director of naval intelligence and operations, Commodore Ranjit Rai, 'the protection of ethnic communities outside of India had become a factor in New Delhi's calculations'.[38]

In 1983, for instance, India was extremely concerned about the welfare of the ethnic Indians of Mauritius – 70 per cent of the local population – after a coup by factions favouring Creole and Muslim minorities, though a military intervention was aborted at the last moment in favour of a diplomatic approach.[39] India's military intervention in Sri Lanka later in four years later was influenced by Sri Lanka's crackdown on Tamil groups, the flow of refugees into India and protests by Indian Tamils at their co-ethnics' treatment by Colombo.[40] And in 1987 and again in 2006, Fiji experienced coups intended to remove ethnic Indians from

---

[34] International Institute for Sustainable Development, *India Energy Subsidy Review: A Biannual Survey of Energy Subsidy Policy* (Vol. 1, No. 1, February 2014), p. 3.

[35] Reuters, 'India to Spend $37 Bln on Major Subsidies in 2015/16', *Yahoo Finance*, 28 February 2015.

[36] Srinath Raghavan, 'The Diaspora and India', *India Review* (Vol. 11, No. 1, January 2012), p. 67.

[37] Devesh Kapur, *Diaspora, Development, and Democracy: The Domestic Impact of International Migration from India* (Princeton, NJ: Princeton University Press, 2010), p. 15.

[38] David Brewster and Ranjit Rai, 'Operation Lal Dora: India's Aborted Military Intervention in Mauritius', *Asian Security* (Vol. 9, No. 1, March 2013), p. 66.

[39] *Ibid.*, pp. 65–70.

[40] Neil DeVotta, 'Sri Lanka's Civil War', in Sumit Ganguly, Andrew Scobell and Joseph Chinyong Liow (eds), *Handbook of Asian Security Studies* (Oxford: Routledge, 2009), p. 164.

power.[41] Despite Prime Minister Indira Gandhi's remark on the former occasion that she felt 'like a mother concerned about the welfare of a daughter who has set up home faraway' – a quintessentially South Asian simile – India's response was tepid.[42] But 62 per cent of Indians polled in 2013 rated the protection of Indian citizens abroad as very important, roughly the same proportion as combating international terrorism or ensuring access to energy supplies (both 63 per cent) and ahead of 'stopping other countries putting pressure on India'.[43]

How is India's diaspora distributed geographically? There are an estimated 25 million overseas Indians, including both Indian nationals and ethnic Indians, with the largest communities in Nepal (6 million), the US (4.5 million), Saudi Arabia (2.8 million), Malaysia (2.2 million), Myanmar (2 million), the UAE (2 million), Sri Lanka (1.6 million) and Thailand (1.6 million).[44] The ratio of Indian nationals (those holding Indian passports) to *ethnic* Indians (those of Indian ancestry, but not a citizen of India) varies greatly in these places. It is especially high in the Gulf states, where Indian nationals travel as workers, and particularly low in places with longstanding settled Indian communities, like Myanmar and Malaysia. As a proportion of native population – an important measure of potential organising power and therefore political significance – Indians are an outright majority in Mauritius (68 per cent), a plurality in Trinidad and Tobago (40 per cent), Suriname (27 per cent), and a significant minority in Fiji (40 per cent), the UAE (32 per cent), Kuwait (22 per cent), Bahrain (19 per cent), Oman (18 per cent) and Qatar (16 per cent). This presence of overseas Indians also results in a substantial annual remittance flow to India, the largest of which comes from the UAE ($12.64 billion), US ($11.18 billion) and Saudi Arabia ($10.74 billion).[45]

Many of the countries with large Indian populations are politically stable and friendly with India, such as the US, Canada and UK. In these places, the Indian diaspora is more important as a community to be

---

[41] Andrew Scobell, 'Politics, Professionalism, and Peacekeeping: An Analysis of the 1987 Military Coup in Fiji', *Comparative Politics* (Vol. 26, No. 2, January 1994); Sina Emde, 'Feared Rumours and Rumours of Fear: The Politicisation of Ethnicity During the Fiji Coup in May 2000', *Oceania* (Vol. 75, No. 4, September–December 2005).

[42] David Brewster, *India as an Asia Pacific Power* (Oxford: Routledge, 2012), p. 126.

[43] Rory Medcalf, 'Facing the Future: India Views of the World Ahead', India Poll 2013, Lowy Institute for International Policy and Australia India Institute, 2013, p. 22.

[44] Ministry of Overseas Indian Affairs, Government of India, 'Population of Overseas Indians', 2015, <http://moia.gov.in/writereaddata/pdf/Population_Overseas_Indian.pdf>, accessed 22 October 2015.

[45] T K Vineeth, 'The Social Construct of India's High-Remittance Story', *Business Standard*, 15 April 2015.

mobilised for lobbying the local government, rather than a group in need of New Delhi's assistance. Other countries are weak, but relatively pliant and proximate, like Nepal. The more interesting cases with regard to power projection are those that are some combination of weak, potentially politically unstable and relatively distant from India. These most resemble the cases seen in the 1980s.

One scenario, tested repeatedly in recent years, is the evacuation of large numbers of Indian nationals in response to a sudden crisis. While Indian transport capabilities worked well in Yemen in 2015 and Libya in 2011, they would be more severely tested by political disorder or violent conflict in the Gulf, involving a much larger outflow of Indians with greater consequences for remittances and therefore domestic politics in key Indian states. India might also be more willing to devote military resources to a multinational campaign if it were seen to contribute to the defence of vulnerable Indian communities abroad. At present, the question of contribution to broader stabilisation efforts is in part obviated by the American and European military presence and willingness to intervene in situations such as Saddam Hussein's invasion of Kuwait (though Indians would point out that Western interventions have frequently *threatened* the security and livelihoods of overseas Indians). But should Western forces retrench in coming decades, this would affect India's calculus. At present, India's primary contribution to stabilisation missions, through UN peacekeeping operations, is largely in areas of secondary strategic importance to India and Indians.

Securing Regional and Global Commons

The regional and global commons are 'areas that belong to no one state and that provide access to much of the globe'.[46] They include the oceans, air, outer space and cyberspace. Over the past decade, many in the US have argued that these commons are becoming 'contested' as a result of challenges including China's attitude towards freedom of navigation and air transit in East Asia, and piracy in crucial shipping lanes.[47] India has good reason to be concerned by such trends. India's trade-to-GDP ratio rose from 30 per cent in 2006 to nearly 43 per cent in 2012, and 90 per cent of that trade by volume (70 per cent by value) is carried over sea.[48]

---

[46] Barry R Posen, 'Command of the Commons: The Military Foundation of U.S. Hegemony', *International Security* (Vol. 28, No. 1, Summer 2003), p. 8.
[47] Michelle Flournoy and Shawn Brimley, 'The Contested Commons', *Proceedings Magazine* (Vol. 135, No. 7, July 2009).
[48] Rajiv K Bhatia and Vijay Sakhuja (eds), *Indo Pacific Region: Political and Strategic Prospects* (Delhi: Vij Books, 2014), pp. 150–51.

Influential Indian voices emphasise India's fundamental interest in an 'open global order' and 'open shipping lanes'.[49] In November 2014, the foreign minister reiterated that 'the safety and security of the sea-lanes is … indispensible for our territorial, economic and energy security.'[50] Indo–US joint statements also increasingly allude to this, the last of which, in January 2015, 'affirm[ed] the importance of safeguarding maritime security and ensuring freedom of navigation and over flight throughout the region' – 'especially', it added pointedly, 'in the South China Sea'.[51]

One implication is that India has an increasing incentive to play what might be termed a constabulary role. Shivshankar Menon, Indian National Security Advisor between 2010 and 2014, writes that 'while the West, particularly the US Fifth Fleet based in Bahrain, has been a traditional provider of security, the situation and local demands are clearly changing'. He argues that 'space is opening up for a greater Indian role in providing maritime security. We should certainly see how the template of our existing maritime security cooperation with Sri Lanka, the Maldives, Mauritius and Seychelles could be extended westwards to Mozambique, the African coast, and partners in West Asia and the Gulf'.[52]

What does maritime security mean in practice? While it includes a variety of domestic coastal-defence tasks, such as preventing terrorist infiltration and interdicting smugglers, the most important mission beyond coastal waters has been anti-piracy.[53] India played a prominent role in anti-piracy operations in the Gulf of Aden in 2008, most notably destroying a pirate 'mother ship'.[54] India has continued cyclic deployment of ships in that area since (some were used in the evacuation of Indian nationals from Yemen in March 2015).[55] But despite a surge in the number of attacks and a widening of the afflicted

---

[49] Sunil Khilnani et al., 'Non-Alignment 2.0: A Foreign and Strategic Policy for India in the Twenty First Century', Centre for Policy Research, 2012, p. 8.
[50] *DNA*, 'Indian Navy Committed to Ensuring Safety of Indian Ocean Sea Lanes Says External Affairs Minister Sushma Swaraj', 3 November 2014.
[51] White House, 'U.S.-India Joint Strategic Vision for the Asia-Pacific and Indian Ocean Region', press release, 25 January 2015.
[52] Shivshankar Menon, 'It's Time for India to Start Looking West Again', *The Wire*, 15 October 2010.
[53] Integrated Headquarters, Ministry of Defence (Navy), 'Freedom to Use the Seas: India's Maritime Military Strategy', May 2007, p. 118.
[54] Hari Kumar and Alan Cowell, 'Indian Warship Skirmishes with Pirates in Gulf of Aden', *New York Times*, 20 November 2008.
[55] Muaz Shabandri, 'Indian Navy Will Support Anti-Piracy Operations', *Khaleej Times*, 17 September 2003; *The Hindu*, 'Indian Warships Sent to Yemen to Provide Anti-Piracy Services', 31 March 2015.

area, India has maintained a cautious approach.[56] Whereas Pakistan has commanded Combined Task Force (CTF) 150, a twenty-five-state, maritime-security coalition, on seven occasions (as many times as Britain), India has never participated.[57] Although this might have as much to do with Pakistani sensitivities as Indian reticence, Harsh Pant and Yogesh Joshi argue that the Indian Navy, 'like those of China and Russia', prefers independent 'national escort missions' rather than integrated multinational coalitions, and has seen infighting between the navy and the foreign ministry over the legality of Indian deployments, given that piracy is not a crime under the Indian Penal Code.[58]

In the longer term, India could also broaden the scope of constabulary missions to address threats that specifically affect India. One model is the Proliferation Security Initiative (PSI), a UN Security Council-backed effort to interdict WMD-related materials, including through the forcible boarding of suspect ships.[59] While India has been wary of the PSI's wide, extra-territorial jurisdiction,[60] it is easy to imagine a larger Indian naval presence in the western Indian Ocean giving New Delhi the opportunity to block the flow of arms or other sensitive goods to Pakistan, anti-Indian militant groups or other adversaries. This would require a much greater intelligence capability than India has evidenced so far and, given the ubiquity of flags of convenience, could bring India into dispute with third parties; but, nevertheless, it would represent another way for India to apply pressure on its adversaries with a smaller risk of escalation than that which accompanies a more direct use of force.

India and Multinational Operations: A Lonely Power?

Coalitions: The New Normal
India's independent approach to anti-piracy connects with an extremely important factor shaping its broader power-projection capabilities. Excluding the US, which is obviously uniquely powerful, today states that

---

[56] On widening attacks, see Natalia Piskunova, 'Pirates of Aden: A Threat Beyond Somalia's Shores?', *Central European Journal of International and Security* (Vol. 9, No. 2, June 2015).
[57] Navaltoday.com, 'Pakistan Hosts CTF 150 Commander', 12 December 2014, <http://navaltoday.com/2014/12/12/pakistan-hosts-ctf-150-commander/>, accessed 22 October 2015.
[58] Harsh V Pant and Yogesh Joshi, 'The American "Pivot" and the Indian Navy: It's Hedging All the Way', *Naval War College Review* (Vol. 68, No. 1, Winter 2015), p. 60.
[59] Mary Beth Nitkitin, 'Proliferation Security Initiative (PSI)', Congressional Research Service, RL34327, June 2012.
[60] A Vinod Kumar, 'India's Participation in the Proliferation Security Initiative: Issues in Perspective', *Strategic Analysis* (Vol. 33, No. 5, July 2009).

routinely project force almost exclusively do so as part of formal coalitions or, at least, with assistance from allies and partners. France's dependence on allies for transportation and ISR in Mali, for instance, was described earlier. The Saudi and UAE-led coalition that intervened in Yemen in 2015 has required extensive American assistance with intelligence, targeting, arms supplies and enforcement of the blockade.[61] Unilateral power projection is unusual, and it is unusual because for non-superpowers it is difficult.

This is reflected in the most basic assumptions of even highly experienced power projectors. Even in the 1990s, when British military forces were larger than today, the UK's chief of the Naval Staff observed that 'it remains conceivable, though unlikely, that British forces would embark on significant action without partners ... multinational forces will be the norm for any future deployment of power'.[62] In 2010, the UK's Strategic Defence and Security Review acknowledged several times that 'we rarely act alone', pointed out the UK had conducted only one significant unilateral operation since the Falklands War and stated that 'we and our NATO Allies consciously depend on each other for particular capabilities'.[63] In 2013, France's White Paper on defence likewise admitted that 'most of our military operations are likely to occur in a multinational framework'.[64]

This assumption does not hold for India. New Delhi does not have meaningful allies and does not want them. 'It would be lazy to choose alliance', declared then-NSA Shivshankar Menon in 2014, 'shirking responsibility for our own fate'.[65] Indian defence debates accordingly proceed largely on the assumption that it will have to go to war alone. But although this is an undeniable constraint on India, it is not an absolute or unchanging one.

The Indo–US Relationship
For one thing, India is forging a strategic partnership with the US to a degree that would seem unimaginable from the vantage point of the early 1990s, let alone the Cold War period of Indian non-alignment. While the full

---

[61] Maria Abi-Habib and Adam Entous, 'U.S. Widens Role in Saudi-Led Campaign against Houthi Rebels in Yemen', *Wall Street Journal*, 13 April 2015; *BBC News*, 'Yemen Conflict: US Boosts Arms Supplies for Saudi-Led Coalition', 8 April 2015.

[62] Andrew Dorman, Mike Lawrence Smith and Matthew Uttley, 'Jointery and Combined Operations in an Expeditionary Era: Defining the Issues', *Defense Analysis* (Vol. 14, No. 1, April 1998), p. 6.

[63] HM Government, *Securing Britain in an Age of Uncertainty: The Strategic Defence and Security Review* (SDSR), Cm 7948 (London: The Stationery Office, October 2010).

[64] President of the Republic, 'The French White Paper on Defence and National Security', English version, 2013, p. 21.

[65] Shivshankar Menon, 'Speech by National Security Advisor at IAFAC on "India in the 21st Century World"', 12 February 2014.

implications of this alignment remain unclear, it is becoming increasingly plausible that India and the US could offer limited military assistance to one another in a variety of regional scenarios. This does not mean that India would, for instance, participate in a war over Taiwan or the South China Sea. But New Delhi could, for instance, offer logistical assistance or access to Indian facilities.[66] There is precedent for such lower-level co-operation. As early as 2001, after the 9/11 attacks, India offered the use of its bases to Washington. The next year the Indian Navy escorted US ships carrying high-value cargo for operations in Afghanistan, freeing US Navy vessels for other tasks.[67] Conversely, Washington could fill in crucial gaps in Indian capability outlined in previous chapters, particularly around intelligence – something that could be shared unobtrusively. This is not as fanciful at it might sound. India gave consideration to joint air strikes with Israel, against Pakistani nuclear facilities, in the 1980s.[68] If it could discuss such operations with a country with which it lacked full official relations at the time, it is unlikely to have compunctions about doing so with an increasingly important partner today. As the US and Pakistan drift further apart, with the former decreasingly dependent on the latter as American troops depart Afghanistan, this becomes even more likely. 'Military or civilian, active or retired, from every political party, Indian, American or of another nationality', notes a recent study by the RAND Corporation, 'almost all interviewees saw a deep congruence of interests in Southeast Asia between the two nations'.[69] While this is true only of that particular sub-region, it suggests that future military co-operation is certainly feasible.

---

[66] The question of whether and how far India would support the US in a conflict with China was debated between the author and Australian academic Hugh White on the Lowy Institute's blog, *The Interpreter*, between 6 February and 13 March 2015. See Hugh White, 'A Second Look at Obama's Visit', *The Interpreter*, 6 February 2015; Shashank Joshi, 'The US-India Convergence', *The Interpreter*, 13 February 2015; Hugh White, 'Obama's India Visit Reveals Weakness of US Position in Asia', 16 February 2015; Shashank Joshi, 'The Consequences of the Strengthening US-India Partnership are Still Uncertain', *The Interpreter*, 10 March 2015; Hugh White, 'Would India Go to War with China to Help America?', *The Interpreter*, 13 March 2015.

[67] Amit Baruah, 'Only "Escort Duties" in Malacca Straits', *The Hindu*, 23 April 2002.

[68] George Perkovich, *India's Nuclear Bomb: The Impact on Global Proliferation* (Berkeley: University of California Press, 2002), pp. 240–41, 257–59, 283; P R Kumaraswamy, *India's Israel Policy* (New York, NY: Columbia University Press, 2010), pp. 229–30; Sergey Radchenko, 'India and the End of the Cold War', in Artemy M Kalinovsky and Sergey Radchenko (eds), *The End of the Cold War and The Third World: New Perspectives on Regional Conflict* (Oxford: Routledge, 2011), p. 175.

[69] Jonah Blank, Jennifer D P Moroney, Angel Rabasa, and Bonny Lin, *Look East, Cross Black Waters: India's Interest in Southeast Asia* (Santa Monica, CA: RAND Corporation, 2015), p. 10.

Multinational Exercises

In addition to the bilateral US-India relationship, the last twenty-five years have seen a flourishing of multinational naval exercises between India, the US and a variety of the Asian allies of the US. The most important of these include the *Malabar* series, which began as a bilateral Indo–US exercise in 1992, and grew to include Australia, Singapore and Japan in 2007; and the *Milan* series, which began in 1995 and has grown to include fifteen nations.[70]

In keeping with its emphasis on strategic autonomy and aversion to formal alliances, India has been extremely careful in how these exercises have been portrayed. After 2007, Chinese sensitivities led to a downgrading of the *Malabar* series. Japan was excluded (until 2014), the number of ships fell from their peak, and Indian aircraft carriers have stopped participating.[71] Nevertheless, the US and India agreed in 2014 to upgrade the exercises and in 2015 Japan was extended a permanent invitation, institutionalising *Malabar* as a multilateral exercise. This pace and scale of military exercises far exceeds that which India achieved even with the Soviet Union at the height of their partnership in the 1970s and 1980s.

Such exercises are a reflection of gradual strategic convergence, and not a precursor to formal alliance. Nevertheless, they have two important long-term effects. One is to deepen interoperability between Indian and foreign militaries, including in complex tasks like ASW. A second is to foster a climate where Indian military activism does not have the stigma it might have done in previous eras, in turn making it easier – though not easy – for India to extend various types of security assistance to these partners in times of conflict.[72] In the short-term, of course, this interoperability is likeliest to be tested in situations involving soft-power projection, such as HADR, rather than in scenarios requiring the use of force. This could include deeper integration of tsunami-relief efforts in the Pacific or anti-piracy operations in Southeast Asia. But, over time, multinational exercises and real-world HADR are likely to be mutually reinforcing, with each side growing progressively more comfortable operating with the other. China's expanding footprint could also accelerate this process. For instance, a future crisis over a Chinese military

---

[70] Sushant Singh, 'Exercise Malabar: Japan Navy to Join India, US in Bay of Bengal', *Indian Express*, 30 June 2015; *Business Standard*, 'India, 16 Others Take Part in "Milan 2014" Naval Exercise', *Standard*, 9 February 2014.
[71] Shashank Joshi, 'Malabar: Modi Government Misses an Opportunity as Annual Exercise Slumps', *The Interpreter*, 9 October 2015.
[72] Gurpreet S Khurana, 'Malabar Naval Exercises: Trends and Tribulations', Issue Brief, National Maritime Foundation, August 2014, pp. 1–2.

Figure 9: Perceptions of India in Selected States of Asia and the US, 2006–15.

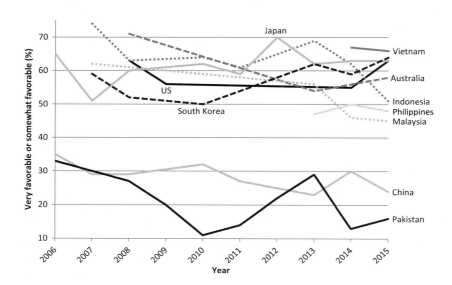

Source: *Bruce Stokes, 'How Asia-Pacific Publics See Each Other and Their National Leaders', Pew Research Center, September 2015, pp. 12–13. Missing data is interpolated.*

presence on Myanmar's Coco Islands, located just north of India's Andaman Islands, could involve a multinational response involving India, Australia and the US.[73] While Indian discomfort with formal coalitions will probably persist into the long term, its deepening military-to-military relationships across Asia are likely to expand its options for power projection throughout the Indo-Pacific.

Responses to Indian Power Projection

How will other states respond to growing Indian capabilities? Perceptions of India by its smaller neighbours grew more unfavourable in the 1980s, when India was at its most interventionist. People would speak of the 'Ugly

---

[73] While there have been rumours of Chinese signals-intelligence facilities on the Coco Islands, one study concludes 'there is minimal physical evidence to suggest that the facilities being developed … will be used to encircle India and support a PLA effort to conduct conventional war in South Asia'. See Christopher D Yung, 'Chinese Overseas Basing Requirements for the Twenty-First Century', in Peter A Dutton and Ryan D Martinson (eds), *Beyond the Wall: Chinese Far Seas Operations* (Newport, RI: US Naval War College, 2015), p. 58.

Indian', or the 'bad boy of the region'.[74] This image improved when New Delhi, under the so-called Gujral Doctrine, took a more restrained approach in the 1990s.[75] Less remembered today is that Indian procurement in the late 1980s, especially of strike aircraft and submarines, also raised concern in more distant powers, particularly Indonesia and Australia.[76]

India undoubtedly sees itself as a benign actor, and many countries largely agree. Across the Asia-Pacific, about half (51 per cent) see India in a positive light, including 66 per cent of Vietnamese, 64 per cent of South Koreans and 63 per cent of Japanese. Only in Malaysia and the Philippines is favourability below 50 per cent. However, Japan (71 per cent) and, perhaps surprisingly, China (57 per cent) both have higher favourability ratings, with far fewer rating Japan unfavourably (13 per cent) than India (31 per cent).

Pakistan's security establishment, of course, views India as predatory, aggressive and expansionist.[77] India's smaller neighbours tend to have within them a range of views of India, often corresponding to whether New Delhi's diplomatic and intelligence efforts help or hinder their particular faction or party. Although less time-series data are available, they are likely to show a more ambiguous and volatile set of attitudes than those in the larger East and Southeast Asian states. But even in a country like Bangladesh, which has swung between pro- and anti-Indian governments, 70 per cent of the population express favourable views of India, the highest such rating of India anywhere in Asia.[78] India is viewed more favourably than China in Japan, the Philippines, South Korea and Vietnam.[79] In the special case of Afghanistan, which has experienced decades of Pakistani subversion, pro-Indian sentiment is exceptionally high at all levels.[80]

---

[74] Ramachandra Guha, *India after Gandhi: The History of the World's Largest Democracy*, 1st ed. (New York, NY: Ecco, 2007), p. 588.

[75] I K Gujral, *Matters of Discretion: An Autobiography* (New Delhi: Hay House, 2011), ch. 58.

[76] Mohammed Ayoob, *India and Southeast Asia: Indian Perceptions and Policies* (London: Routledge, 1990), chs. 2–3; Sayan Majumdar, '"Bears" to "Blackjacks" – A Possibe Logical Progression?', India Defence Consultants, 31 March 2006, <http://www.indiadefence.com/Tu-160.htm>, accessed 22 October 2015; Kunwar Rajendra Singh, *Navies of South Asia* (Delhi: Rupa & Co., 2002), p. 126.

[77] Fair, *Fighting to the End*, pp. 154–73.

[78] Pew Research Center, 'Global Opposition to U.S. Surveillance and Drones, but Limited Harm to America's Image', p. 38.

[79] *Ibid.*, p. 37.

[80] Zach Warren 'Afghanistan in 2014: A Survey of the Afghan People', Asia Foundation, 2014, pp. 73–75; Larry Hanauer and Peter Chalk, *India's and*

These data are indicative but potentially misleading.[81] More broadly, threat perceptions of India at the official and elite level – in governments, think tanks and the intelligentsia – tend to be low, although the long-term effect of actions such as India's special forces raid into Myanmar in June 2015, and Indian officials' subsequently bellicose rhetoric, is yet to be seen. Much of this is likely a function of India's relative detachment from the region's maritime disputes, its democratic status, its growing proximity to the US and a belief in Indian 'strategic restraint'.[82] But even Russia, while cultivating new ties to both China and Pakistan in the aftermath of the Ukraine crisis, has continued to provide India with highly sensitive military technology and welcomed its prospective entry to the Shanghai Cooperation Organisation.[83] Moscow is not cheering India's rise in the manner of Washington, but it has given few signs of concern and many of implicit support.

How resilient is this relatively benign image? Indians are aware that this favourable regional reputation might be sensitive to stronger capabilities and greater military activity. As the Indian Navy's former western commander notes, the prime minister's office and foreign ministry 'have always been wary about discussing expeditionary capabilities, considering the implications of such operations and India's carefully nurtured image of a country with no belligerent ambitions'.[84] When discussing these topics in New Delhi, this author was told by a retired officer to avoid the term 'expeditionary warfare', which was deemed overly provocative. These sensitivities reflect a curious paradox: Indian analysts will frequently lament that India is a 'soft' country without the stomach to retaliate against provocations and project force, but will also invoke India's purportedly restrained heritage as proof of its benign intentions. This contradictory rhetoric will become increasingly difficult to sustain if India does become more active.

There are some ways in which India could mitigate this. One Indian defence analyst, writing with an American colleague, notes that non-combat missions, such as 'observation flights of the sea lines of commerce and communication, disaster response, and humanitarian missions', could

---

Pakistan's Strategies in Afghanistan: Implications for the United States and the Region (Santa Monica, CA: RAND Corporation, 2012), p. 23.

[81] Rani D Mullen, 'India's Soft Power', in David M Malone, C Raja Mohan, and Srinath Raghavan (eds), *Oxford Handbook of Indian Foreign Policy* (Oxford: Oxford University Press, 2015), p. 198.

[82] Sunil Dasgupta and Stephen P Cohen, 'Is India Ending its Strategic Restraint Doctrine?', *Washington Quarterly* (Vol. 34, No. 2, Spring 2011).

[83] Tanvi Madan, 'Mr. Putin Goes to India: Five Reasons the Russian President Will Be Welcomed There', Up Front, Brookings, 9 December 2014.

[84] Shiv Aroor, 'Army and Navy Plan to Set Up a Marine Brigade', *India Today*, 9 June 2010.

'project India's military power without necessarily upping the ante'.[85] This only works up to a point. Some threats require force. But strong Indian relationships with states like Japan, South Korea, Australia, Indonesia, Vietnam and other ASEAN countries – what Rory Medcalf and C Raja Mohan call 'middle power coalitions'[86] – could blunt, though not eliminate, international concern about Indian power-projection potential before it even develops. This will not be easy. To the east, India will resist being pulled into East Asian disputes, while its interlocutors 'will expect India to act as a regional partner'.[87] To India's west, the interests of middle powers are frequently dissonant. One enumeration of India's key partners in the Middle East lists Iran, Saudi Arabia, Egypt and the Gulf States.[88] It would be hard to think of a less-harmonious group of states. India could muddle through unobtrusively, but this will involve a deliberate effort to maintain restraint in the face of ambitious rhetoric and domestic and foreign pressures to protect Indian interests.

Ambition, Arms and Influence

India's relationship to power projection is an ambivalent one. Much of India's intellectual and political elite vehemently rejects what they see as Western-style military intervention, in theory and in practice. But India's elected leaders have marked out a wide area of strategic interest, approved the acquisition of military platforms with longer reach, embraced the role of net provider of security 'in our immediate region and beyond' (as the Indian prime minister put it in 2013), and allowed the Indian armed services to accord increasingly central roles to power-projection missions in their doctrines and strategies. 95 per cent of the Indian public views the military as very important to achieving the country's foreign-policy goals, a higher ranking than any other instrument of the state and 27 percentage points above the foreign ministry. Moreover, most of the public's stated goals go

---

[85] Adam B Lowther and Rajeswari Pillai Rajagopalan, 'Building a Partnership between the United States and India: Exploring Airpower's Potential', *Air and Space Power Journal* (March–April 2015), pp. 35–36.

[86] Rory Medcalf and C Raja Mohan, 'Responding to Indo-Pacific Rivalry: Australia, India and Middle Power Coalitions', Analysis, Lowy Institute for International Policy, August 2014, pp. 1–2.

[87] David Brewster, 'Indian Strategic Thinking about the Indian Ocean: Striving Towards Strategic Leadership', *India Review* (Vol. 14, No. 2, April 2015), p. 234. As Jonah Blank et al. note, 'Southeast Asia sees India primarily as a security partner, while India primarily sees Southeast Asia as a trade partner'. *Look East, Cross Black Waters: India's Interest in Southeast Asia*, p. xxii.

[88] Menon, 'It's Time for India to Start Looking West Again'.

well beyond the narrow Pakistan- or China-specific scenarios that we instinctively associate with Indian defence policy.[89]

To be sure, after an interventionist spell in the 1980s, India has shied away from serious power projection in recent years, notably rejecting US requests for participation in the stabilisation of Iraq after 2003 and shunning overt intervention in Afghanistan even after repeated attacks on its interests and personnel. India's defence posture remains dominated by Pakistan and China, and some of India's interest in power projection ought to be seen as a response to a perceived broadening of Sino–Indian rivalry from land borders to the Indian Ocean as a whole. 'There is a demand that India be a net provider of security', as former NSA Menon acknowledged in 2014, but as for 'the basic decision on how far we are willing to assume these functions ... we have not decided'.[90]

Predicting the targets and shape of future power projection is difficult. But this chapter's survey of Indian interests suggests a variety of scenarios that could persuade future Indian governments to overcome traditional reticence over the use of military force – not necessarily in the short-run, but in the years and decades ahead. India is widely associated with caution and restraint.[91] But a large recent part of the reason for this – successful nuclear deterrence by Pakistan – would not necessarily apply in many of the areas outlined here.

As for Indian capabilities themselves, this study highlights areas of strength and weakness. India has acquired the nucleus of a substantial capability, but it remains limited in number and in terms of specific enablers. A comparison with two other middle powers, France and Britain, is instructive. These countries – which spend not dissimilar amounts to India on defence – have extremely limited *independent* power-projection capabilities. But compared to India, they have greater operational experience, access to a wide range of foreign basing, and a proven ability to draw on allied resources as part of formal and ad hoc coalitions. This last factor is perhaps the most profound constraint on Indian power projection. Notionally independent operations, such as France's in Mali, have in fact relied hugely on the support of multiple allies in crucial areas. France and Britain are members of deeply rooted and decades-old military alliance with historically unparalleled levels of interoperability, and enjoy other partnerships, such as those with Gulf states, that bring basing rights and other benefits. India has no such partnerships with large powers and, despite the huge leaps forward

---

[89] Rory Medcalf, 'Facing the Future: India Views of the World Ahead', India Poll 2013, Lowy Institute for International Policy and Australia India Institute, 2013, p. 7.
[90] *Business Standard*, 'India Needs to Decide on Net Security Provider Role: NSA', *Business Standard*, 12 February 2014.
[91] Dasgupta and Cohen, 'Is India Ending its Strategic Restraint Doctrine?'.

in the Indo–US relationship over the past decade, faces domestic political sensitivities in pursuing these. India is likely to continue to forge co-operative security arrangements with other powers in Asia, but if these are to transcend occasional exercises and arms sales, and facilitate Indian power projection in more substantive ways, they would raise major strategic questions that India is not yet prepared to answer with clarity.

In the absence of coalitions, unilateral power projection is both militarily difficult and reputationally hazardous. The line between net provider of security and meddlesome hegemon is a blurred one – as Indian elites themselves have often argued in relation to Western intervention. While the US, UK and France can at least put forward legitimating UN resolutions in the Security Council, even if in anticipation of a Russian or Chinese veto, India has no such institutional power, until such a time that the Security Council is reformed.[92] If Indian power projection merely takes the form of increased participation in multinational operations, perhaps starting with the least controversial, such as anti-piracy – a sort of 'peacekeeping-plus' – then this problem is slight. This is probably what the US has in mind when it has spoken of net security provision. But this would only go so far in protecting the Indian interests described earlier in this chapter. Independent Indian power projection could be relatively uncontroversial in the international community were it confined to South Asia (excepting Pakistan, of course, where the nuclear risks multiply the stakes), but less so beyond this. India has long proclaimed the virtues of a multi-polar world, seeing itself as one of those poles; but amongst others, and despite the relatively benign view Asian elites have of India, there is no guarantee that Indian military activism will be seen as a force for stability irrespective of the forms that it takes.

These are medium- to long-term challenges. India's relationship with Pakistan has worsened over 2014–15 and there are few signs that the border dispute with China is about to be resolved. Increased resources have done little to improve India's viable military options against Pakistan, while the gap between India and China is growing rather than narrowing. In the short term, then, power projection will remain a second-tier concern. The contradiction between the civilian language of an extended neighbourhood and the military's embrace of power projection on the one hand, and the reality of political and diplomatic caution on the other, will prevail until external circumstances – a challenge to one of the interests outlined in this chapter – forces a response from India. At that point, this broad but diffuse effort will begin to come into sharper focus.

---

[92] David M Malone and Rohan Mukherjee, 'Dilemmas of Sovereignty and Order: India and the UN Security Council', Waheguru Pal Singh Sidhu, Pratap Bhanu Mehta and Bruce Jones (eds), *Shaping the Emerging World: India and the Multilateral Order* (Washington, DC: Brookings Institution Press, 2013).